SAP® BEx Simplified

Business Explorer for End-Users

Arshad Khan

SAP® BEx Simplified

Business Explorer for End-Users

Arshad Khan

BPB PUBLICATIONS
B-14, CONNAUGHT PLACE, NEW DELHI-1

FIRST INDIAN EDITION 2007

ISBN 81-8333-180-7

Original English Language Edition Published & Copyright © by ARSHAD H. KHAN, Original ISBN : 0-9772838-2-8

Printed in India under arrangement with Independent Publishers Group, Chicago, USA.

All rights reserved. No part of this publications may be reproduced, in any form or by any means without permission in writing from Publisher

Other product names mentioned are used for identification purpose only and may be trademarks of their respective companies.

All trademarks referred to in the book are acknowledged as properties of their respective owenrs.

AUTHORIZED EDITION FOR SALE IN INDIAN SUBCONTINENT, MIDDLE EAST & SOUTH EAST ASIA ONLY.

Distributors:

BPB PUBLICATIONS
B-14, Connaught Place, **NEW DELHI-110001**
Phone: 23325760, 23723393, 23737742

COMPUTER BOOK CENTRE
12, Shrungar Shopping Centre, M.G. Road,
BANGALORE-560001 Phone: 5587923, 5584641

MICRO BOOKS
Shanti Niketan Building, 8, Camac Street,
KOLKATTA-700017 Phone: 22826518, 22826519

BUSINESS PROMOTION BUREAU
8/1, Ritchie Street, Mount Road,
CHENNAI-600002 Phone: 28410796, 28550491

DECCAN AGENCIES
4-3-329, Bank Street,
HYDERABAD-500195 Phone: 24756400, 24756967

MICRO MEDIA
Shop No. 5, Mahendra Chambers, 150 D.N. Road, Next to Capital Cinema V.T. (C.S.T.) Station,
MUMBAI-400001 Ph.: 22078296, 22078297

INFO TECH
G-2, Sidhartha Building, 96 Nehru Place,
NEW DELHI-110019
Phone: 26438245, 26415092, 26234208

INFO TECH
Shop No. 2, F-38, South Extension Part-1
NEW DELHI-110049
Phone: 24691288, 24641941

BPB BOOK CENTRE
376, Old Lajpat Rai Market,
DELHI-110006 PHONE: 23861747

Published by **Manish Jain for BPB Publications**, B-14, Connaught Place, New Delhi-110 001 and Printed by him at Akash Press, Delhi.

"SAP", mySAP.com, mySAP Business Suite, and SAP NetWeaver are trademarks of SAP Aktiengesellschaft, Systems, Applications and Products in Data Processing, Neurottstrasse 16, 69190 Waldorf, Germany. The publisher gratefully acknowledges SAP's kind permission to use its trademark in this publication. SAP AG is not the publisher of this book and is not responsible for it under any aspect of press law.

The following are some of SAP AG's trademarks (or registered trademarks), along with their corresponding descriptor and registration status, in the USA:
ABAP/4® programming language
ABAP™ programming language
Accelerated R/3™
AcceleratedSAP™ methodology
Accelerated <anything>™ software
ASAP™
EnjoySAP™
Business Framework
BW Explorer
mySAP.com™
mySAP Business Suite™
mySAP CRM™
mySAP PLM™
mySAP SCM™
R/2™
R/3™
SAP™
SAPPHIRE® conference
SAP™ R/3® software
SAP™ R/2™ software
SAP™ BW software
SAP APO™
SAP B2B™
SAP EarlyWatch™
SAP NetWeaver®

CONTENTS

Introduction xv

Exercise Scenarios xvii

Chapter 1: Overview of Data Warehousing and BW 1
Data warehousing 1
   Background and overview 1
   Fundamental concepts 1
   Benefits 2
Business Warehouse (BW) 3
   What is the Business Warehouse 3
   BW and SAP R/3 relationship 4
   BW data characteristics 4
   BW queries 5
BW architecture and components 6
   Business Explorer 6
   Business Warehouse Server 7
   Source Systems 7
BEx architecture and components 7
   Business Explorer Browser (BEx Browser) 8
   Business Explorer Analyzer (BEx Analyzer) 8

Chapter 2: Impact of BW implementations 10
New reporting and analysis paradigm 10
BW access methods and process 11
   Access methods 11
   Who can access BW reports 12
   Roles and authorizations 12
   IDs and passwords 12

| Which BW system to use | 13 |

Functional areas covered by the BW system *13*
    Report Tree 13
    How to view the InfoProviders 15

Miscellaneous *17*
    Knowing the limitations 17
    Role of the legacy reporting tools 18

Getting help *18*
    Online help 18
    Company support/Help Desk 18

Chapter 3: Launching a BW report via the Analyzer 19

How to launch the Analyzer *19*
Displaying the available reports *21*
How to select a report for execution *27*
How to find a report *27*
How to launch a selected report *31*
How to enter values in the Query Selection window *32*
How to execute the report *33*
How to refresh a report *33*

Chapter 4: Specifying selection criteria for reports 36

Query Selection window components *36*
Minimum input requirements *37*
Entering values in the Query Selection window *37*
Using drop-down menus *38*
Filters *40*
How to specify include filters *40*
How to specify exclude filters *42*
Using operators on the web *44*
Using include/exclude filters on the web *45*
Adding values and ranges on the web *46*

Chapter 5: Launching a BW report via the Browser/Portal 48
How to launch the Browser *48*
Browser windows *49*
Browser Toolbar *50*
How to navigate to a specific report *51*
How to find a report *51*
How to select a report for execution *53*
How to launch a selected report *54*
How to specify the selection criteria for a report *55*
How to execute a report *55*
Working with Browser windows and folders *56*
    Moving and organizing reports 57
    Enhancing displays 58
    Adding an Internet address 61
    Creating a new folder 64
    Deleting a folder 65
    Rearranging groups 66
How to access BW reports via the Portal *68*

Chapter 6: Anatomy of Excel and Web reports 69
Excel report anatomy *69*
Web report anatomy *70*
How to analyze BW (Excel and Web) reports *72*

Chapter 7: Analyzer tools and techniques 73
BEx Toolbar *73*
Context Menu *73*

Chapter 8: Web reporting tools and techniques 77
Web Toolbar *77*
Generic Navigation Block *77*
Drill-down characteristics *78*
Context Menu *78*

Chapter 9: Basic navigation and analysis functions 80
Most commonly used functions *80*
    Back 80
    Back to Start 80
    Keep Filter Value 81
    Select Filter Value 81
    Other functions 81
Using common functions in Excel *81*
    Back 83
    Back to Start 84
    Keep filter value 85
    Select filter value 88
    Remove filter value 93
Using common functions on the web *95*
    Back 96
    Back to Start 97
    Keep filter value 98
    Select filter value 99
    Remove filter value 103

Chapter 10: Slicing, dicing, and drilling 104
What is slicing and dicing *104*
What is drill-down *105*
Example of drill-down *105*
What is drill-across *107*
Example of drill-across *107*

Chapter 11: Analysis using the Analyzer 109
Drill-down and drill-across *109*
    How to drill-down using the Context Menu 109
    How to drill-across using the Context Menu 111
    How to remove drill-down 113
    Drill-down by double-clicking 115

  Reversing a drill-down by double-clicking 117
Filter and drilldown according to *118*
How to swap axes *121*
  What is swapping 121
  How to swap 121
How to sort *124*
Working with hierarchies *126*
  What is a hierarchy 126
  Expanding a hierarchy 127
  Collapsing a hierarchy node 129
  Deactivating a hierarchy 131
How to jump *131*

Chapter 12: Miscellaneous functions using the Analyzer 133
How to export report results to Excel *133*
How to add a report to the favorites *134*
How to delete a report from the favorites folder *137*
How to print a report *139*
How to e-mail a report *141*
How to receive a report via e-mail *141*
How to logoff *142*
How to create a variant *144*
  What is a variant 144
  Creating a variant 144
How to retrieve a variant *147*
How to delete a variant *148*

Chapter 13: Analysis on the web 151
Drill-down and drill-across *151*
  How to drill-down from the Navigation Area 152
  How to drill-down from the Results Area 153
  How to drill-across 154
  How to remove drill-down or drill-across 155

How to filter by a characteristic *157*
    Using the Context Menu to filter 157
    Using the Navigation Block to filter 159
How to filter and drilldown according to *162*
How to swap axes *163*
    What is swapping 163
    How to swap 164
How to sort *165*
Working with hierarchies *167*
    What is a hierarchy 167
    Expanding a hierarchy 167
    Expanding a hierarchy node 168
    Collapsing a hierarchy node 169
    Deactivating a hierarchy 170
How to use the jump function *171*

Chapter 14: Miscellaneous functions on the web **172**
How to export report results to Excel *172*
How to add a report to the favorites (Bookmark) *174*
How to delete a report from the favorites folder *175*
How to print a report *176*
How to e-mail a report *178*
How to logoff *182*
How to create, retrieve, and delete a variant *182*

Chapter 15: Changing properties (Excel) **183**
Query Designer *183*
    Launching the Query Designer 183
    Query Designer windows 184
How to change properties *185*
    How to change the properties of characteristics 185
    How to change the properties of key figures 190
    How to change the row display order 195

| How to add an attribute | 197 |
| Currency translation | 200 |

Chapter 16: Changing properties (Web) 201
How to change properties 201
    How to change the properties of characteristics 201
    How to change the properties of key figures 205
    Currency translation 212

Introduction

SAP BEx Simplified: Business Explorer for End-Users will introduce you to SAP's powerful and flexible reporting and analysis tool. It covers both Excel-based as well as web-based BEx reporting. SAP provides other reporting tools, such as Crystal formatted reporting and the Web Application Designer, which are not covered in this book.

The topics covered in *SAP BEx Simplified: Business Explorer for End-Users* include an overview of data warehousing and the Business Warehouse (BW), how to launch reports (via the Analyzer, web or Portal), how to specify report selection criteria, anatomy of Excel and web reports, tools and techniques (Excel and web), working with the BEx Browser, navigation and analysis functions, and customizing query properties. The execution of various functions is demonstrated in a step-by-step manner, with liberal use of screenshots.

Most end-users do not use both Excel and web-based reports because most organizations prefer to use only a single method for the majority of their users. Hence, all the chapters in this book will not be of interest to all end-users, with the exception of those who use both Excel- and web-based reports. Therefore, if you want to read only the chapters of interest to you, here are some guidelines that you can follow:

- For those who use only Excel-based reporting, read the following chapters:
    - 1-4, 6, 7, 9-12, and 15
- For those who use only web-based reporting, read the following chapters:
    - 1, 2, 4-6, 8-10, 13, 14, and 16

You should be aware that the Business Explorer is a very versatile business intelligence tool, which is packed with functions. Most users will execute only a few of its primary functions, which are covered in this book. The objective of *SAP BEx Simplified: Business Explorer for End-Users* is to introduce you to these primary functions, so that you can start working with the tool. You should realize that a fair amount of hands-on practice is required to master the Business Explorer. Therefore, after reading this book, you should practice the techniques demonstrated on a real BW system.

Happy reading!

Arshad Khan

EXERCISE SCENARIOS

SAP BEx Simplified contains many exercises, which are demonstrated in a step-by-step manner. These exercises cover some basic scenarios, which are most commonly used, that will help you become familiar with the application of the BEx tool. It is suggested that you refer to this section before starting a new chapter.

The following are the scenarios, in sequence, which are demonstrated in the hands-on chapters of this book:

- Chapter 3: Demonstrates how to launch the BEx Analyzer, display the available reports, find a specific report, select and launch a report, enter values before executing a report, and refresh a report.
- Chapter 5: Demonstrates how to launch the BEx Browser, navigate to and find a specific report, select and launch a report, and execute a report. It also demonstrates how to move a report from one folder to another, enhance the window background, add an internet address, create and delete a folder, and rearrange groups.
- Chapter 9: Demonstrates the execution of the following widely-used functions in Excel: *Back, Back to Start, Keep Filter Value, Select Filter Value,* and *Remove Filter Value.* Also demonstrates the execution of each of these functions on the web.
- Chapter 10: Demonstrates the effect of drill-down and drill-across operations. The drill-down example is shown in Excel, while the drill-across example is demonstrated on the web.
- Chapter 11: Demonstrates how drill-down and drill-across can be performed using the BEx Analyzer's Context Menu tool (on characteristic *Calendar Year/Month*), which is followed by the drill-down reversal. A secondary method for drill-down (and its reversal), by double-clicking, is also demonstrated. This chapter also demonstrates how to execute the *Filter and drill-down according to, swap, and sort* functions as well as working with hierarchies (expand a hierarchy, collapse a hierarchy node, and deactivate a hierarchy).

- Chapter 12: Demonstrates how to use the BEx Analyzer to export report results to an Excel file, add/delete a report to/from the favorites, print a report, e-mail and receive a report, and logoff. Also demonstrates the creation, retrieval, and deletion of variants.
- Chapter 13: Demonstrates how to execute various functions on the web. Shows how to drill-down and drill-across. Demonstrates techniques for drilling-down from the Navigation Area as well as the Results Area. Also shows how to remove drill-down or drill-across using the Context Menu and the Navigation Block. It also demonstrates how to filter by a characteristic, use the Context Menu to filter, use the Navigation Block to *filter, filter and drilldown according to, swap*, and *sort*. This chapter also shows how to work with hierarchies (expand a hierarchy, expand a hierarchy node, collapse a hierarchy node, and deactivate a hierarchy).
- Chapter 14: Demonstrates how to perform miscellaneous functions on the web. Shows how to export report results to an Excel file, add/delete a report to/from the favorites, print a report, e-mail a report, and logoff.
- Chapter 15: Demonstrates how to change query properties in Excel reports. Shows how to change the properties of a characteristic (sold-to-party), change the properties of a key figure (order dollars), re-arrange the rows and columns (display), add an attribute, and perform currency translation.
- Chapter 16: Demonstrates how to change query properties in web reports. It shows how to change the properties of a characteristic (sold-to-party), change the properties of a key figure (order dollars), and perform currency translation.

Chapter 1: Overview of Data Warehousing and BW

Data warehousing

Background and overview

In the past couple of decades, especially in the past few years, a number of factors have led companies to analyze their current and historical data. The aim has been to make their employees more productive and achieve a competitive edge in the market. One of the most important tools used for this objective has been the data warehouse, which can store huge amounts of data that can be accessed and analyzed easily and quickly. Data warehouses are provided by a number of vendors, including SAP. SAP's data warehouse is called the Business Information Warehouse. It is more popularly known as the Business Warehouse (BW).

Fundamental concepts

A data warehouse, including the Business Warehouse, is characterized by four unique characteristics: Subject-oriented, integrated, time variant, and non-volatile.

Subject-oriented
The data in a data warehouse is organized according to subjects such as customer, vendor, orders, and products. This contrasts with classical applications that are organized by business functions such as loans, finance, inventory, etc.

Integrated

The data in a data warehouse is always integrated—without any exception. The source data from multiple systems is consolidated in a data warehouse after undergoing various operations such as extraction, transformation, and loading.

Time variant

Data warehouse data is accurate as of a moment in time, while transactional (operational) data is accurate as of the moment of access. The data in a data warehouse consists of a lengthy series of snapshots, at various points in time, which can cover a very lengthy period that can stretch 10-20 years. In contrast, typical transaction databases retain data for only a 6-24 month period.

Non-volatile

The data stored in a data warehouse remains static. Any new data, which is typically introduced periodically, is appended. Data warehouse data is subjected to regular access and analysis. However, activities such as insertions and deletions, which occur routinely with operational systems, do not occur in a data warehouse which loads fresh data from its source systems only periodically.

Benefits

The benefits obtained from BW are the same as those provided by a conventional data warehouse. Despite being a superior data warehouse, BW does not require a large team of top-notch professionals to build or maintain it. It provides all the benefits that are associated with the implementation of conventional data warehouses, which are listed below:

- Facilitates integration in an environment characterized by un-integrated applications
- Integrates enterprise data across a variety of functions
- Integrates external as well as internal data
- Supports strategic and long-term business planning
- Supports day-to-day tactical decisions
- Enables insight into business trends and business opportunities
- Organizes and stores historical data needed for analysis, especially trend analysis
- Provides more accurate and complete information
- Improves knowledge about the business

- Enables cost-effective decision making
- Enables organizations to understand their customers, and their needs, as well competitors
- Enhances customer service and satisfaction
- Provides competitive advantage
- Helps generate new revenue (new customers), reduces costs (improved processes), and improves the bottom line (profits)
- Streamlines business processes and provides decision support for various business processes
- Provides easy reporting access for end-users
- Provides timely access to corporate information
- Enables users to analyze data from different angles, using powerful front-end access tools
- Reduces users' dependency on IT as they can quickly create their own reports
- Generates ROI of 100-400 percent in the first year if the data warehouse is well-designed and implemented

In organizations that have implemented SAP, BW provides tight integration with its primary source system, the SAP R/3 transaction system, and also helps overcome its reporting limitations.

Business Warehouse (BW)

What is the Business Warehouse

The Business Warehouse is a data warehousing application platform, which includes a back-end development platform and front-end reporting tools. It provides a strategic as well as operational decision support and reporting solution, which is closely integrated with SAP's flagship product—SAP R/3. BW enables easier, flexible, and powerful reporting and analysis. It can be used by a variety of users ranging from end-users (with limited skills) to power-users (with sophisticated skills and the ability to customize their reports). Strategic as well as operational users can use BW.

BW can be used to analyze current and historical data in SAP R/3 as well as non-SAP systems. It uses OLAP technology, which enables it to analyze data in many different dimensions, as well as non-OLAP technology. This versatility makes it a very powerful tool.

BW and SAP R/3 relationship

The BW system is tightly integrated with the SAP R/3 transaction system, which runs the business operations. With the growing importance of business intelligence, BW has been gaining in importance over the years. It has developed into an enterprise-wide information hub in SAP's overall enterprise architecture, enabling organizations to analyze data from SAP R/3 applications, non-SAP applications, as well as miscellaneous external data sources (such as databases and the Internet).

BW data characteristics

Data differences: SAP and BW

An operational system like SAP R/3 captures real-time data whenever a business transaction is executed. For example, purchase orders and sales orders are added, deleted, and changed routinely during business hours, which can cover 24 hours for some organizations. In contrast, a BW system contains read-only data. Once data has been loaded into a BW system, it is not changed unless there are errors that need to be rectified.

A BW system stores data for a longer period, typically 3-5 years, though many companies store 10-20 years of data, which enables greater strategic trend analysis. This contrasts with the 6-24 months of data that is typically stored in transaction systems.

Data is loaded into the BW system, from its source systems, at a predetermined frequency. Typically, this is done once per day (usually at night). During some periods, like month-end closing, data loading is done more frequently, upon request. Some organizations load data in real-time, though this is not the norm. Hence, it is important that BW users should be aware of the data load schedule or they may be unpleasantly surprised. The reason is that when BW and SAP R/3 reports are executed, their results may not be in sync because they may not be accessing the same data. Unless both the BW and SAP R/3 reports are executed immediately after data is loaded into the BW system, which is the only period when both systems contain the same data, the two results will be different. For example, if BW data is loaded at 2am and the SAP R/3 and BW reports are executed at 11am, their results will not match. While the BW system will have remained static from 2am to 11am, the dynamic SAP R/3 system will have processed hundreds of transactions in the intervening 9 hours and, hence, will be out of sync with the BW system.

Structure of BW data

BW and SAP R/3 data structures are quite different. BW data is structured in a multi-dimensional format, which enables analysts to analyze its data in various dimensions such as by region, product, and period. This is in contrast to the SAP R/3 system, with an online transaction processing system (OLTP) structure, which is optimized for capturing business data rather than analyzing it. Table 1 highlights the differences between BW (data warehouse) data and SAP R/3 transaction (OLTP) data.

Table 1	
Data Warehouse (BW)	Traditional OLTP database (SAP R/3)
Used for data retrieval and analysis	Used to run daily business transactions
Integrated data	Application specific data
Historical and descriptive data	Current, changing, and incomplete data
Organized by subjects	Organized for performance
Non-volatile data	Data that is updated constantly
Relational database structure	Relational database structure
Multi-dimensional format, with redundant data, which is optimized for queries.	Structure that requires fast access to non-redundant data (data is fragmented in many different tables)
Fewer but larger tables	Greater number of smaller tables
Data for analyzing the business	Data for running the business
Summarized and/or detailed data	Raw data
Contains data and metadata (data about data)	Contains only data
Queries are unplanned and cannot be easily or quickly optimized	Queries are pre-defined and can be optimized
Time element is contained in the key structure	Time element may or may not be contained in the key structure

BW queries

A query is a report that can retrieve and analyze data based on a selection of variables, which can be specified at run time. Every BW system contains a large number of queries, delivered as standard Business Content, which can be customized using a variety of techniques and functions. New queries can be built using the Query Designer, which can be launched through the BEx Analyzer—one of the BW reporting tools.

BW architecture and components

The BW system has been developed on a 3-tier (3-layer) architecture, Figure 1, which includes the following components:

- Source system: Data is loaded into BW from this component.
- BW Server: Data loaded into BW is stored in this component. It also contains the OLAP Processor, where the query processing logic is executed.
- Business Explorer: Tool which enables the stored data to be accessed and analyzed.

Figure 1: BW 3-layer architecture

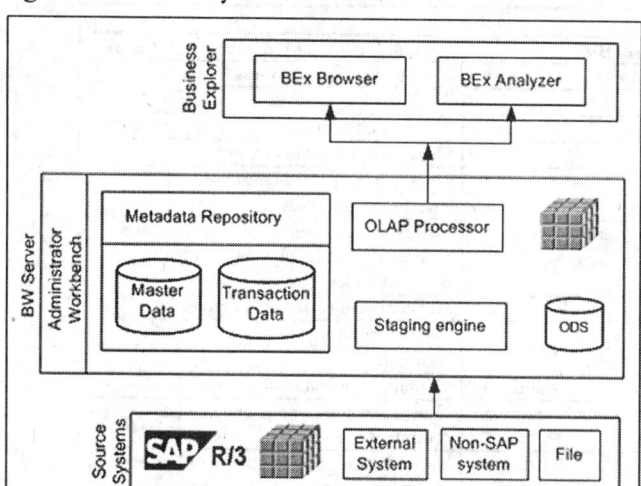

Business Explorer

The Business Explorer (BEx) is the top layer in the BW architecture. It is characterized by an easy-to-use graphical interface. The Business Explorer supports both MS-Excel and web interfaces for its reporting and analysis. It is used for both strategic as well as operational reporting.

Business Warehouse Server

The BW Server is the middle layer. Its primary tasks are:

- Data storage: The data storage structures, called InfoProviders (such as InfoCubes and ODS objects), are located in this component. InfoCubes contain detailed, summarized or aggregated data. They are the basis for BW reporting and analysis.
- Data warehouse management and administration. It includes the Administrator Workbench, which is the tool used to create the BW objects like InfoCubes, specify loading routines, etc.

Source Systems

The bottom layer consists of the source system(s). These can be quite diverse and include any or all of the following systems: SAP R/3, external systems, flat files/spreadsheets, and other BW system(s).

BEx architecture and components

Figure 2 provides an overview of the BEx architecture and components. Queries are defined in the highlighted area.

Figure 2: BEx architecture

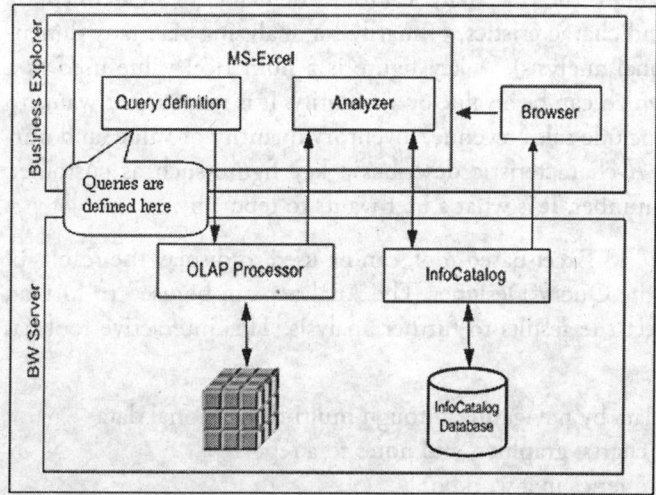

The Business Explorer consists of the following components:
- BEx Browser: Used to retrieve and execute queries
- BEx Analyzer: Used to create and execute queries

Another component, called BEx Web, enables access to BW data using a web browser, such as Netscape or the Internet Explorer, without requiring any special software like the SAP GUI. It can be used to publish BEx Analyzer queries on the Internet or Intranet.

Business Explorer Browser (BEx Browser)

The BEx Browser is a graphical interface that can organize BW reports and manage workbooks (which display the results of queries). It enables BW reports to be accessed through the web, eliminating the need to have the SAP client software installed on the desktop. The Browser can access various document types assigned to a role or stored in the user's favorites. Document types that can be accessed through the BEx Browser include workbooks, links (references to file system, shortcuts), links to internet sites (URLs), web applications, etc. The BEx Browser can copy documents and folders (from one role to another).

Business Explorer Analyzer (BEx Analyzer)

The BEx Query Designer is the BW analytical tool where queries are defined, by selecting key figures and characteristics, primarily for analyzing via many dimensions (multi-dimensional analysis). A key figure is a numerical value used as a measure in a report, which can be a value or a quantity. It is what a user wants to report on. Examples include sales revenue, inventory quantity or value, and purchase order quantity. A characteristic describes a key figure such as customer, vendor, and material number. It is what a user wants to report by.

The BEx Analyzer, an MS Excel-based tool, can be used to display the results of queries developed in the Query Designer. The Analyzer can be used to format, manipulate, and subject the results to further analysis. This interactive tool has the ability to:

- Analyze selected data by navigating through multi-dimensional data
- Add calculations, charts, graphics, and notes to a report
- Combine various queries in a workbook

- Distribute reports via e-mail
- Provide navigation abilities that can provide different views of the data
- Perform drill-down or drill-across
- Perform other functions such as filter, sort, cumulate, etc.

The BEx Toolbar, which is activated when the Analyzer is launched, is used to execute various navigation and analysis functions and features. Many of these functions will be demonstrated, in a step-by-step manner, in subsequent chapters.

CHAPTER 2: IMPACT OF BW IMPLEMENTATIONS

New reporting and analysis paradigm

The overall reporting process in a BW system using the Business Explorer, which is similar to conventional reporting, is shown on Figure 3:

Figure 3: Reporting process

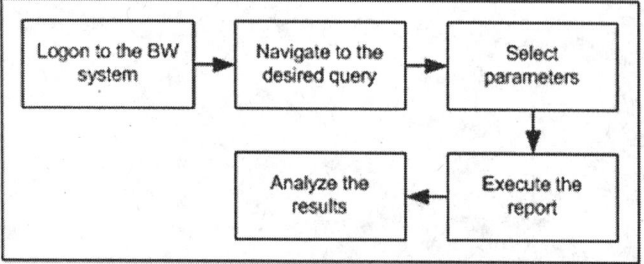

The introduction of the Business Explorer tool, with the implementation of a BW system, provides analytical capabilities to a very large number of users who previously had to depend on IT for their reporting needs. After an implementation, such users have access to a reporting tool and the data it can access, which provides them with capabilities that they could not have visualized with their legacy reporting system. Hence, they tend to become more inquisitive and analytical and, consequently, more productive.

Most users end up executing queries that have been created by the BW project team (before implementation) or by skilled business analysts/developers (after go-live). A small group of users, known as super-users or power-users, also quickly develop the skills to create and modify queries that can be quite powerful. They help reduce IT's report development workload.

BW access methods and process

Access methods

BW reports can be accessed through the:

- Analyzer
- Browser
- Formatted reporting (such as Crystal Reports or other SAP-certified third-party reporting tools, which are not covered in this book)
- Organization's Website or Portal

The BEx access method used depends on whether the BW reports are to be executed and/or displayed in Excel, on the web, or via formatted reporting. In some cases, all four access methods can be used. Most organizations permit only one access method to be used by most users. Usually, an exception is made for a select group of power-users who are allowed to use more than one access method. Therefore, you should determine which access method you are required to use. The access method and procedure are often communicated to the users before the BW system goes live.

<u>Access via the Analyzer and Browser</u>

These BEx Analyzer Excel-based and web-based access methods are described comprehensively in Chapters 3 and 5. These chapters contain procedures that describe, in a step-by-step manner, how BEx Analyzer reports can be located, selected, and executed in Excel and on the web.

<u>Access via a Portal</u>

As companies rollout portals, this access method is becoming more popular. The content as well as look and feel for these portals can vary significantly from company to company. Typically, to access BW reports via a portal, a user has to:

- Logon to the company portal using the portal ID and password
- Navigate to the desired report via a menu, hyperlinks, or buttons (which are typically organized by functions such as Finance, Accounts Payable, Purchasing, Sales, Manufacturing, etc.)
- Select the report
- Execute the report

When a BEx Analyzer report is executed through a portal, it launches the BEx web tool. The report thus launched is displayed on the web.

Who can access BW reports

Only authorized users can access the BW system, launch the Business Explorer, and execute reports. Typical users include executives, senior managers, middle managers, line managers, business analysts, functional staff, clerks, project team members, etc. Access can very restricted, limited, or minimally restricted depending on the user's function and assigned role. The level of access permitted to each user group depends on their function and assigned role.

Roles and authorizations

The level of authorizations is dependent on roles that have been defined in the BW system. This enables the system to restrict a user to the specific reports assigned to his role and prevent access to unauthorized reports. For example, a buyer assigned the purchasing role will be unable to access reports assigned to the finance manager role or the accounts payable role. Typically, reports that are made available to users are grouped and displayed according to function and/or roles such as Finance, Human Resources, Purchasing, Purchase-to-Pay, Order-to-Cash, etc.

IDs and passwords

To access the BW system, you will need a User ID and password.

- If access is through the company portal, the portal User ID and password can be used. A prerequisite is that you should be authorized by the security and authorizations team to access the BW system.
- If access is through the Analyzer or Browser, you will require the BW system User ID and associated password, which will be different than the portal User ID and password.

SAP users often have a misconception that they can use their SAP User ID and password to access the BW system. It is possible that the User IDs may be the same for SAP R/3 and BW. However, you will need specific authorization to access BW, even if you currently have SAP R/3 access, because SAP R/3 and BW authorizations are independent of each other. An SAP R/3 user may not be permitted to access the BW system and vice versa.

Which BW system to use

A BW system typically has many environments, or "boxes," such as production, testing (quality assurance), development, and training. The authorizations for each BW system are different. Therefore, you must determine which system(s) you are authorized to access before trying to login. Typically, during and immediately after training, you will be provided access to the BW training system. Later on, after certain prerequisites have been met, you will be provided access to the BW production system.

Keep in mind that the level of authorization permitted in each system, such as production and training, can be different. For example, in the training system, a user may have unrestricted access to a wide variety of roles. However, in the production system, minimal access is provided due to security considerations. Invariably, an authorization for the training system will not enable a user to access the production system.

Functional areas covered by the BW system

The functional areas (also known as application areas) for which reports are available in the BW system, which BEx can access, depend on the scope of the implementation and the subsequent addition of queries. When BW is initially implemented, the scope of the functional areas covered is usually limited for a number of reasons. Later on, queries for additional functional areas are developed. Typically, after some period has elapsed, BW reports are available for all/most of the functional areas that have been implemented during the company's SAP project.

Report Tree

BW reports are usually displayed to end-users in a report tree structure. Though such structures can vary, they are typically organized according to various processes, departments or functions.

Analyzer report tree

The Analyzer report tree structure is based on the needs of the organization and the functional modules that have been implemented. For example, an organization has structured its reports under three headings (folders): Purchase-to-Pay

(P2P, Order-to-Cash (OTC), and Finance. Each of these areas is divided into sub-folders, which are further sub-divided into lower level folders. BW reports are located in the lowest sub-folder. To access a particular P2P report, a user needs to drill-down to the lowest P2P sub-folder, where the desired report is displayed. For example, to access a purchase order report, a user needs to drill-down two levels:

Purchase-to-Pay > Purchasing > Purchase Order report

Figure 4 is an example of the report tree that is displayed when the BEx Analyzer is launched. To display the *Purchasing Overview* report, drilling has been performed via:

SAP Demo > SAP Demo Purchasing > Purchasing Data > Purchasing Overview

After a report is displayed, it can be selected (by clicking on it) or launched (by double-clicking on it).

Figure 4

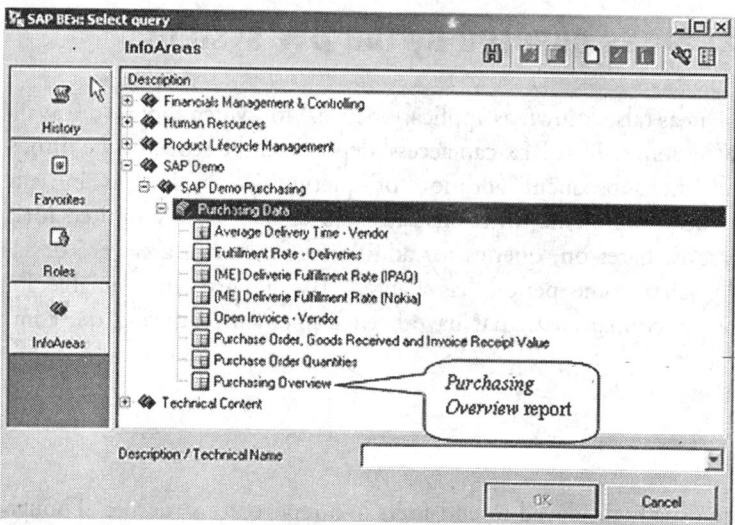

Copyright SAP AG

Portal/Web report tree

The report tree structures for the portal and the Analyzer can be identical or different. Drill-down in a portal structure can be performed through hyperlinks or buttons. In the organization referred to in the previous section, the Analyzer and portal (web) report tree structures are different. While the Analyzer top-level structure contains only P2P, OTC and Finance folders, its portal/web reports are structured at the top-level according to various functions (Product Sales, Logistics, PO Analysis, Tax, AP Payment, etc.). The reports in each functional area can be displayed by drilling down, via buttons, to lower levels where they are located. For example, if the Income Statement button is clicked, it displays the following reports: Annual Income Statement, Quarterly Income Statement, Monthly Income Statement, and Comparison Report (previous versus current year). After the desired report is displayed, it can be launched by clicking on it.

How to view the InfoProviders

An InfoProvider is the source from which a query retrieves its data. Every query is associated with an InfoProvider. A query cannot reference and retrieve its data from more than one InfoProvider because it can point to only one InfoProvider. However, an InfoProvider can provide data to many different queries. For example, a billing InfoProvider can feed its data to a P2P query as well as an OTC query, provided both the P2P and OTC queries reference the same billing InfoProvider.

Viewing and navigating through the InfoProvider list, which is typically organized by functions in InfoAreas (Figure 5), provides a good overview of the functions covered by the BW system and the organization of its reports.

Figure 5

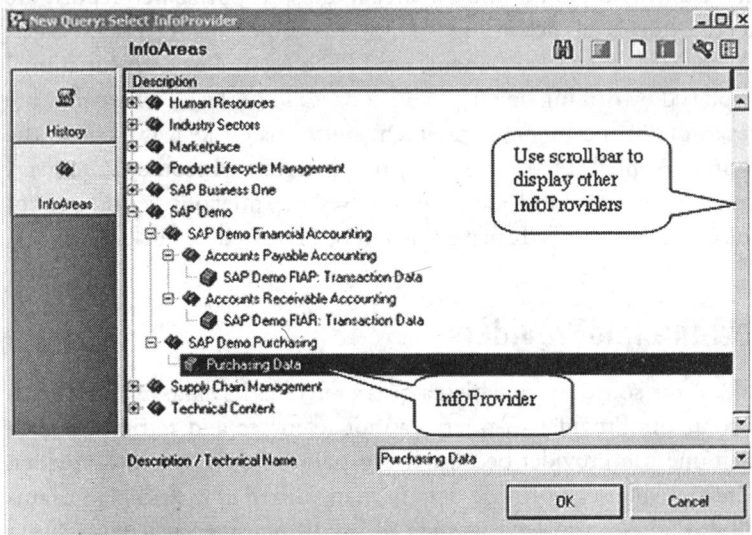

Copyright SAP AG

Figure 5 provides a view of the InfoProviders available in the BW system. To view the complete list of available InfoProviders, move the scroll bar up/down. Drilling down to the lowest level in the structure will display the available reports, which are shown on Figure 6:

Figure 6

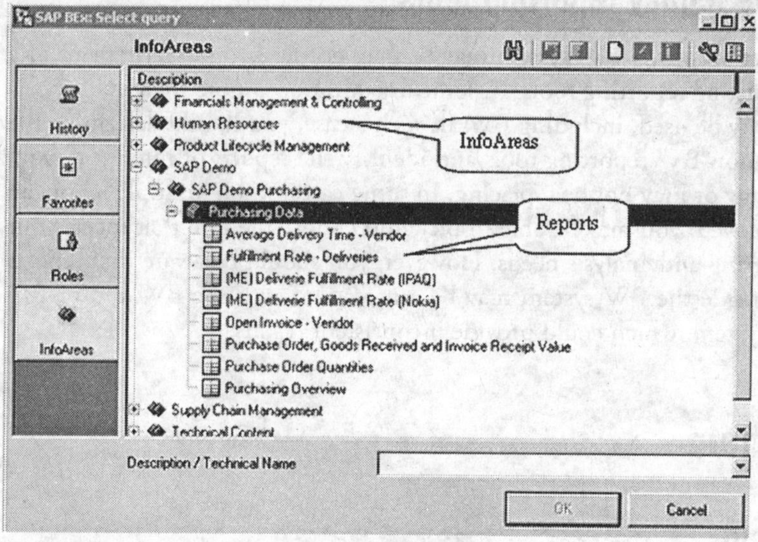

[Screenshot of SAP BEx Select query dialog showing InfoAreas tree with Financials Management & Controlling, Human Resources, Product Lifecycle Management, SAP Demo (expanded to SAP Demo Purchasing > Purchasing Data with reports: Average Delivery Time - Vendor, Fulfilment Rate - Deliveries, (ME) Deliverie Fulfilment Rate (IPAQ), (ME) Deliverie Fulfilment Rate (Nokia), Open Invoice - Vendor, Purchase Order, Goods Received and Invoice Receipt Value, Purchase Order Quantities, Purchasing Overview), Supply Chain Management, Technical Content. Annotations point to "InfoAreas" and "Reports".]

Copyright SAP AG

InfoAreas can be structured very differently across organizations. For example, an InfoArea structure, based on financial reporting, contains Cost Center Accounting, General Ledger, Internal Orders, Profit Center Accounting, and Strategic Enterprise Management. In contrast, another organization's structure is based on P2P, OTC, and Finance.

Miscellaneous

Knowing the limitations

The BW system receives its data periodically from its sources. Therefore, it is usually out of sync with the source systems' data, which is changing constantly. Hence, you should be aware of the differences due to the BW data load schedule. Keep yourself informed of the data load and refresh schedule. If you are not well-informed, and the SAP R/3 and BW reports are executed with a time difference, you may be surprised when analyzing the results because the two reports will return results that do not match.

Role of the legacy reporting tools

The introduction of the BW system may or may not lead to the retirement of a company's existing reporting tools. In some organizations, more than one reporting system may be used, including BW. In such a case, you should determine the status of the non-BW reporting tools and identify the reports of interest to you, which BW may or may not be replacing. In some cases, when multiple reporting tools are deployed, you may be able to pick and choose the tool that meets your unique reporting and analysis needs. However, you should be aware that reports generated outside the BW system may be out of sync with the BW and/or R/3 transaction system, which could provide inconsistent results.

Getting help

Online help

The SAP company website has a wealth of information that is available to anyone with internet access. You can access BW documentation and obtain help from the SAP help website at www.help.sap.com.

Company support/Help Desk

BW users are provided support internally through a number of ways. The first line of support is the company Help Desk. Additionally, power-users are assigned within the different functional groups to help end-users. Another source of help is the company intranet, where reference and training documentation, FAQs, job aids, etc. may be available. You should identify such resources within your organization and/or functional area so that you can obtain support when needed.

CHAPTER 3: LAUNCHING A BW REPORT VIA THE ANALYZER

How to launch the Analyzer

To launch the BEx Analyzer, navigate via the Windows menu, Figure 7, using the following menu path:

- Start > Programs > Business Explorer > Analyzer

Figure 7

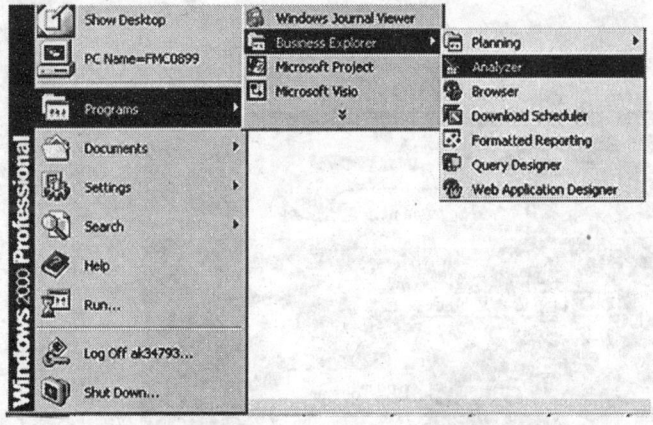

This will lead you to the following pop-up window (Figure 8):

Figure 8

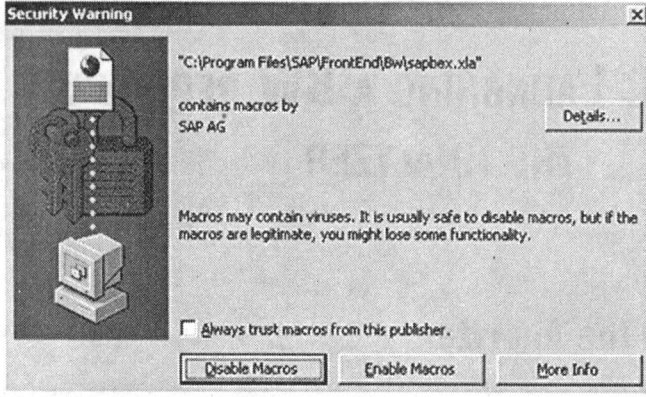

- Click the *Enable Macros* button

This will lead you to the next window, Figure 9, which shows the familiar Excel spreadsheet. The differences to be noted, which are highlighted, are the additional add-in menu item (Business Explorer) and the Business Explorer Toolbar (BEx Toolbar).

Figure 9

The BEx Toolbar is usually displayed in the middle of the blank screen, as shown on Figure 9. However, in some cases, you might find it displayed on the side, as shown on Figure 10. You can drag the Toolbar, using the mouse, to any preferred location on the screen.

Figure 10

The important features of the BEx Toolbar are described in Chapter 7.

Displaying the available reports

After the BEx Analyzer has been launched, you can navigate to the report(s) that you want to execute. There are two ways in which the BW reports can be accessed. Some organizations prefer their users to access the reports via *Workbooks*, while others prefer that users access them via *Queries*. Both these options are available via the drop-down menu shown on Figure 11. We will use the *Queries* option in order to navigate to the desired reports. This requires executing the following steps, which are also highlighted on Figure 11, using the BEx Toolbar:

- Click the *Open* icon

This will display the menu shown on Figure 11.

Figure 11

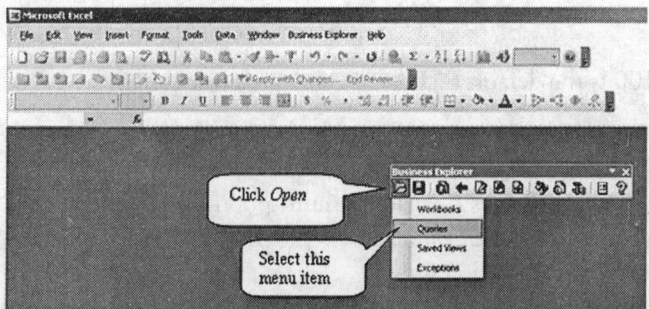

- Select the menu item *Queries*

The previous procedure, to access the queries or workbooks, can also be performed via the Business Explorer add-in menu, as shown on Figure 12:

Figure 12

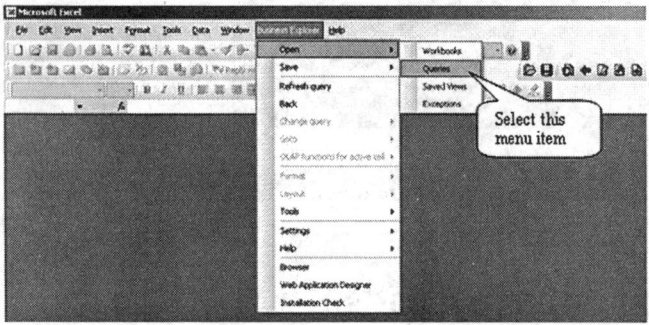

After *Queries* has been selected from the drop-down menu, the SAP Logon window will pop-up (Figure 13):

Figure 13

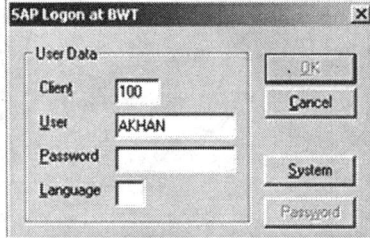

Copyright SAP AG

On Figure 13, enter:

- Client number (100 is the default that can be changed, if required)
- User ID
- Password

Note that, usually, the *Client* and *User ID* fields are auto-populated by the system. You can accept the defaults, for the *Client* and *User ID*, and only enter the password provided by the BW authorization group.

Observe that the *OK* button is grayed out on Figure 13. After you enter the required fields, the button will no longer be grayed out. After the field entries have been made:

- Click the *OK* button

This will lead to the next window (Figure 14):

Figure 14

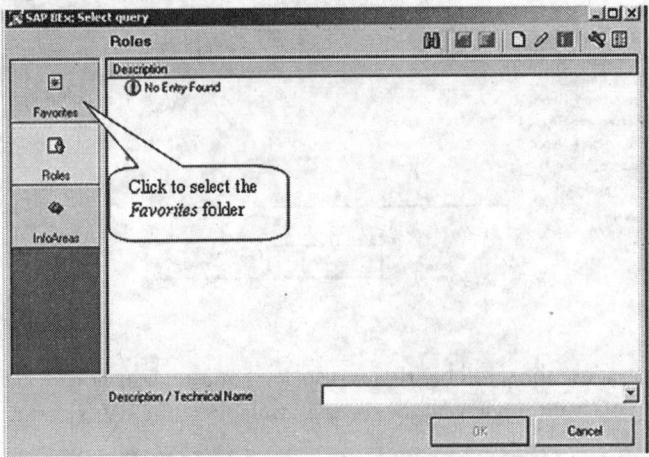

Copyright SAP AG

On Figure 14, the *Roles* button is highlighted. The "No Entry Found" text indicates either that no queries have been saved to a role or that authorization to save any role(s) has not been provided. If some roles had been defined, they would have been displayed in a tree structure similar to the one shown on Figure 6.

To display the queries which are available in the favorites folder:

- Click the *Favorites* button

This will lead to the next window, Figure 15, where the favorite reports are listed:

Figure 15

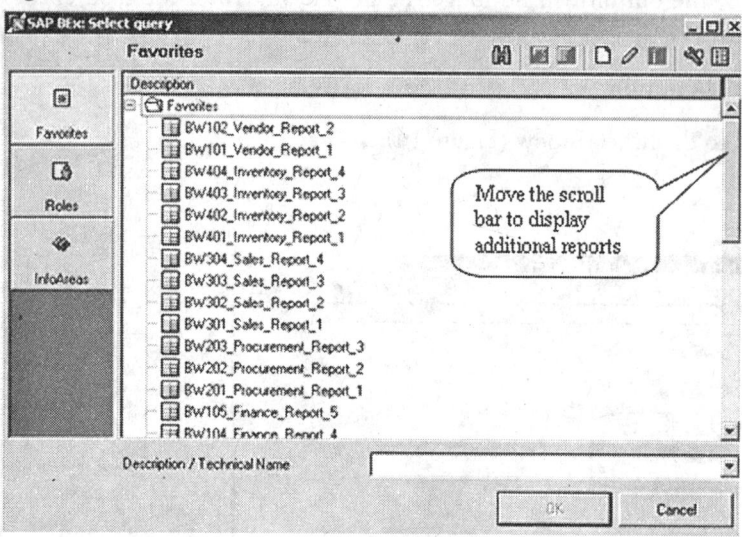

Copyright SAP AG

To view additional reports, use the scroll bar that is displayed on the right side of the window (Figure 15). If you want to view all the queries available in the BW system:

- Click the *InfoAreas* button

This will lead to Figure 16, where the InfoAreas button is highlighted:

Figure 16

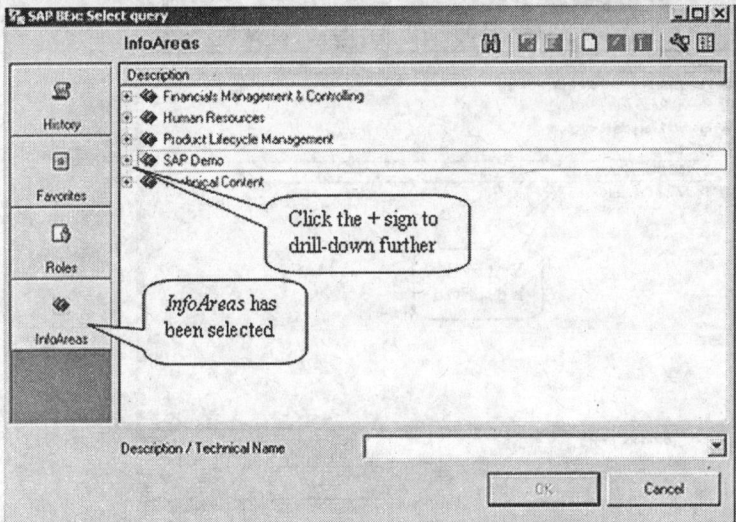

Copyright SAP AG

Note: InfoAreas are used to organize various BW objects, such as InfoProviders and InfoCubes, in a tree structure or directory. You will notice that Figure 15 has three buttons while Figure 16 has four buttons—the extra one being *History*. The difference can be attributed to the two figures being captured on different systems. Depending on the settings at your organization, either three or four buttons may be displayed.

Initially, only the top level node, under *Roles* or *Favorites*, is usually displayed. To view lower levels:

- Click the + sign next to the node, as highlighted on Figure 16

The next window, Figure 17, displays the next level in the InfoArea folder hierarchy after a drill-down on *SAP Demo*:

Figure 17

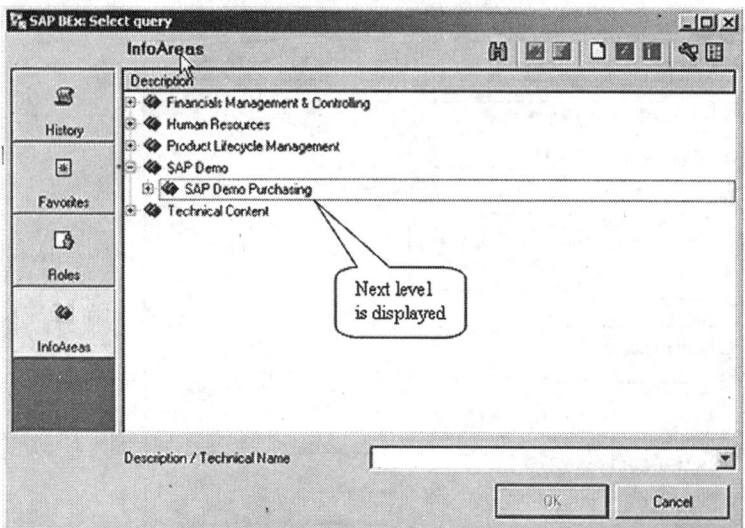

Copyright SAP AG

The next window, Figure 18, displays the results after further drilling has been performed:

Figure 18

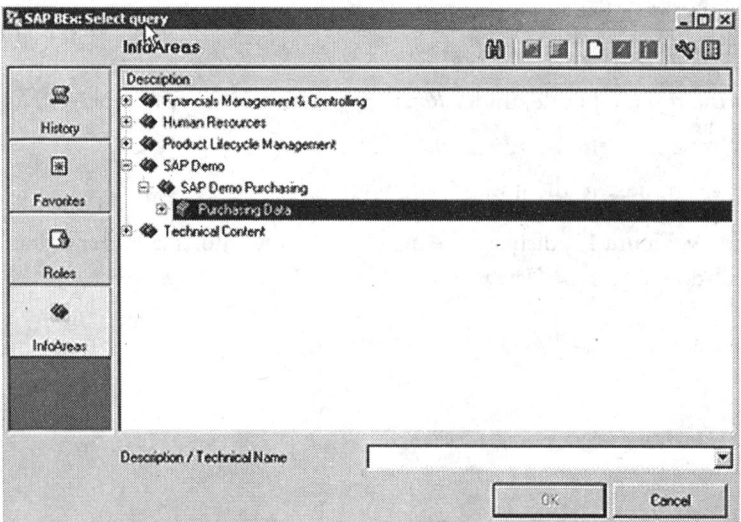

Copyright SAP AG

The drill-down process can continue until the lowest level folder is reached, where the reports contained in that folder will be displayed, as shown on Figure 19.

Figure 19

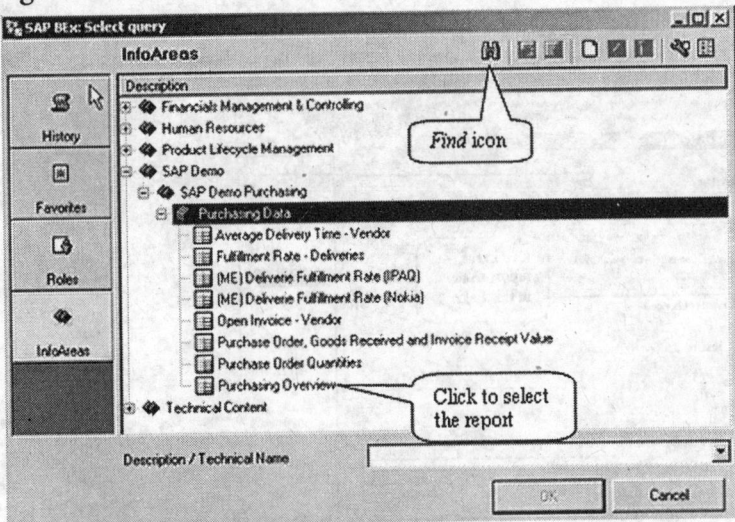

Copyright SAP AG

How to select a report for execution

To select a report:

- Navigate to the folder where the report is located
- Click the report

This action will highlight the report and select it. For example, to select the *Purchasing Overview* report:

- Click the report *Purchasing Overview*, as shown on Figure 19

How to find a report

To locate a report whose folder location is known, drill-down into the InfoArea folders step-by-step (down each level) until the desired report is displayed. If you do not know where a report is located, use the *Find* function for quick retrieval. To use this feature:

- Click the binoculars icon, which is highlighted on Figure 19

This will cause the *Search for Queries* window to pop-up (Figure 20):

Figure 20

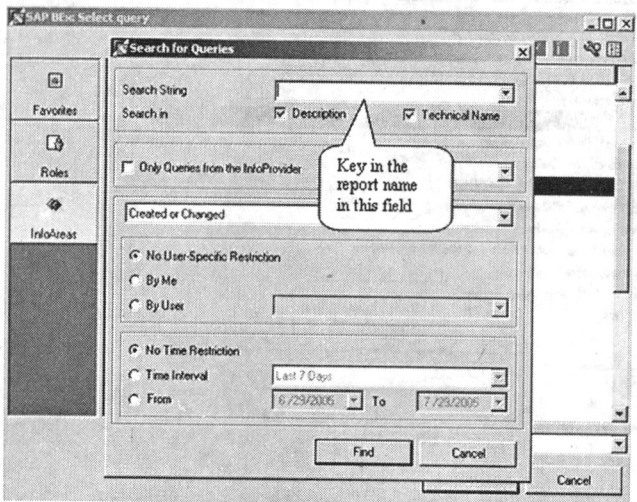

Copyright SAP AG

To find a report:

- Key in the report's name, or just a part of the name, in the *Search String* field, which is highlighted on Figure 20

To search for a report whose name includes the string *Procurement*:

- Type *Procurement* in the *Search String* field, as shown on Figure 21

Figure 21

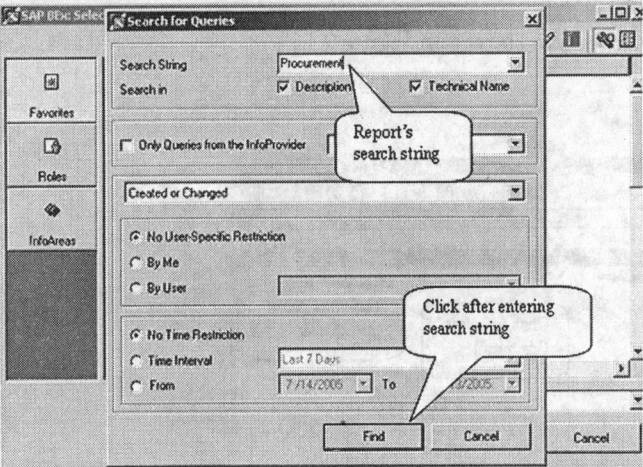

Copyright SAP AG

- Click the *Find* button

This will cause all the reports meeting the search criteria (*Procurement*) to be displayed, as shown on Figure 22, where three reports are listed:

Figure 22

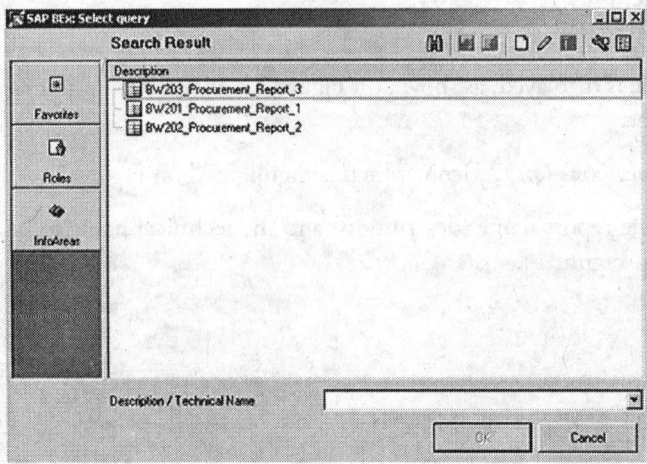

Copyright SAP AG

To select the *BW201_Procurement_Report_1* report:

- Click the desired report, as shown on Figure 23

Figure 23

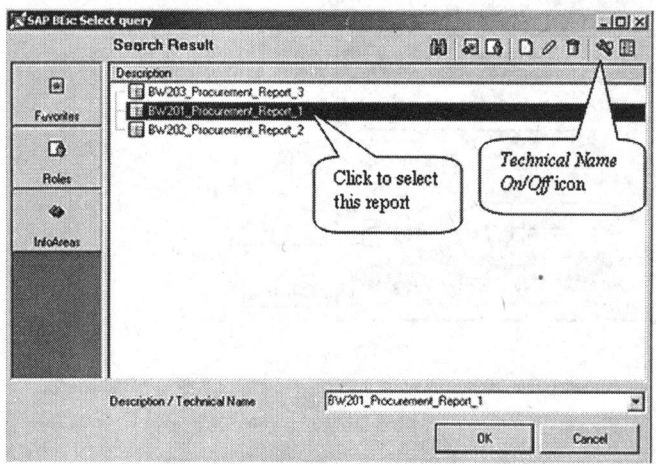

Copyright SAP AG

The reports which are listed can be displayed using two options:

- Text (report name) only
- Text and technical name

If only the report name is displayed, as shown on Figure 23, and you want to display the technical name:

- Click the *Technical Name On/Off* icon, which is highlighted on Figure 23

This will cause both the report name (description) and the technical name to be displayed, as shown on Figure 24.

Figure 24

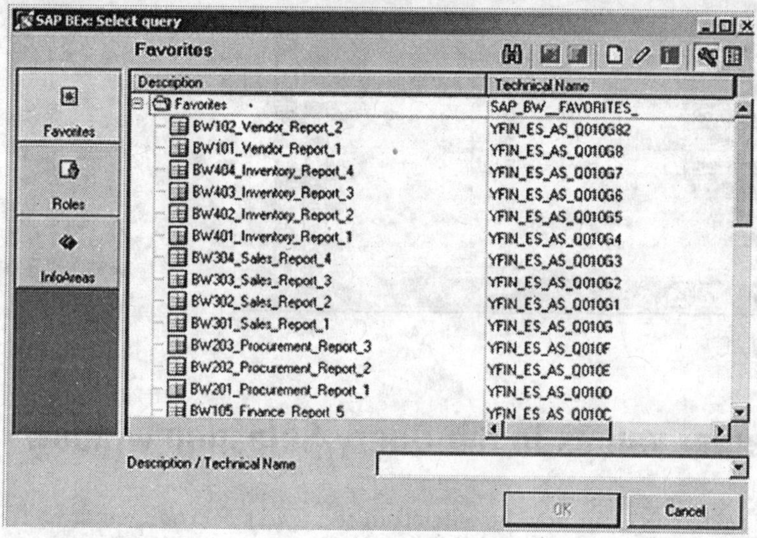
SAP BEx: Select query
Favorites
Description
Technical Name
Favorites
SAP_BW__FAVORITES_
BW102_Vendor_Report_2
YFIN_ES_AS_Q010G82
BW101_Vendor_Report_1
YFIN_ES_AS_Q010G8
BW404_Inventory_Report_4
YFIN_ES_AS_Q010G7
BW403_Inventory_Report_3
YFIN_ES_AS_Q010G6
BW402_Inventory_Report_2
YFIN_ES_AS_Q010G5
BW401_Inventory_Report_1
YFIN_ES_AS_Q010G4
BW304_Sales_Report_4
YFIN_ES_AS_Q010G3
BW303_Sales_Report_3
YFIN_ES_AS_Q010G2
BW302_Sales_Report_2
YFIN_ES_AS_Q010G1
BW301_Sales_Report_1
YFIN_ES_AS_Q010G
BW203_Procurement_Report_3
YFIN_ES_AS_Q010F
BW202_Procurement_Report_2
YFIN_ES_AS_Q010E
BW201_Procurement_Report_1
YFIN_ES_AS_Q010D
BW105 Finance Report 5
YFIN ES AS Q010C
Favorites
Roles
InfoAreas
Description / Technical Name
OK
Cancel

Copyright SAP AG

If the report's name as well as its technical name are being displayed, the technical name display can be suppressed. To remove the technical name from the display:

- Click the *Technical Name On/Off* icon

How to launch a selected report

To launch a report after it has been selected:

- Double-click on the selected report

This will cause a *Query Selection* window to pop-up (Figure 25):

Figure 25

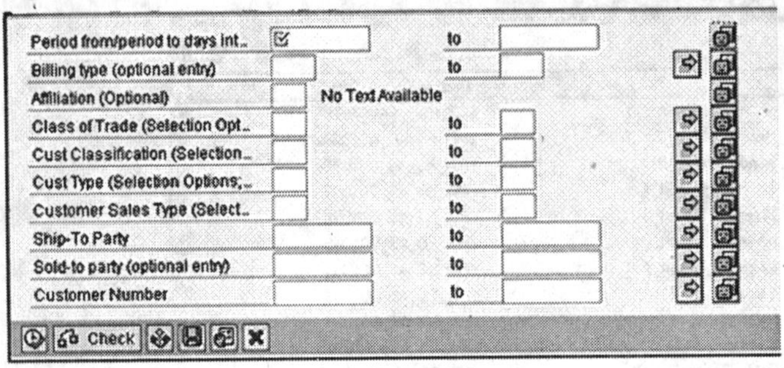

```
Period from/period to days int..  ☑           to
Billing type (optional entry)                  to
Affiliation (Optional)           No Text Available
Class of Trade (Selection Opt..                to
Cust Classification (Selection..               to
Cust Type (Selection Options;..                to
Customer Sales Type (Select..                  to
Ship-To Party                                  to
Sold-to party (optional entry)                 to
Customer Number                                to
```

Copyright SAP AG

How to enter values in the Query Selection window

Appropriate field values can now be entered in the *Query Selection* window. To make a field entry:

- Click on the field
- Type in the appropriate value for that field

The next window, Figure 26, shows entries that have been made in two fields (*Period from/period to days*), which will cause results for the January 1, 2005 to July 7, 2005 period to be returned when the report is executed:

Figure 26

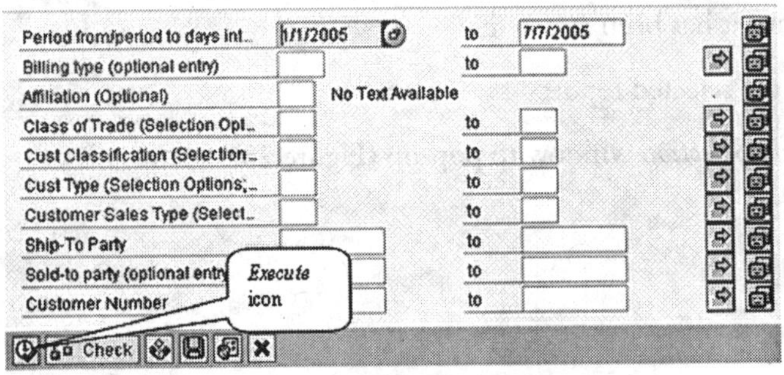

```
Period from/period to days int..  1/1/2005      to   7/7/2005
Billing type (optional entry)                   to
Affiliation (Optional)           No Text Available
Class of Trade (Selection Opt..                 to
Cust Classification (Selection..                to
Cust Type (Selection Options;..                 to
Customer Sales Type (Select..                   to
Ship-To Party                                   to
Sold-to party (optional entry)    Execute       to
Customer Number                   icon          to
```

Copyright SAP AG

The various features of the *Query Selection* window, and how to enter values in the appropriate fields, are explained in detail in subsequent sections of this chapter.

How to execute the report

The final step is report execution. To execute the report:

- *Enter the appropriate field values in the *Query Selection* window (Figure 26)
- Click the *Execute* icon

This will execute the report and display the results, an example of which is displayed on Figure 27.

Figure 27

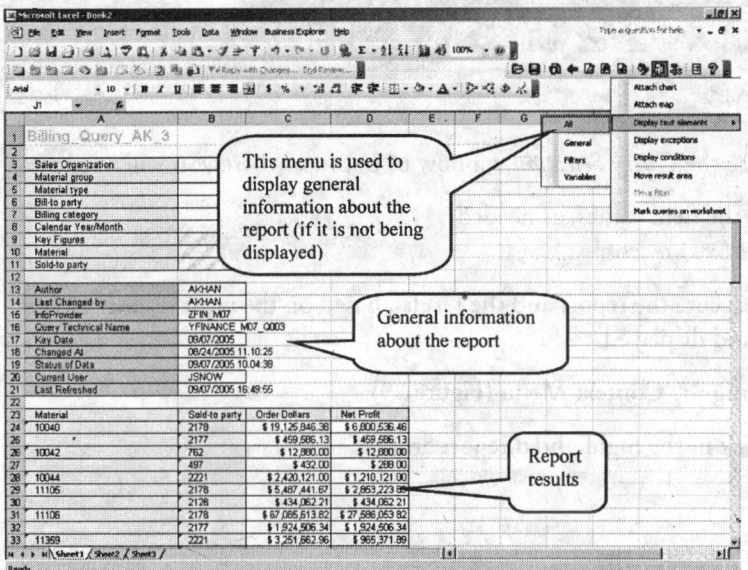

Copyright SAP AG

This Excel-based report contains various sections, which are explained in detail in Chapter 6.

How to refresh a report

The *Refresh* function is used to ensure that the report results are based on the latest available data. When this function is executed, the *Query Selection* window pops-up, where the input parameters (field values) can be re-entered and the report re-executed.

There are two methods for refreshing a report: using the BEx Toolbar or the Context Menu.

To refresh using the BEx Toolbar (Figure 28):

- Click the *Refresh* icon (third icon from the left on Figure 28)

Figure 28

Copyright SAP AG

This will cause the *Query Selection* window to pop-up, where you will need to:

- Re-enter the field values, as needed
- Click the *Execute* icon

This will re-execute the report and the results, based on the most recent data, will be retrieved and displayed.

To refresh using the Context Menu (Figure 29):

- Right-click in the highlighted report area

Figure 29

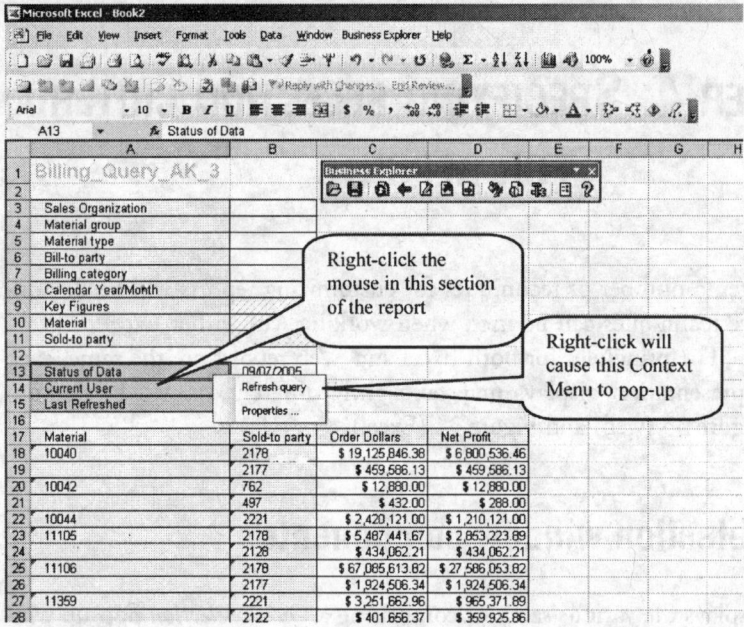

This will cause the Context Menu to pop-up, which is displayed on Figure 29:

- Select the menu item *Refresh Query*

This will cause the *Query Selection* window to pop-up, where you will need to:

- Re-enter the field values, as needed
- Click the *Execute* icon

This will re-execute the report and the results, based on the most recent data, will be retrieved and displayed.

CHAPTER 4: SPECIFYING SELECTION CRITERIA FOR REPORTS

In this chapter, a number of techniques for customizing reports will be demonstrated. These techniques can be used when working with either Excel or Web-based reports. The principles for both Excel and Web reports are the same, even though the presentation displays may be slightly different, as will be demonstrated on Figure 33 (web) and Figure 34 (Excel).

Query Selection window components

Figure 30 displays the various sections comprising a *Query Selection* pop-up window. The fields in this window can be populated in a number of ways, such as selecting variables from a drop-down menu, entering specific values in blank fields, and by overwriting default field values. Some default field values are auto-populated by the system. Depending on the reporting requirements, these values can either be left unchanged or modified before the report is executed.

Figure 30

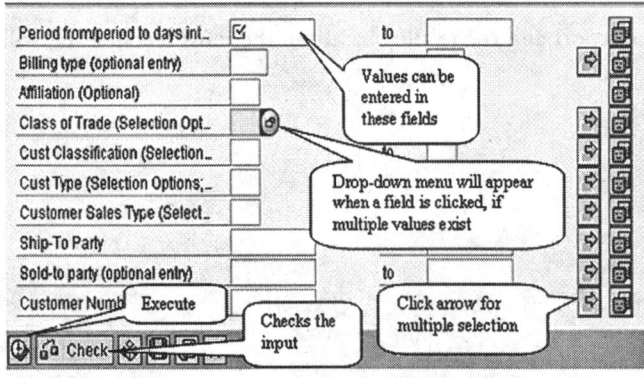

Copyright SAP AG

Minimum input requirements

A report can be executed after appropriate values have been entered in the input fields of the *Query Selection* window. All the fields on this window are optional, meaning that they need not be populated before a report is executed. The only exception applies to fields which are marked by an asterisk (*). Such fields are mandatory and must be populated before the report can be executed. On Figure 31, the *PO Doc Date* is a mandatory field and, therefore, must be populated before the report can be executed.

Figure 31

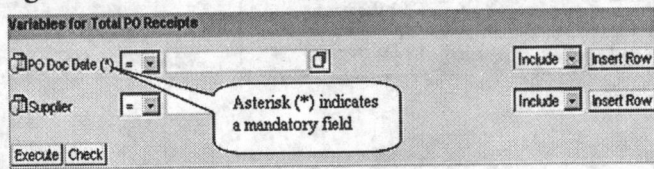

Copyright SAP AG

Entering values in the Query Selection window

Report results can be narrowed or broadened through the selective use of selection criteria or filters. Greater the number of fields that are filled before a report is executed, narrower will be the result. If all the available fields are left blank prior to report execution, the results will encompass all the available data relevant to the fields in the *Query Selection* window.

For example, suppose there are three fields in a *Query Selection* window: company code, buyer, and purchase orders. If all three fields are left blank before execution, the report will display all purchase orders for all buyers for all company codes. Now if a single value is entered in the company code field (100), the report will include all purchase orders for all buyers but only for company code 100. The results for all other company codes will be screened out.

The input fields should be used judiciously so that minimum data is displayed in the report. Limiting the results to the essential requirements enables faster query execution.

Using drop-down menus

Drop-down menus are used to view a field's possible values when entering field values prior to executing a query. All fields do not have a drop-down menu. If a drop-down box exists but is not being displayed, click in the appropriate field in order to display it. Suppose you want to view the values that can be selected for the *Department* field on Figure 32:

Figure 32

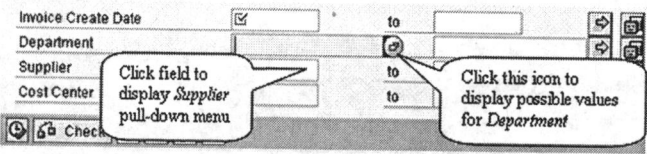

Copyright SAP AG

- Click the pull-down icon for the appropriate field (*Department*), which is highlighted on Figure 32

This will cause a window to pop-up, where the possible values for the selected field (*Department*) will be displayed. The next window, Figure 33, pops-up when the pull-down icon for the *Supplier* field is clicked.

Figure 33

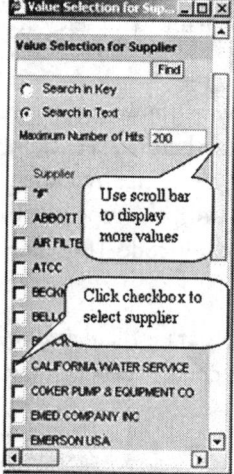

Copyright SAP AG

Figure 33 is displayed when the pull-down menu is clicked on the web (web-based report). The next window, Figure 34, is displayed when the pull-down menu is activated in Excel (Analyzer-based report). Since the same data is being accessed, the content is identical even though the displays differ slightly.

Figure 34

Copyright SAP AG

To select an item from a displayed list of values:

- Click the checkbox next to the item to be selected (on Figure 34, *California Water Service* has been selected)
- Click the checkmark, which is highlighted on Figure 34

This will populate the selected item, *California Water Service*, in the *Supplier* field on the *Query Selection* window.

Filters

A filter, by placing restrictions, enables data meeting certain conditions to be returned when a query is executed. Filters, which can be used to select individual values, supports a number of operators including equal to, greater than, less than, greater than or equal to, less than or equal to, and between. Usually, filters are used to limit the data returned by a query before applying analysis techniques on the report results.

Filters can be defined for the following:

- Include a single value
- Include a range of values
- Exclude a single value
- Exclude a range of values

These filters can determine which results are displayed in the report. It is recommended that filters be used to limit the data that is to be displayed. Subsequently, analytical functions can be performed on the displayed results. This process ensures that the report execution time is minimized.

How to specify include filters

To specify the values/ranges to be included or excluded in the report, click on the multiple selection value arrow that is associated with the appropriate field. For example, if you want to specify values and/or ranges for the *Supplier* field on Figure 35:

Figure 35

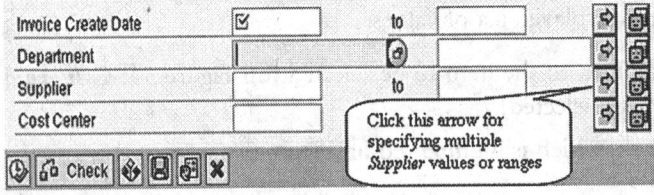

Copyright SAP AG

- Click the third multiple selection arrow, which is highlighted

This will lead to the next window (Figure 36):

Figure 36

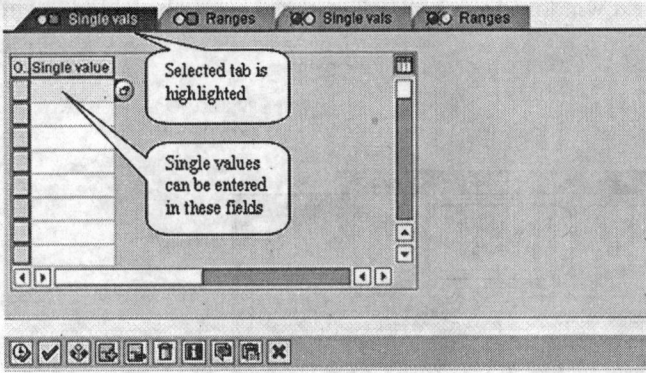

Copyright SAP AG

Notice that the *Single Value* tab is highlighted. On Figure 36, you can enter the single value(s) to be *included* when the query is executed.

- Enter three *Supplier* values that are to be included, as shown on Figure 37

Figure 37

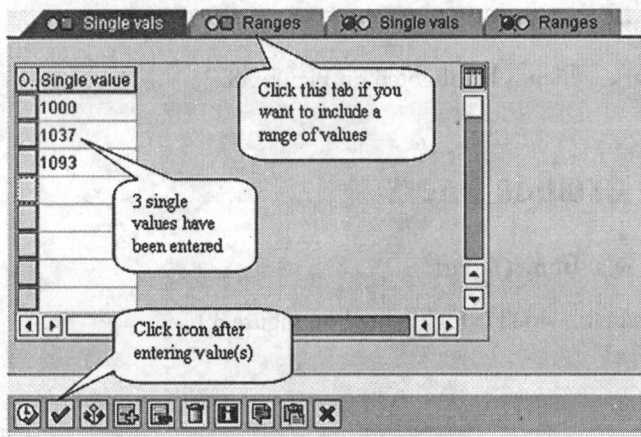

Copyright SAP AG

After entering the required value(s):

- Click the checkmark, which is highlighted on Figure 37

To specify a range to be included:

- Click the *Ranges* tab, as instructed on Figure 37

This will lead to the next window, Figure 38, where the ranges to be included can be specified:

Figure 38

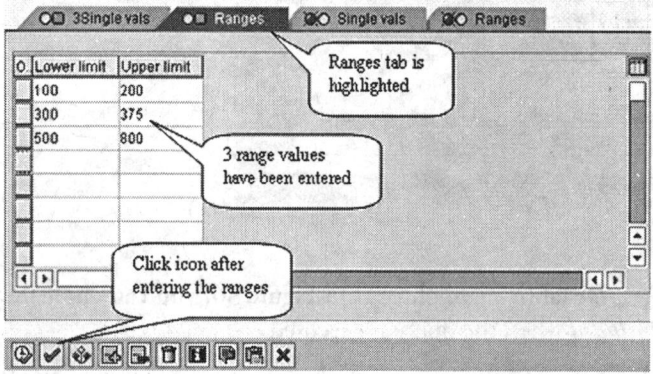

Copyright SAP AG

- Enter the ranges to be included in the report, as shown on Figure 38

After entering the required range(s):

- Click the checkmark, which is highlighted on Figure 38

How to specify exclude filters

To exclude a single value(s) from a report:

- Click the *Single vals* tab, which is highlighted on Figure 39

Figure 39

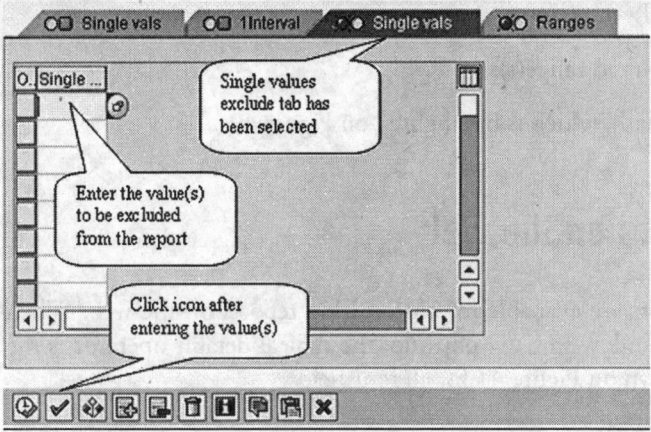

Copyright SAP AG

- Enter the value(s) to be excluded, as shown on Figure 39

After entering the required value(s):

- Click the checkmark, which is highlighted on Figure 39

To exclude a range (or ranges) from a report:

- Click the *Ranges* tab, which is highlighted on Figure 40

Figure 40

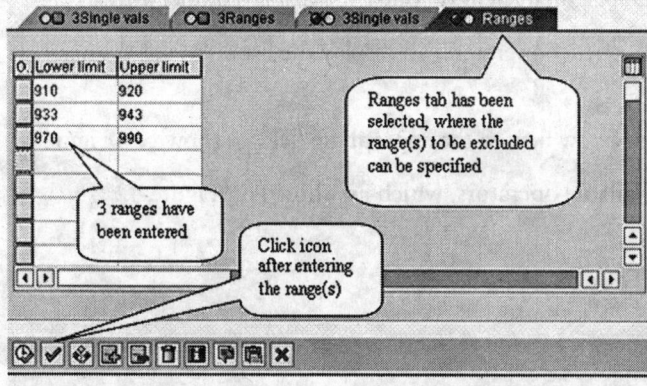

Copyright SAP AG

- Enter the range(s) to be excluded, as shown on Figure 40 (where three ranges have been entered)

After entering the required range(s):

- Click the checkmark, which is highlighted on Figure 40

Using operators on the web

A number of operators are available for customizing reports on the web. When the *Query Selection* window initially pops-up, the typical default operator is the equal (=) sign, as shown on Figure 41 for all four fields.

Figure 41

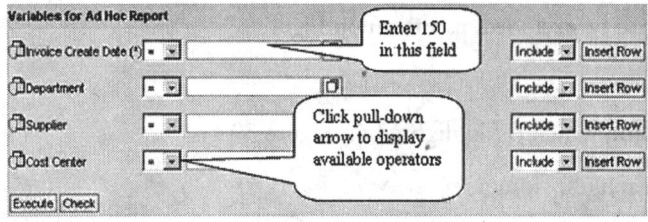

Copyright SAP AG

Suppose you want the report results to be limited to *Department 150*:

- Enter 150 in the Department field (because the displayed operator is "=")

It is also possible to select other operators. To display the list of available operators that can be selected:

- Click the pull-down arrow next to the appropriate field, as shown on Figure 41

This will display the available operators, which are shown on Figure 42.

Figure 42

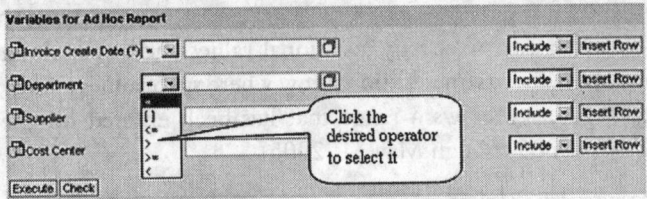

Copyright SAP AG

To select a particular operator on the displayed list:

- Click the desired operator

This will replace the previously selected operator (=) with the newly selected operator.

Suppose you want to analyze the results for all departments with numbers greater than 150:

- Enter 150 in the *Department* field
- Select the ">" operator, which is highlighted on Figure 42

Using include/exclude filters on the web

The *include/exclude* operators can be accessed in a different way on the web. A pull-down menu, which is highlighted on Figure 43, is used to specify and select the include and exclude functions. The default function is *include*, which can be changed to *exclude* by selecting it from the drop-down menu.

Figure 43

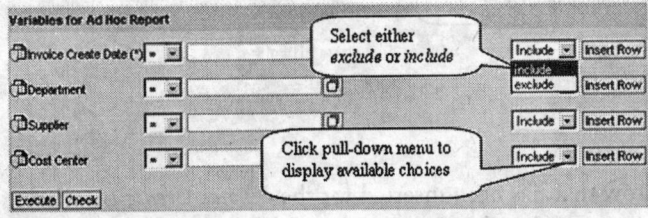

Copyright SAP AG

Adding values and ranges on the web

The *Insert Row* button can be used to specify additional values and/or ranges in the *Query Selection* window. It inserts an additional row where such values and/or ranges can be entered. Figure 44 shows a range that has been entered for the *Invoice Create Date* (May 1, 2005 though May 31, 2005).

Figure 44

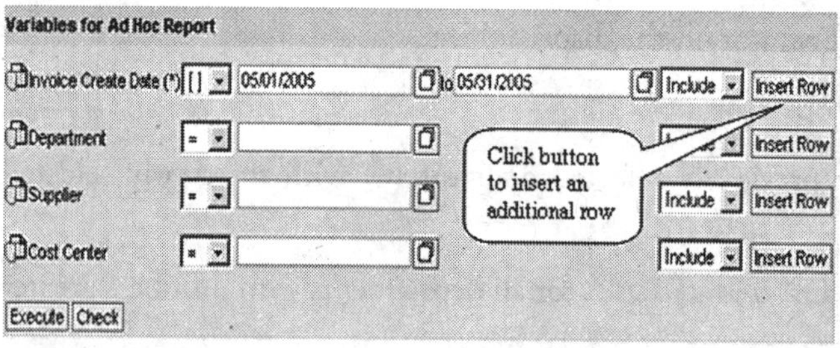

Copyright SAP AG

Now suppose you want to specify another date for inclusion in the report (in addition to the previously specified date range: May 01, 2005 though May 31, 2005):

- Click the *Insert Row* button, as shown on Figure 44

This will lead to the next window (Figure 45).

Figure 45

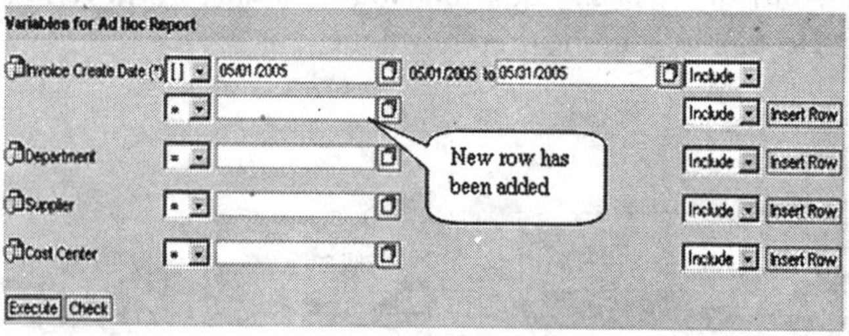

Copyright SAP AG

Notice the additional row that has been inserted for the *Invoice Create Date* field. Suppose you want to enter another date, April 30, 2005, that is to be included in the report:

- Enter the desired date (4/30/2005) in the appropriate field, as shown on Figure 46

Figure 46

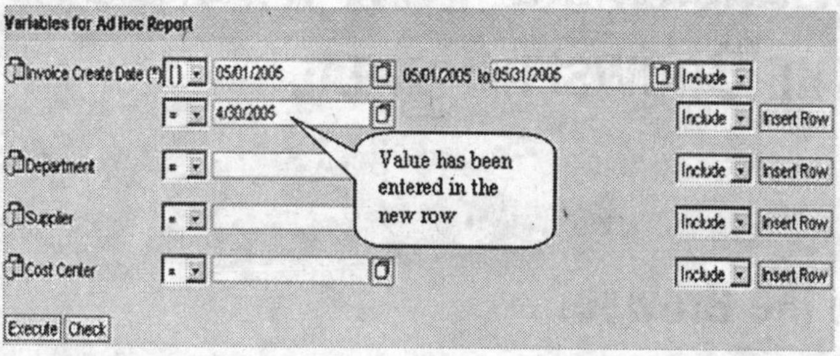

Variables for Ad Hoc Report				
Invoice Create Date (*) [ ] ▼	05/01/2005	📅 05/01/2005 to 05/31/2005	📅	Include ▼
	= ▼ 4/30/2005	📅 *(Value has been entered in the new row)*		Include ▼ Insert Row
Department	= ▼			Include ▼ Insert Row
Supplier	= ▼			Include ▼ Insert Row
Cost Center	= ▼	📅		Include ▼ Insert Row
Execute Check				

Copyright SAP AG

After the field value has been entered:

- Click the *Execute* button

CHAPTER 5: LAUNCHING A BW REPORT VIA THE BROWSER/PORTAL

How to launch the Browser

To launch the BEx Browser, navigate via the Windows menu, Figure 47, using the following menu path:

- Start > Programs > Business Explorer > Browser

Figure 47

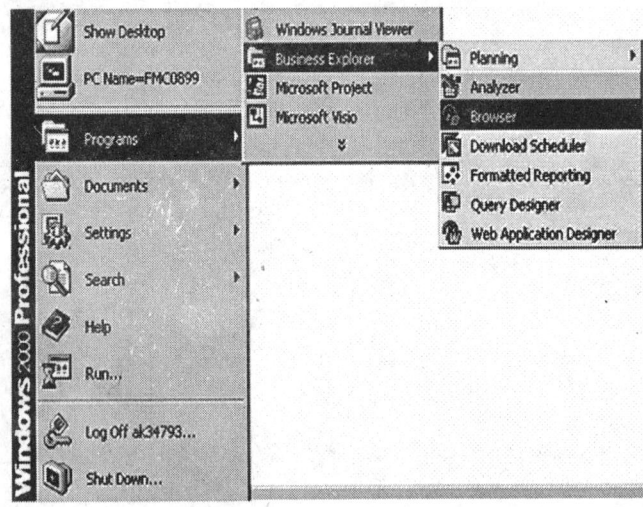

This will lead to the following SAP Logon pop-up window (Figure 48):

Figure 48

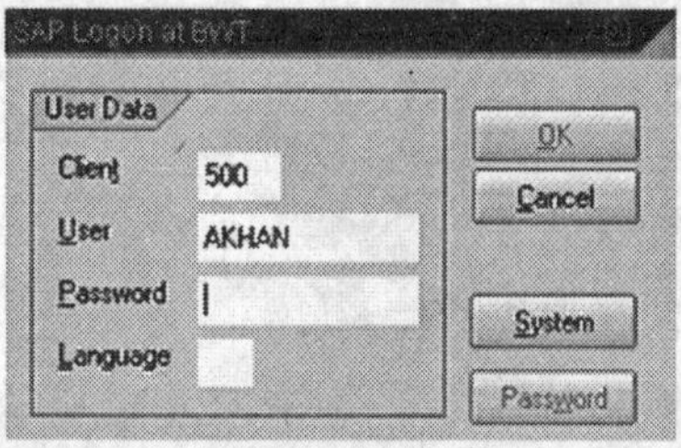

Copyright SAP AG

On Figure 48, enter:

- Client number (500 is the default that can be changed, if required)
- User ID
- Password

Note that, usually, the *Client* and *User ID* fields are auto-populated by the system. You can accept the defaults, for the *Client* and *User ID*, and only enter the password provided by the BW authorization group.

Observe that the *OK* button is grayed out on Figure 48. After you enter the required fields, the button will no longer be grayed out. After the field entries have been made:

- Click the *OK* button

This will lead to the next window, Figure 49, where the Browser is displayed:

Browser windows

The Browser window includes the following components, which are highlighted on Figure 49:

- Browser Toolbar
- Main window, on the right, where the queries are displayed
- Smaller window, on the left, where the *Roles and Favorites* are displayed
- *Find* window (small box located in the bottom left corner)

Figure 49

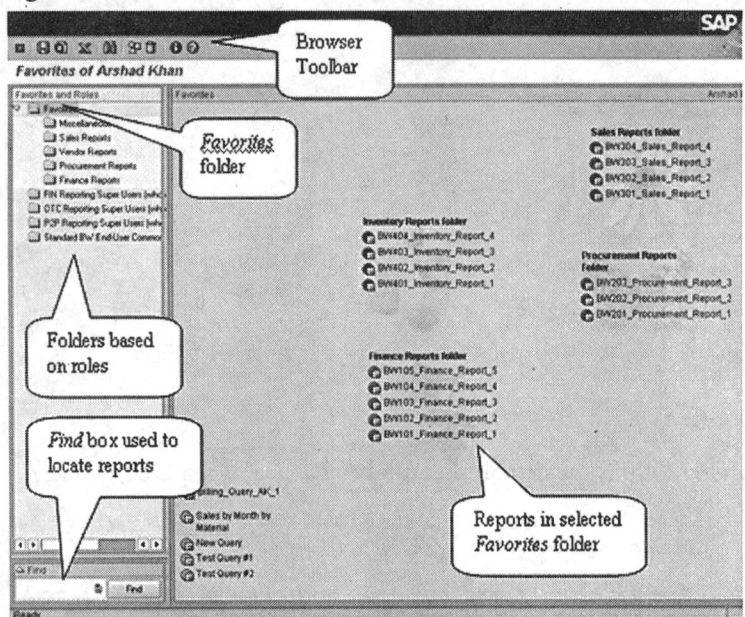

Copyright SAP AG

Browser Toolbar

The Browser window contains a toolbar, Figure 50, which can be used to execute a number of functions.

Figure 50

Copyright SAP AG

The Browser Toolbar icons, shown on Figure 50, represent the following functions from left to right: Exit, Save, Refresh, Start BEx Analyzer, Find, New Folder, Delete, Information (BW Browser), and Help.

How to navigate to a specific report

The BEx Browser can be used to navigate to the desired report(s). To navigate to a particular report:

- Click the appropriate folder in the *Favorites and Roles* window

This will display the reports contained in the selected folder in the main Browser window (located on the right-hand side). On Figure 51, the *Miscellaneous Reports* folder has been selected and the reports contained in it are displayed in the right-hand window.

Figure 51

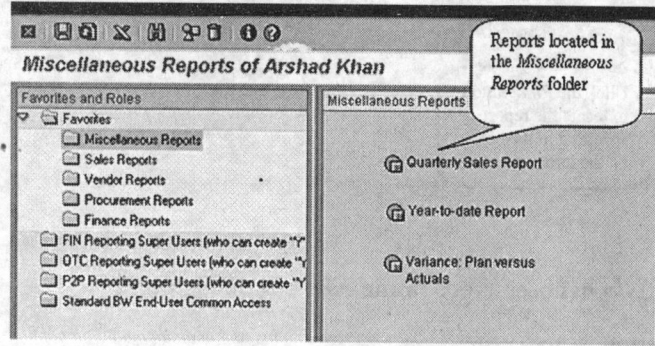

Copyright SAP AG

If the desired report is not located in the selected folder, click on another folder to display the reports contained in it. This process can be continued until the desired report is displayed. Since this can be a tedious process, another method for quickly locating a report is explained in the next section.

How to find a report

An efficient method for finding a report uses the *Find* function. To quickly locate a report:

- In the *Find* box, enter the text (string) or number that is contained in the report title, as shown on Figure 52

Figure 52

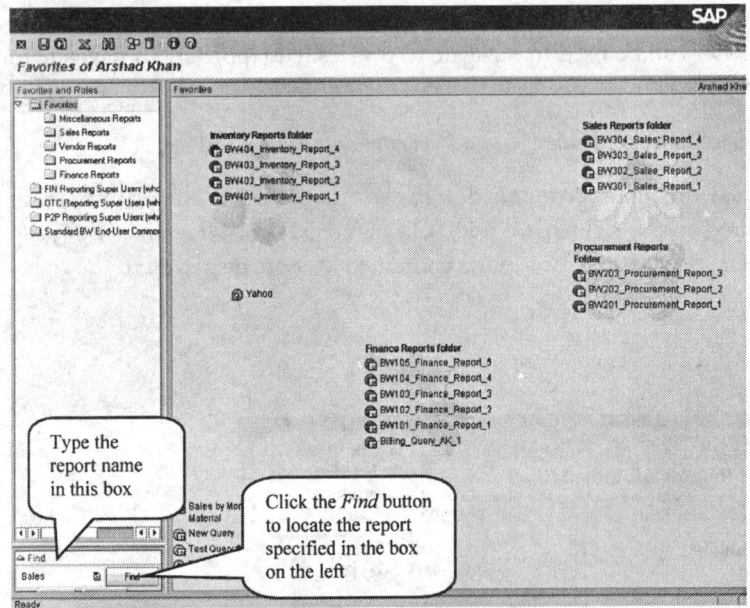

Copyright SAP AG

Notice that the word *Sales* has been typed in the *Find* box on Figure 52.

- Click the *Find* button

This will cause all the reports meeting the search criteria (*Sales* in the report title) to be listed, as shown on Figure 53.

Figure 53

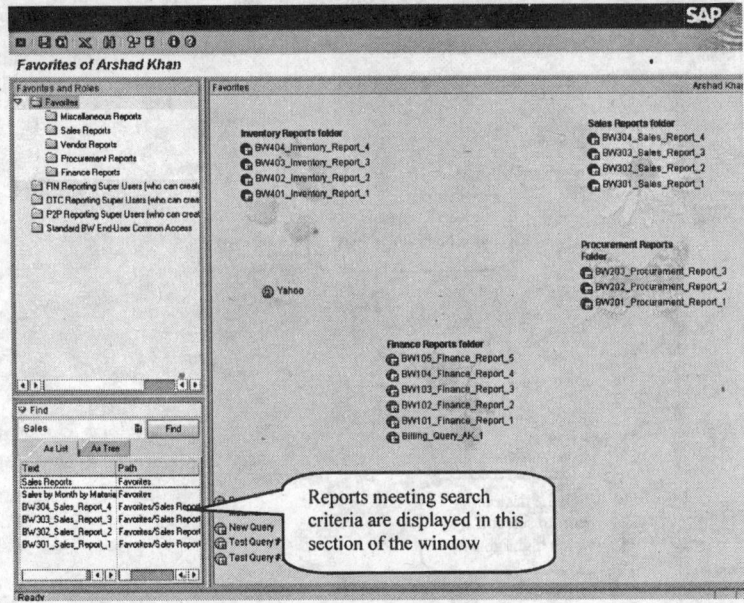

Copyright SAP AG

How to select a report for execution

To select a report that is displayed in the main Browser window or in the *Find* box:

- Click the desired report

This will select the report shown on Figure 54, where *BW303_Sales_Report_3* has been selected.

Figure 54

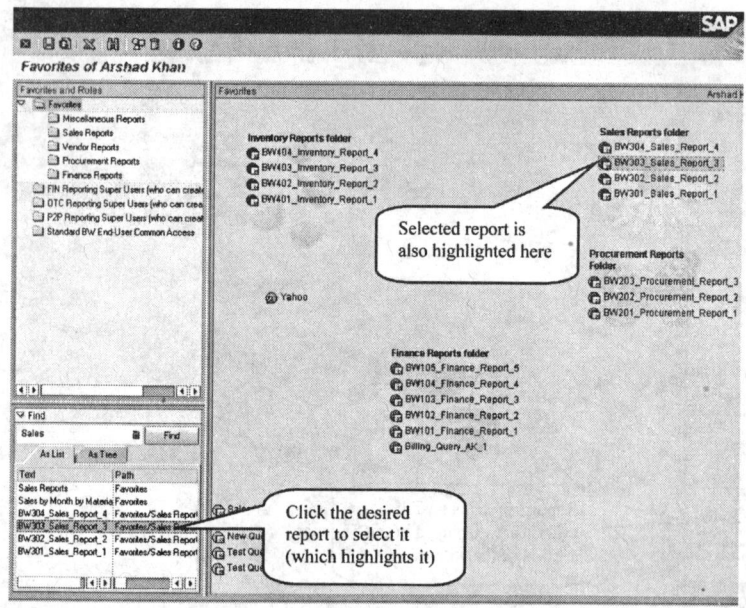

Copyright SAP AG

How to launch a selected report

To launch a report in the BEx Browser:

- Double-click the selected report

This will typically cause the *Query Selection* window to pop-up, where the appropriate field selections/entries will need to be made before the report can be executed.

Figure 55

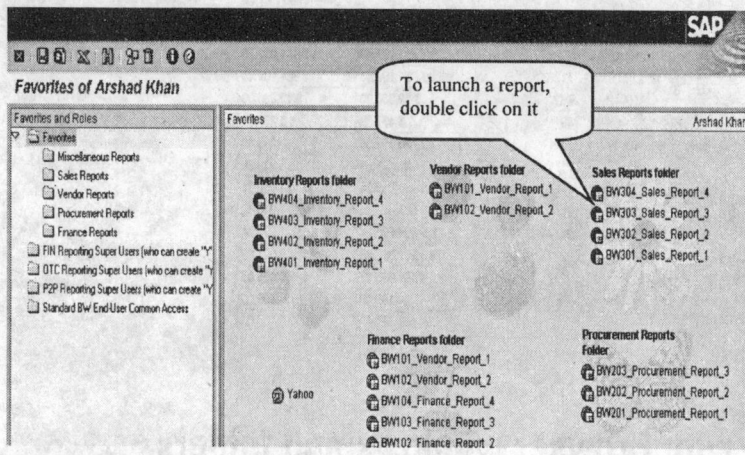

Copyright SAP AG

How to specify the selection criteria for a report

The selection criteria for a report executed via the BEx Browser can be specified in the same manner as demonstrated in Chapter 4. The reason is that the same principles apply for various techniques such as specifying filters, excluding and/or including values and ranges, using drop-down menus, etc.

How to execute a report

After the appropriate entries have been made in the *Query Selection* window, the report is ready to be executed. To execute the report:

- Click the *Execute* icon

Based on the input selection and filter criteria used, the report results will be displayed. The following is an example of the resulting report that is displayed on the web (Figure 56):

Figure 56

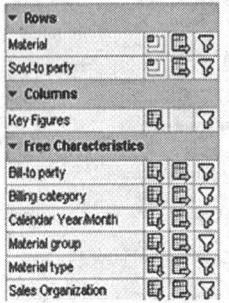

Copyright SAP AG

Working with Browser windows and folders

The Context Menu is the primary tool that is used for working with Browser folders. It can be activated by right-clicking the mouse. Some of the tasks that can be performed by the Context Menu in the Browser include:

- Managing folders (creating, renaming, and deleting)
- Moving and grouping reports
- Moving reports among folders
- Changing background themes
- Saving reports to favorites

In this chapter, various Browser functions will be demonstrated, using Figure 57 as the starting point.

Figure 57

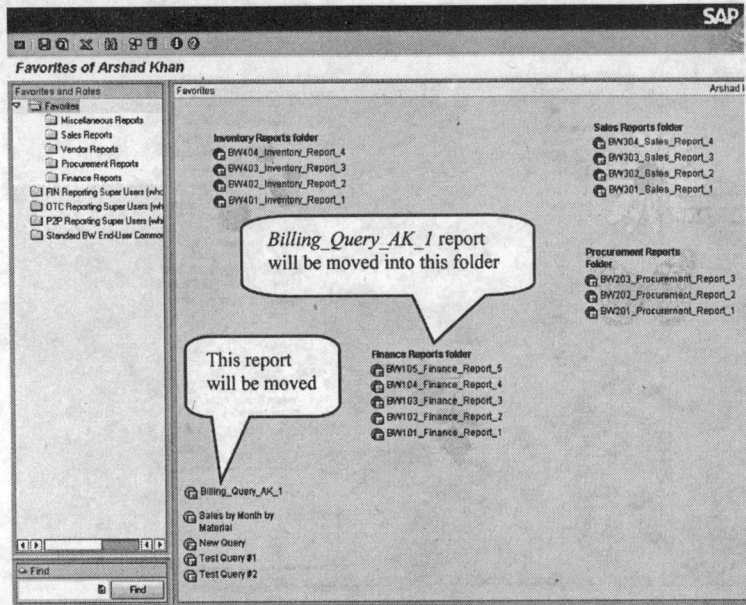

Copyright SAP AG

Moving and organizing reports

We will now move the report *Billing_Query_AK_1*, from its highlighted location on Figure 57, to the *Finance Reports folder*. To move the report:

- Drag and drop the report, using the mouse, to the desired location

Figure 58 highlights the report's new location.

Figure 58

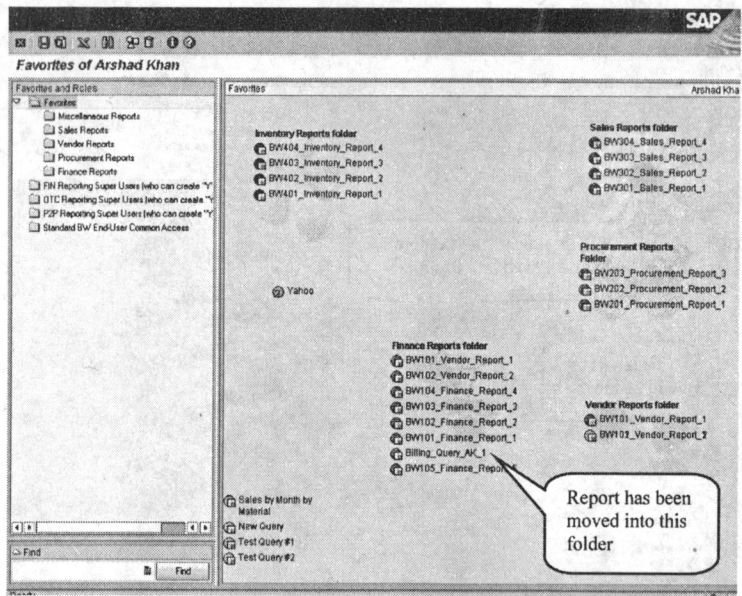

Copyright SAP AG

Enhancing displays

We will now change the background symbol for the *Procurement Reports folder* (Figure 59).

Figure 59

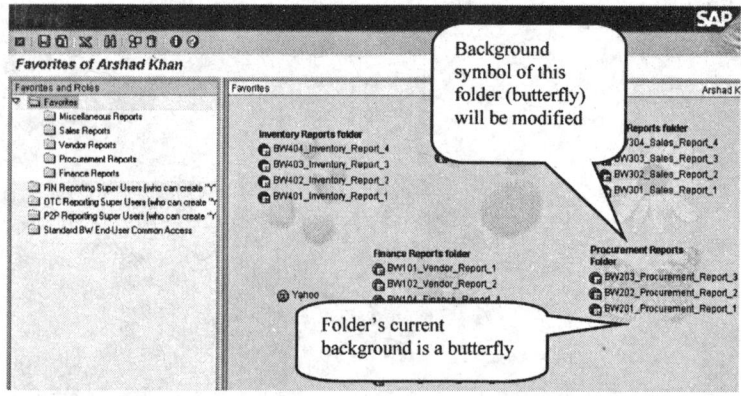

Copyright SAP AG

- Right-click anywhere in the Butterfly area of the *Procurement Reports folder*

This will activate the Context Menu, which is shown on Figure 60:

Figure 60

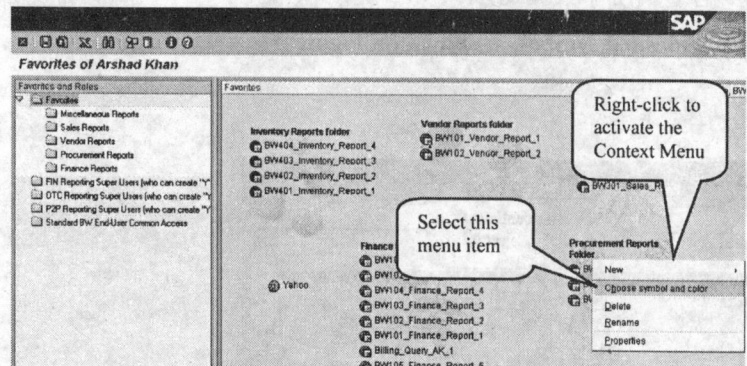

Copyright SAP AG

- Select the menu item *Choose symbol and color*

This will cause a window to pop-up, which is displayed on Figure 61.

Figure 61

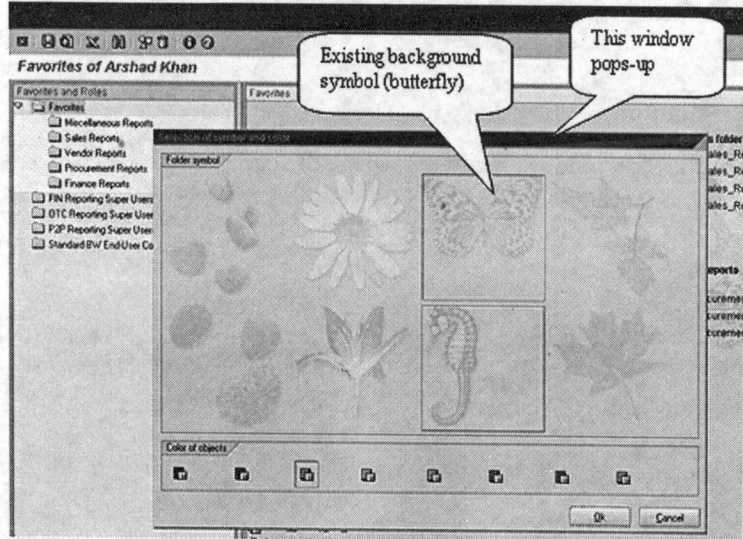

Copyright SAP AG

Note that the butterfly symbol, the current setting, is highlighted by the square box.

To select the new symbol, *Sunflower*, which is located to the left of the butterfly symbol:

- Click the *Sunflower* symbol (Figure 62)

This will select the desired symbol, as shown on Figure 62:

Figure 62

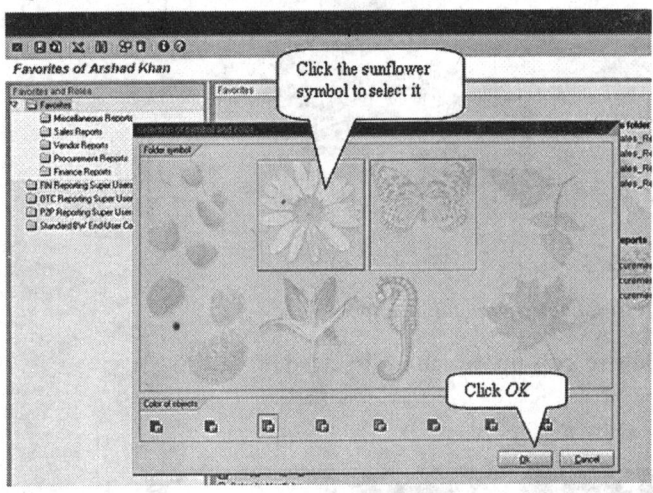

Copyright SAP AG

- Click the *OK* button

This will lead to the next window, Figure 63, where the background has changed from the butterfly to the sunflower.

Figure 63

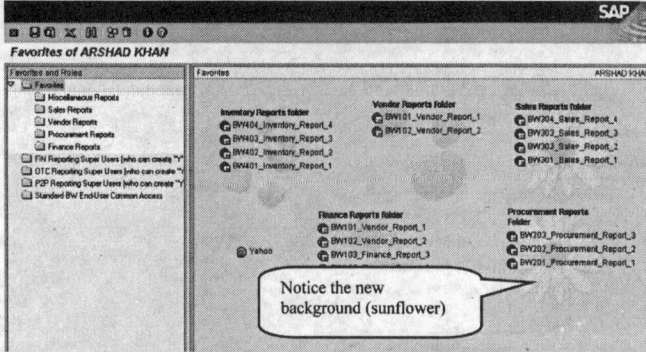

Copyright SAP AG

Adding an Internet address

We will now add an internet URL to the following Browser window (Figure 64):

Figure 64

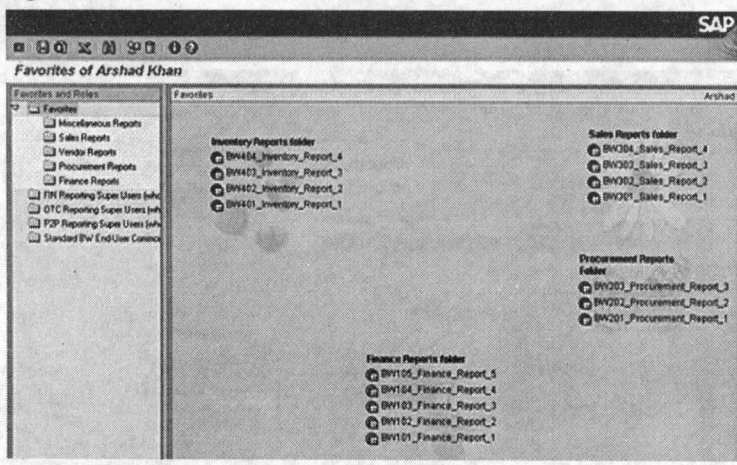

Copyright SAP AG

- Right-click in the Browser window

This will activate the Context Menu, which is shown on Figure 65.

Figure 65

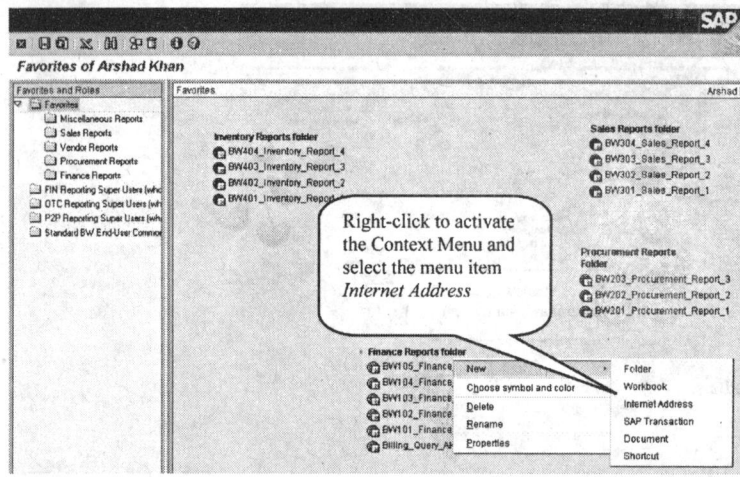

Copyright SAP AG

- Navigate via the menu path *New > Internet Address*, as shown on Figure 65

This will cause the *Properties* window to pop-up, as shown on Figure 66.

Figure 66

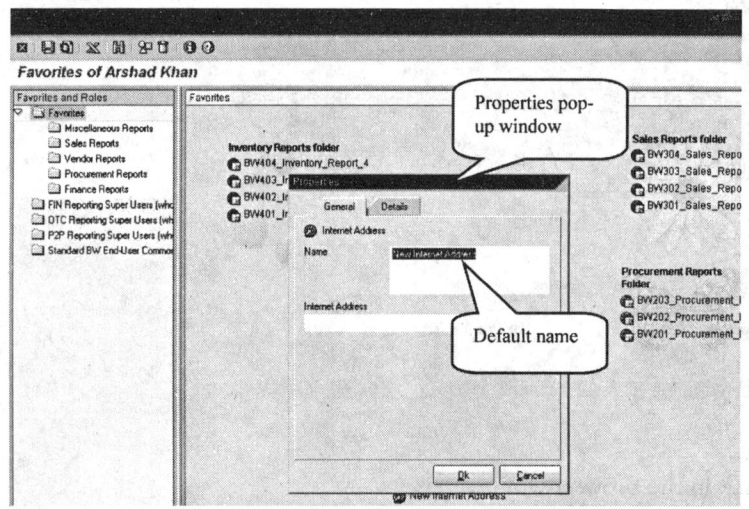

Copyright SAP AG

As shown on Figure 67:

- Enter the *Name* (*Yahoo*)
- Enter the *Internet Address* (*www.yahoo.com*)

Figure 67

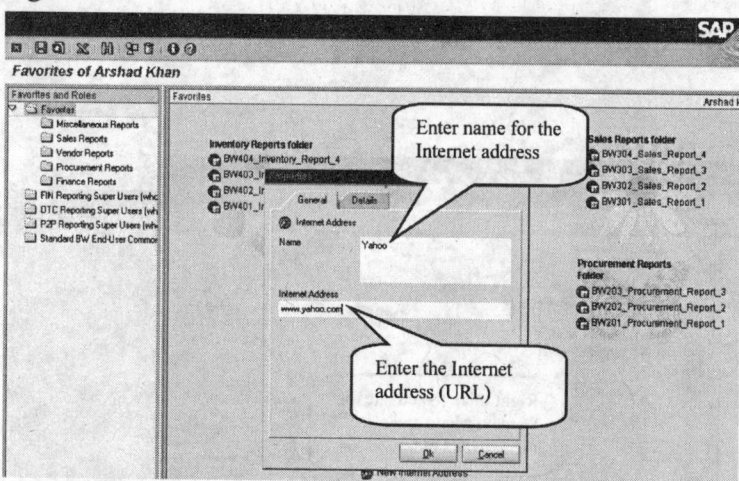

Copyright SAP AG

- Click the *OK* button

This will add the *Yahoo* URL to the Browser window, as shown on Figure 68.

Figure 68

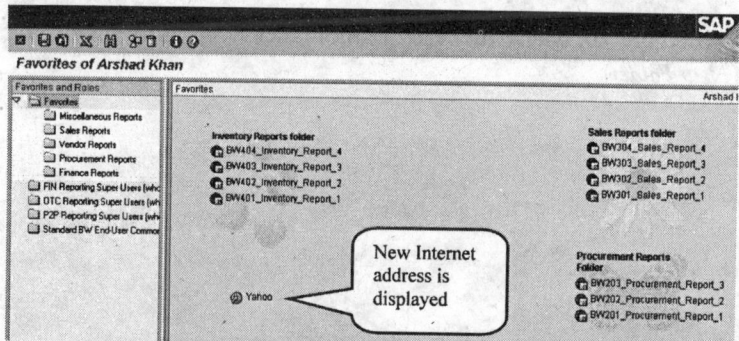

Copyright SAP AG

Creating a new folder

We will now add a new folder in the Browser window. To start the process:

- Right-click anywhere in the Browser window

This will cause the Context Menu to pop-up, as shown on Figure 69.

Figure 69

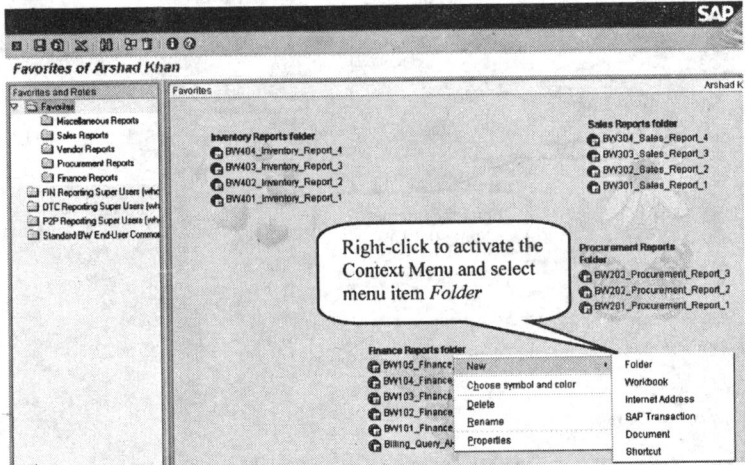

Copyright SAP AG

- Navigate via the menu path *New > Folder*, as shown on Figure 69

This will lead to Figure 70, where the system automatically provides the default folder name (*New Folder*).

Figure 70

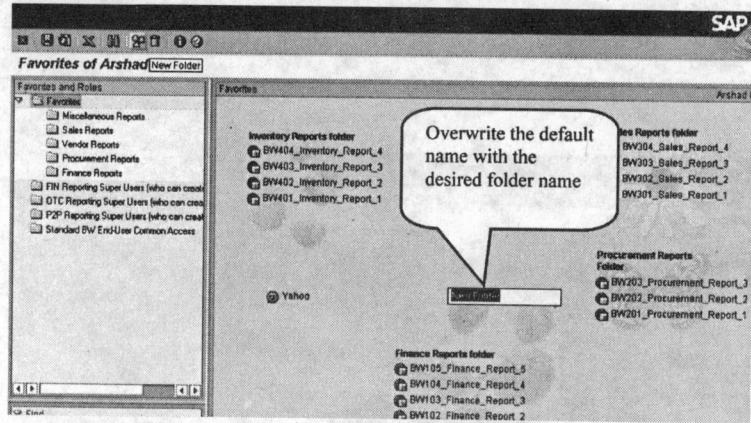

Copyright SAP AG

- Overwrite the default *New Folder* name with the desired folder name

Deleting a folder

We will now delete a folder. To start the process:

- Right-click on the folder to be deleted

This will cause the Context Menu to pop-up, as shown on Figure 71.

Figure 71

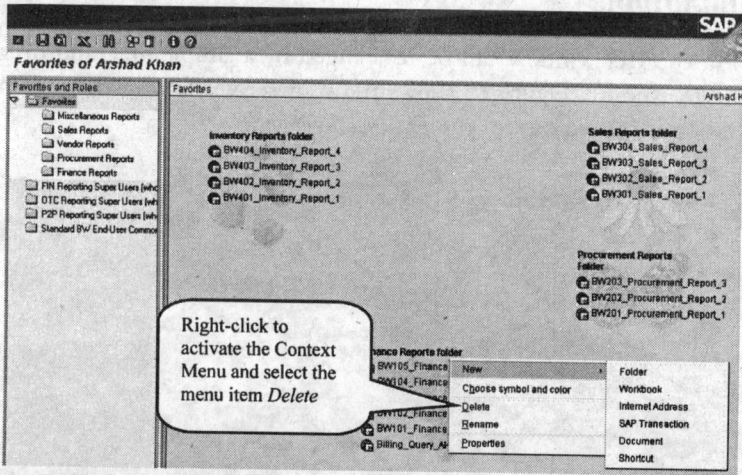

Copyright SAP AG

- Select the menu item *Delete*

This will cause a warning pop-up box to appear, as shown on Figure 72.

Figure 72

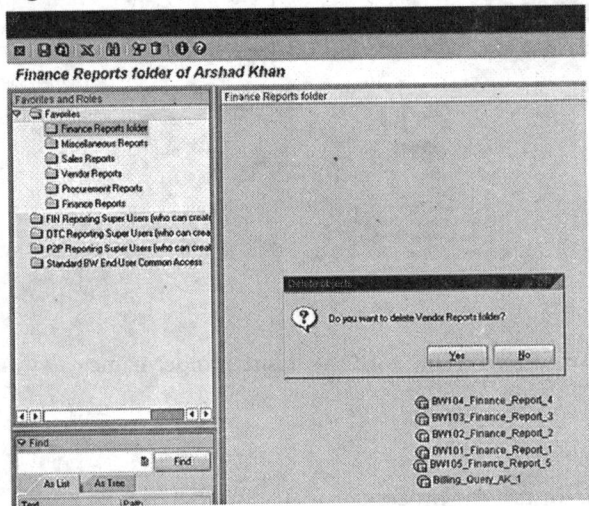

Copyright SAP AG

- Click the *Yes* button to delete

Rearranging groups

The groups in a Browser window can be rearranged by a simple drag and drag operation using the mouse. Figure 73 shows the Browser window before a drag and drop operation is carried out for the *Finance Reports folder*.

Figure 73

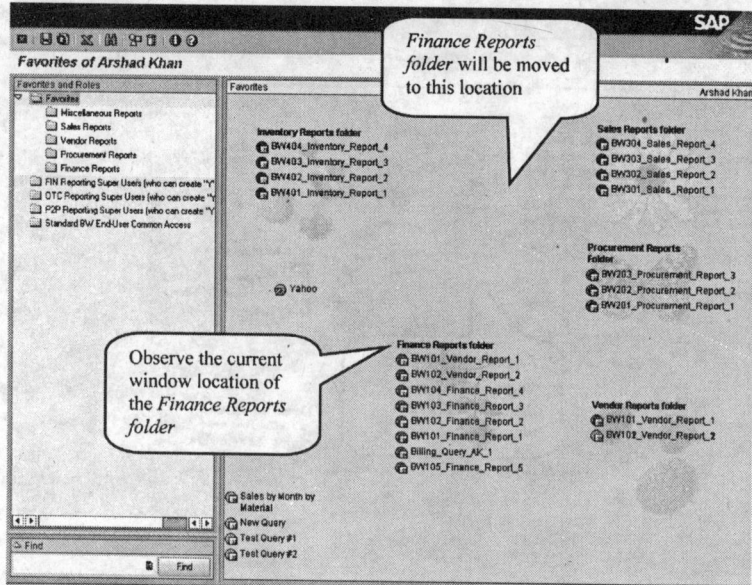

Copyright SAP AG

- Use the mouse to drag the *Finance Reports folder* to the top of the window area (between inventory and sales reports).

After the drag and drop operation has been completed, the window display will be as shown on Figure 74:

Figure 74

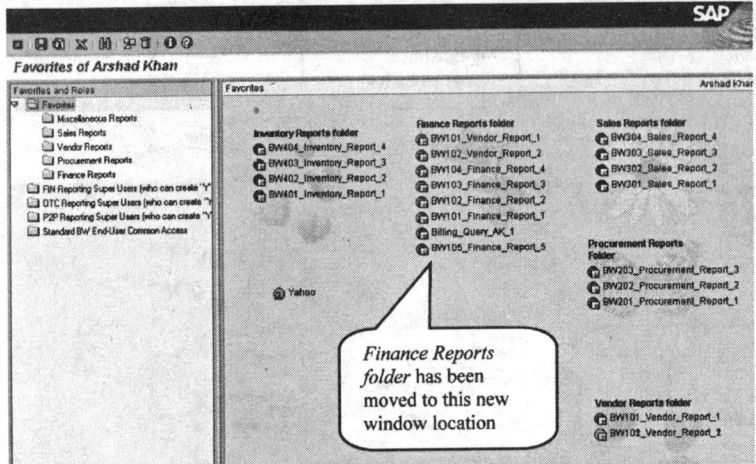

Copyright SAP AG

How to access BW reports via the Portal

The Portal appearance, i.e., its look and feel as well as content, at every company is different as it is customized to reflect the organization's own unique applications and requirements. The commonly used method to access BW reports via the Portal involves the following steps:

- Launch the Internet Explorer browser
- Enter the portal User ID
- Enter the password

This will lead the user to the portal's welcome page. In some cases, a link is provided to the BW reports. In others, the BW reports menu is listed on the portal's welcome page. These reports are typically organized by functions such as Finance, Human Resources, Purchasing, Sales, Purchase-to-Pay, Order-to-Cash, etc. To access and execute a report, a user has to:

- Click on the appropriate top-level report folder
- Drill-down into the sub-folders, if they exist, until the desired report is found
- Double-click to execute the report

CHAPTER 6: ANATOMY OF EXCEL AND WEB REPORTS

Excel and web-based reports access the same BW data. However, they display the reports somewhat differently. Also, the techniques used for navigation and analysis can vary. In this chapter, the various components of Excel and web-based reports are identified and described.

Excel report anatomy

An Excel report contains the following elements, which are highlighted on Figure 75:

- Report title: This identifies the report name
- Drill-down characteristics: These are the slice and dice elements, which can be used to analyze the report in greater depth though various techniques
- Results Area: This is the section where the report results are displayed
- BEx Toolbar: An additional toolbar that is displayed when the BEx Analyzer is activated

Figure 75

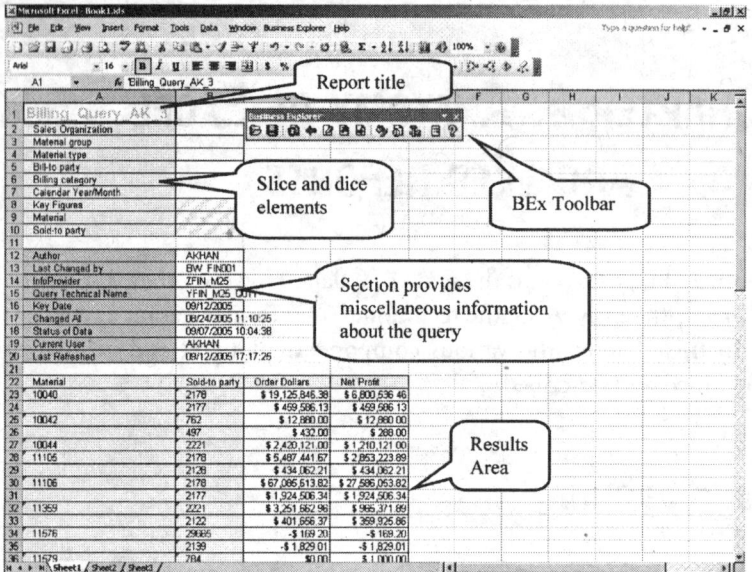

Web report anatomy

A BW web report contains the following elements, which are highlighted on Figure 76:

- Report title: This identifies the report name
- Drill-down characteristics: These are the slice and dice elements, which can be used to analyze the report in greater depth though various techniques
- Results Area: This is the area where the report results are displayed
- Web Toolbar: An additional toolbar that is displayed when viewing web reports

The Generic Navigation Block, located above the Results Area, is a powerful tool that can be used to analyze the displayed results, using various techniques such as drill-down and drill-across, filtering, etc.

Figure 76

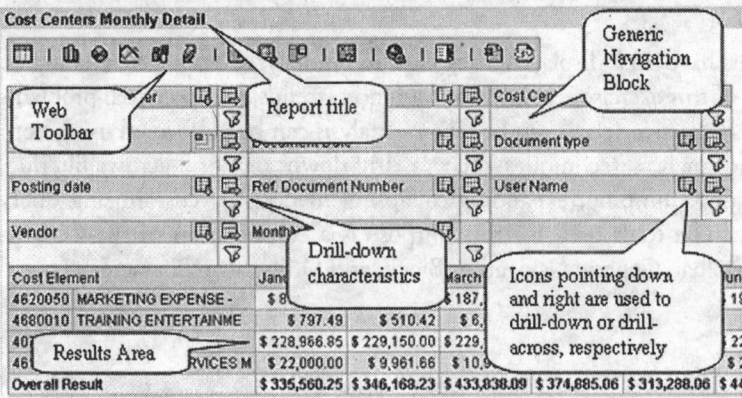

Copyright SAP AG

Web report displays are often customized and, hence, can vary from one project implementation site to another, even though their basic functionality is the same. Figure 77 displays a different version of a web report, where the Generic Navigation Block is located on the left-hand side of the window.

Figure 77

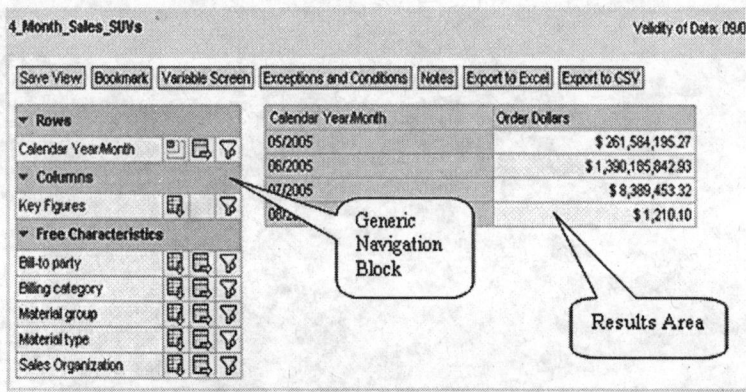

Copyright SAP AG

How to analyze BW (Excel and Web) reports

After the results have been displayed, they need to be analyzed from different angles. The objective of this exercise is to identify variances, trends, and potential problems so that timely corrective action can be taken. Analysis can be performed using both navigation and analysis techniques such as drill-down and drill-across, filtering, swapping, sorting, jumping, expanding/collapsing hierarchies, customizing query properties, etc. The tools used for this purpose is a combination of the Context Menu, Web Toolbar, Generic Navigation Block, and Drill-down Characteristics.

Chapter 7: Analyzer Tools and Techniques

BEx Toolbar

The BEx Toolbar, Figure 78, is an additional toolbar that is displayed when the BEx Analyzer is launched. It is a versatile tool that can be used to perform both navigation and analysis functions. The BEx Toolbar can perform OLAP functions, open queries, create new queries, or change/delete existing queries. It also has formatting capabilities. When used in conjunction with the Context Menu, it can provide power analytical capabilities to Business Explorer users.

Figure 78

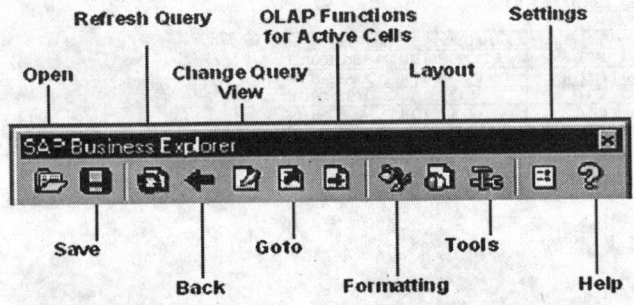

Copyright SAP AG

Context Menu

The Context Menu is another versatile tool that can be used when working with the Business Explorer. It also supports both navigation and analysis functions. The Context Menu, Figure 79, can be activated by right-clicking the mouse. The functions available when the Context Menu is activated depend on the report area where the mouse is clicked. For example, the Context Menu will display different menu items when activated from the Results Area or the Drill-down Characteristics area. Figures 79-81 show three variations of the Context Menu. These variations were activated due to the mouse being clicked in three different report areas.

Figure 79

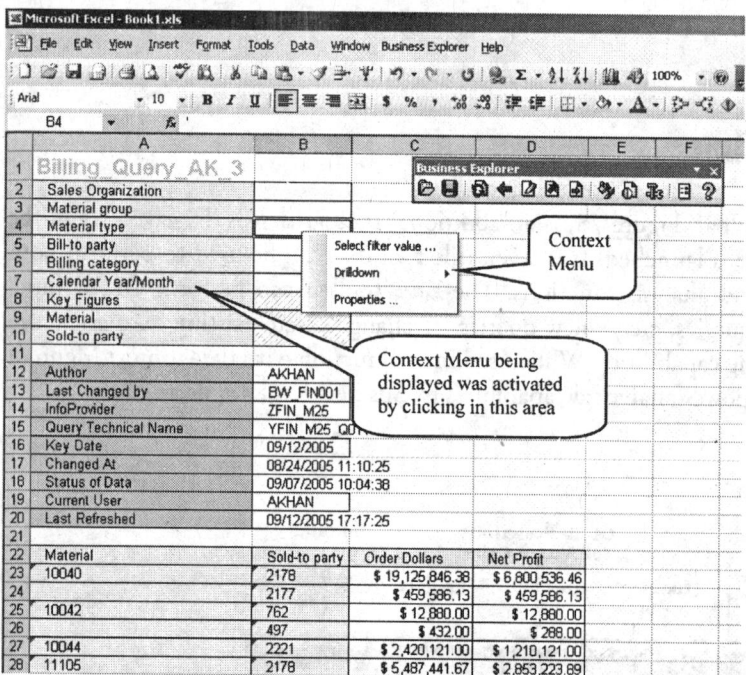

Copyright SAP AG

Figure 80

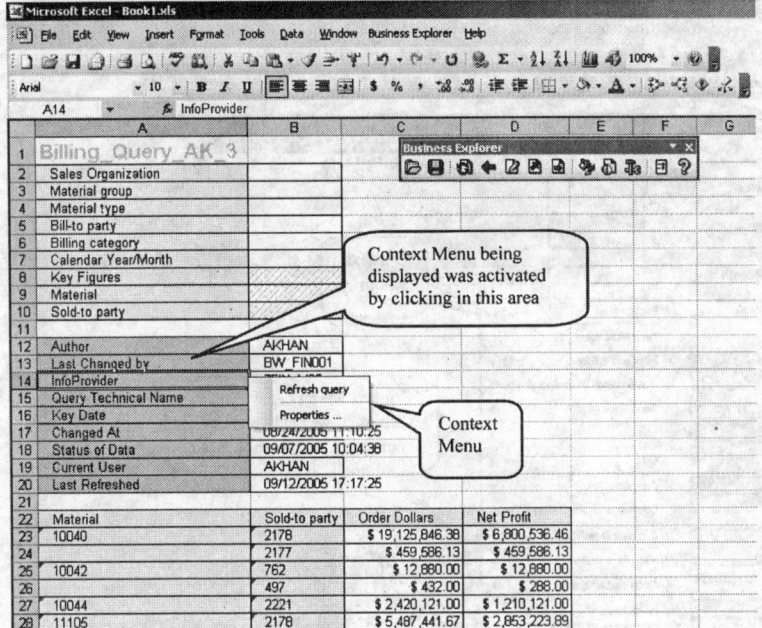

Copyright SAP AG

Figure 81

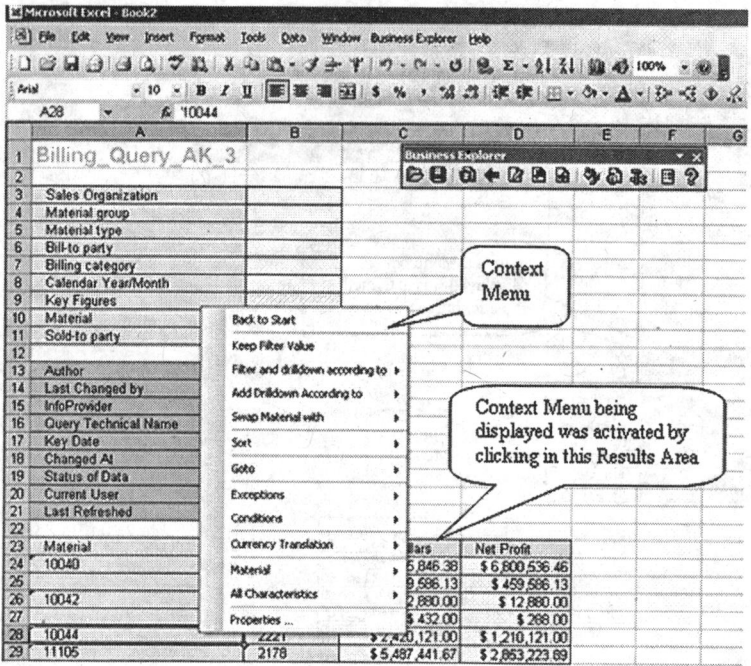

Copyright SAP AG

There exist two Context Menu versions: Basic Menu and Enhanced Menu. The Basic Menu, with a limited number of functions, is a subset of the Enhanced Menu. Within the Context Menu, it is possible to toggle between the two menus (Enhanced Menu and Basic Menu).

The Context Menu contains many functions and features, ranging from basic to very advanced. They include basic navigation techniques (such as back, forward, and back to start), filtering, drilling down, drilling across, removing drill-down, swapping axes, expanding/collapsing/deactivating hierarchies, sorting, currency translation, exporting to Excel, and changing query properties.

Chapter 8: Web Reporting Tools and Techniques

Web Toolbar

The Web Toolbar, Figure 82, is a feature-rich and powerful tool that enables users to easily navigate though and analyze BW data and reports through a mouse click. It allows users to quickly change views (table vs. graphic), place additional filters and export the data to an MS-Excel spreadsheet. It also enables access to the Ad-Hoc Query Designer, where queries can be created or modified.

Figure 82

Copyright SAP AG

Some of the functions available through the Web Toolbar include:

- Create various types of charts
- Swap the query axes: rows (characteristics) with columns (key figures):
- Define, change, delete, and activate/deactivate exceptions and conditions
- Provide query information
- Launch the Ad-Hoc Query Designer
- Export query data to MS-Excel or a comma separated value (CSV) file
- Support bookmarks, which are displayed in the browser's address line

Generic Navigation Block

The Generic Navigation Block, which is displayed in the form of a table, presents the current navigational state of a report as shown on Figure 83. In addition to displaying characteristics and structures, it also displays any filters. The Generic Navigation Block permits rows and columns to be swapped, filters to be added or removed, and drill-down or drill-across functions to be executed. The query results are displayed in the Results Area.

Figure 83

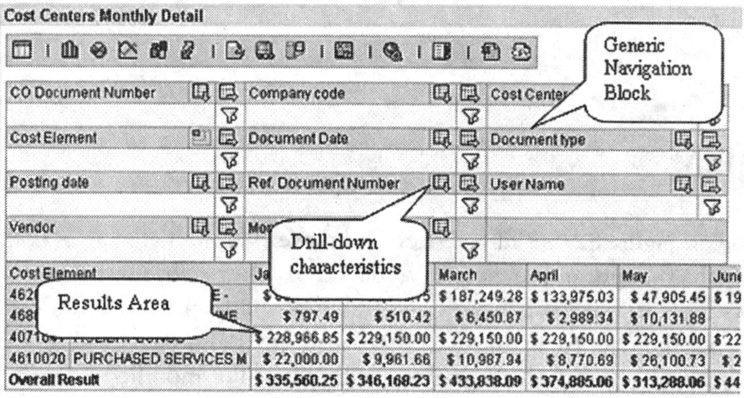

Copyright SAP AG

Drill-down characteristics

Drill-down characteristics permit both navigation as well as execution of various analytical functions, such as drilling (down and/or across), filtering, etc. They can be in collapsed or expanded mode. When the drill-down characteristics are expanded, various operations can be performed such as filtering, slicing, and dicing. To meet individual requirements, report displays can be modified by selecting different values in the drill-down characteristics, which lead to different results being displayed in the rows and columns.

Context Menu

The Context Menu is also available on the web. It serves the same purpose and provides the same functionality as the Context Menu in the BEx Analyzer, which was explained in Chapter 7. It supports both navigation and analysis functions. Figure 84 shows the Basic Menu version of the Context Menu on the web.

Figure 84

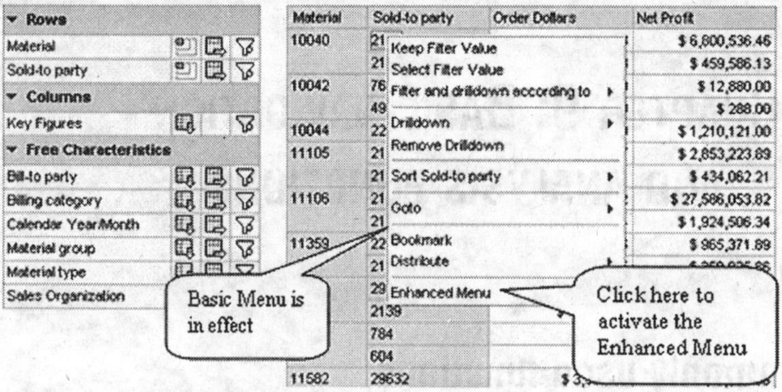

Copyright SAP AG

Figure 85 shows the Enhanced Menu version of the Context Menu. When the Enhanced Menu is in effect, the option to revert back to the Basic Menu is available, as shown on Figure 85.

Figure 85

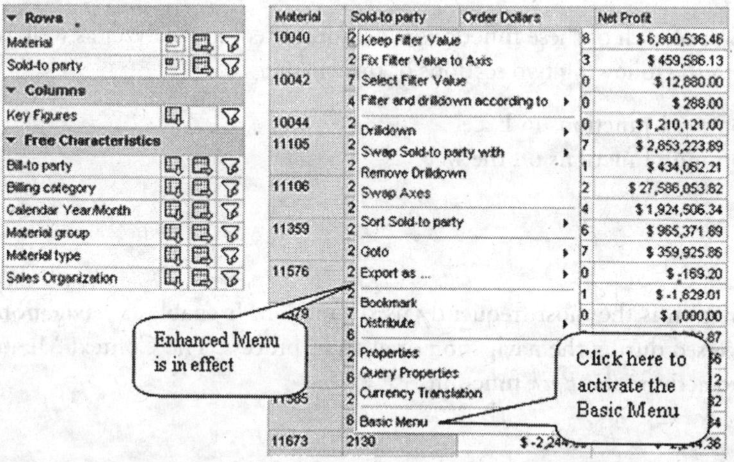

Copyright SAP AG

The Context Menu can be activated in web reports by right-clicking the mouse, just like in Analyzer reports. However, there exist older BW installations where the Context Menu is activated by left-clicking the mouse. Therefore, if you try to activate the Context Menu with a right-click and it does not pop-up, try the left-click.

CHAPTER 9: BASIC NAVIGATION AND ANALYSIS FUNCTIONS

Most commonly used functions

The basic functions covered in this chapter are:
- Back
- Back to Start
- Keep filter value
- Select filter value
- Remove filter value

The application of each of these functions is demonstrated, in Analyzer as well as web reports, in the following two sections of this chapter:

- Using common functions in Excel
- Using common functions on the web

Back

The *Back* function is the most frequently used function. It enables a navigation step to be reversed during the navigation or analysis process. The Context Menu can be used to activate the *Back* function.

Back to Start

The *Back to Start* function reverses all the previously executed navigation or analysis steps in just one step. When this function is executed, all the steps executed since the report was first run are reversed, causing the original report results to be displayed. The Context Menu can be used to activate the *Back to Start* function.

Keep Filter Value

The *Keep Filter Value* function is used for displaying only the data for a characteristic value, while the characteristic value itself is removed from the drill-down. If *Country* is a report characteristic, *Keep Filter Value* can be used to filter the data for a specific country such as France. Consequently, the characteristic value, France, will no longer be displayed in the drill-down. The status, that the data for France has been filtered, will be displayed on the Navigation Block or in the filter.

Select Filter Value

The *Select Filter Value* function is used for applying a filter for a characteristic (or structure) according to values.

Other functions

The Business Explorer supports a number of additional navigation and analysis functions, such as drill-down and drill-across. Their application will be demonstrated, using screenshots, in subsequent chapters. In some cases, step-by-step procedures for executing these functions will be demonstrated. The functions covered in subsequent chapters include:

- Drill-down
- Drill-across
- Sort
- Swap
- Jump
- Expand/collapse hierarchies

Using common functions in Excel

We will execute various functions on the Excel-based report displayed on Figure 86, which will be our starting point for navigation and/or analysis.

Figure 86

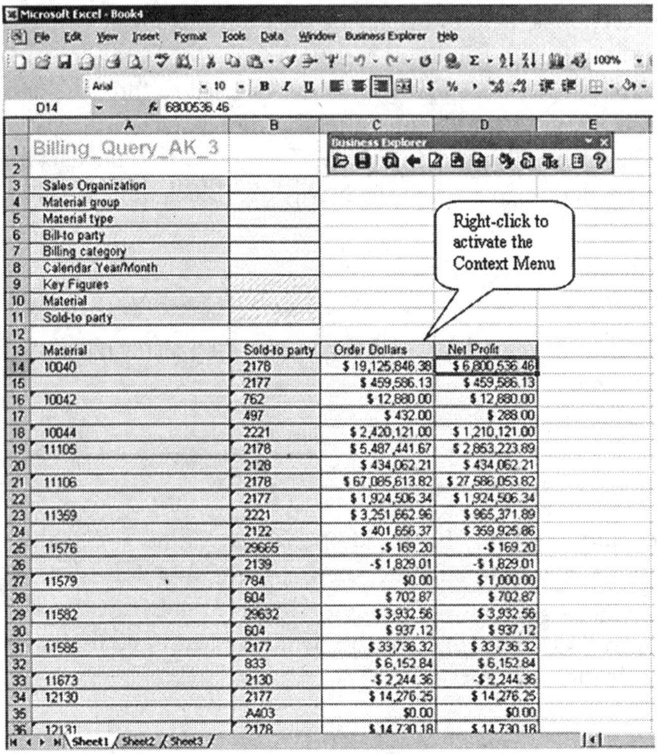

	A	B	C	D	E
1	Billing_Query_AK_3		Business Explorer		
2					
3	Sales Organization				
4	Material group				
5	Material type			Right-click to	
6	Bill-to party			activate the	
7	Billing category			Context Menu	
8	Calendar Year/Month				
9	Key Figures				
10	Material				
11	Sold-to party				
12					
13	Material	Sold-to party	Order Dollars	Net Profit	
14	10040	2178	$ 19,125,846.38	$ 6,800,536.46	
15		2177	$ 459,586.13	$ 459,586.13	
16	10042	762	$ 12,880.00	$ 12,880.00	
17		497	$ 432.00	$ 288.00	
18	10044	2221	$ 2,420,121.00	$ 1,210,121.00	
19	11105	2178	$ 5,487,441.67	$ 2,853,223.89	
20		2128	$ 434,062.21	$ 434,062.21	
21	11106	2178	$ 67,085,613.82	$ 27,586,053.82	
22		2177	$ 1,924,506.34	$ 1,924,506.34	
23	11359	2221	$ 3,251,662.96	$ 965,371.89	
24		2122	$ 401,656.37	$ 359,925.86	
25	11576	29665	-$ 169.20	-$ 169.20	
26		2139	-$ 1,829.01	-$ 1,829.01	
27	11579	784	$0.00	$ 1,000.00	
28		604	$ 702.87	$ 702.87	
29	11582	29632	$ 3,932.56	$ 3,932.56	
30		604	$ 937.12	$ 937.12	
31	11585	2177	$ 33,736.32	$ 33,736.32	
32		833	$ 6,152.84	$ 6,152.84	
33	11673	2130	-$ 2,244.36	-$ 2,244.36	
34	12130	2177	$ 14,276.25	$ 14,276.25	
35		A403	$0.00	$0.00	
36	12131	2178	$ 14,730.18	$ 14,730.18	

In the first step, the Context Menu tool is activated. To activate:

- Right-click in the Results Area, as shown on Figure 86

This will cause the Context Menu to pop-up, which is displayed on Figure 87.

Figure 87

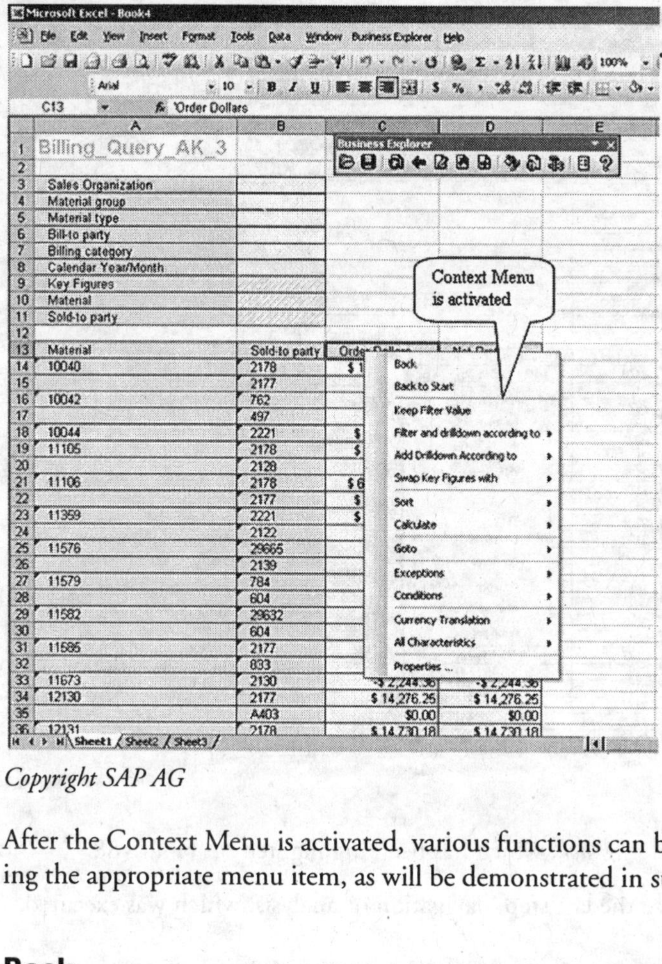

Copyright SAP AG

After the Context Menu is activated, various functions can be executed by selecting the appropriate menu item, as will be demonstrated in subsequent sections.

Back

To execute this function:

- Right-click in the Results Area

This will cause the Context Menu to pop-up, which is displayed on Figure 88.

Figure 88

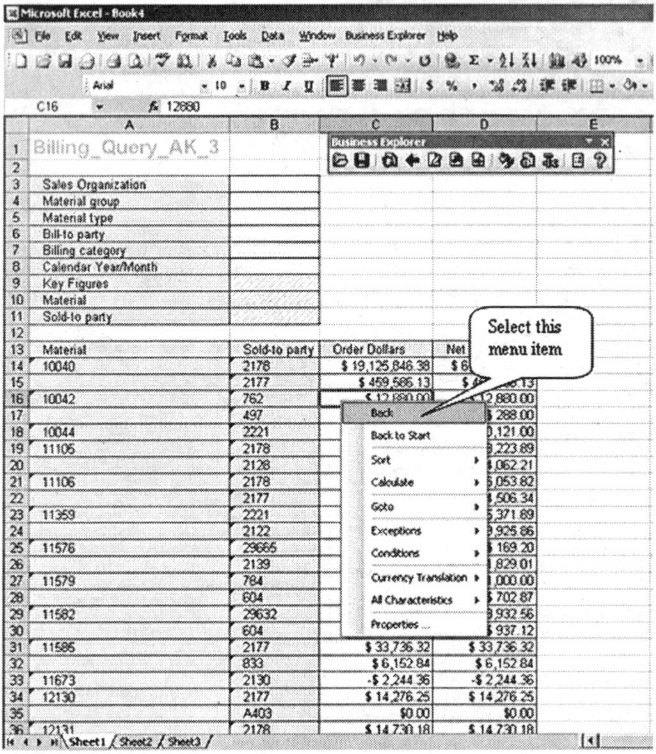

Copyright SAP AG

- Select the menu item *Back*, which has been highlighted on Figure 88

This action will reverse the last step, navigation or analysis, which was executed.

Back to Start

To execute this function:

- Right-click in the Results Area

This will cause the Context Menu to pop-up, which is displayed on Figure 89.

Figure 89

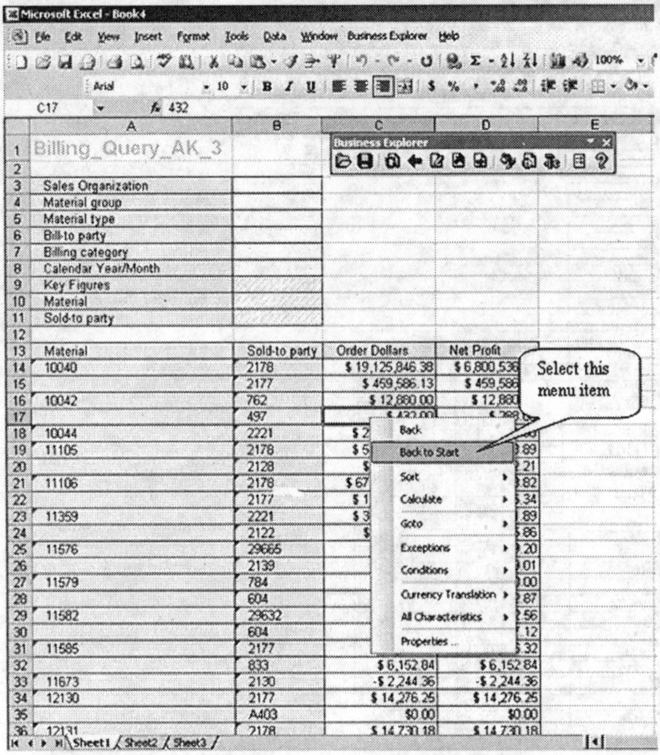

Copyright SAP AG

- Select the menu item *Back to Start*, which has been highlighted on Figure 89

This action will reverse all the steps executed since the report was first run and display the initial report results.

Keep filter value

To execute this function:

- Right-click on *Material 11105*, as shown on Figure 90

Figure 90

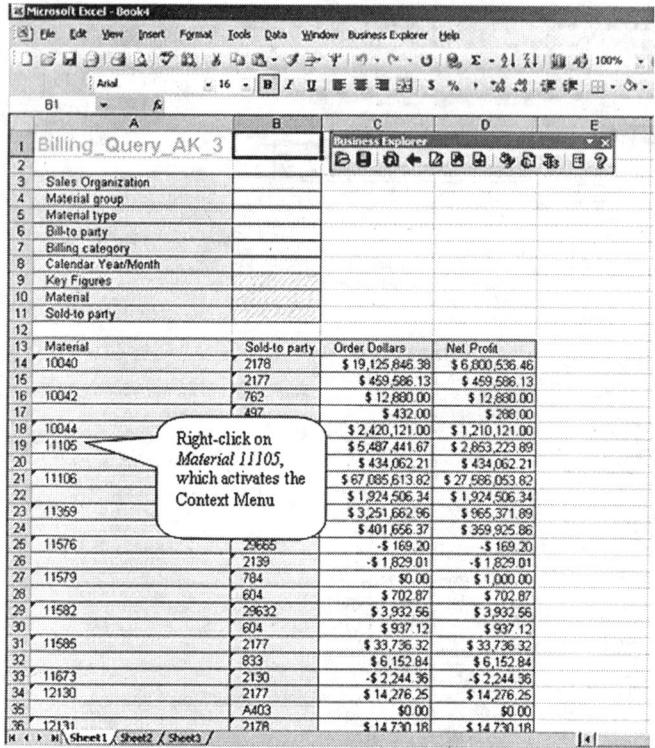

This will cause the Context Menu to pop-up, which is displayed on Figure 91.

Figure 91

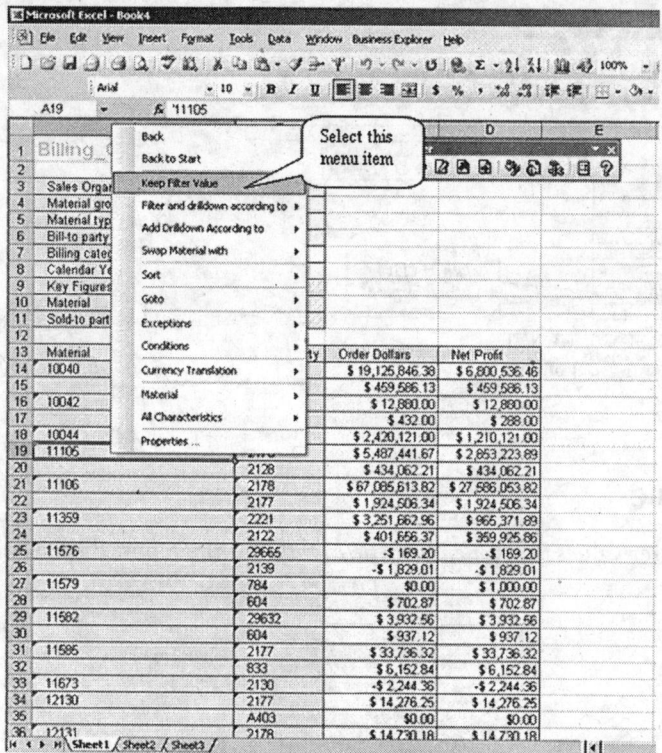

Copyright SAP AG

- Select the menu item *Keep Filter Value*, which has been highlighted on Figure 91

This will execute the function and the report results will be displayed, as shown on Figure 92, where the applied filter for *Material 11105* is highlighted.

Figure 92

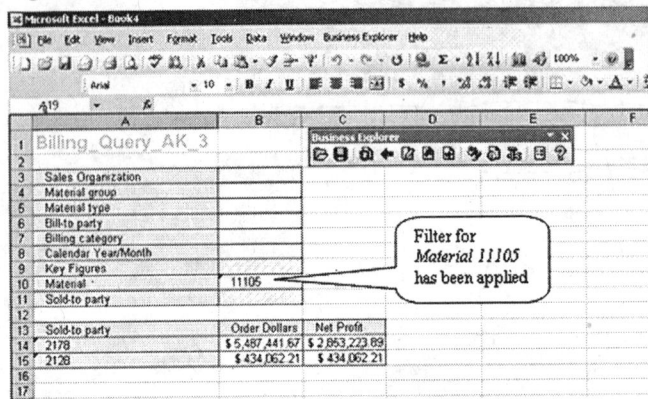

Select filter value

We will now select filter values, for *Calendar Year/Month*, for the report displayed on Figure 93.

Figure 93

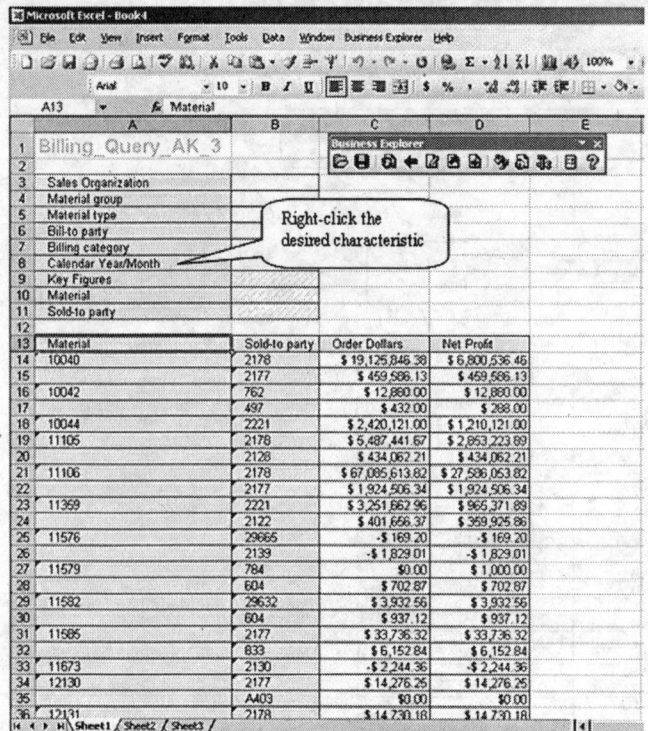

To execute this function:

- Right-click on *Calendar Year/Month* in the shaded *Slice and Dice* area (row #8), as shown on Figure 93

This will cause the Context Menu to pop-up, which is displayed on Figure 94.

Figure 94

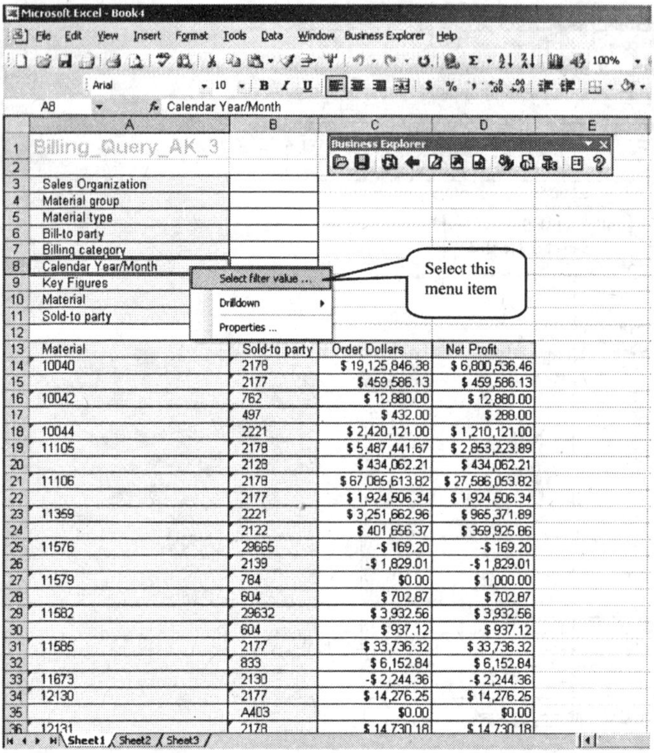
Microsoft Excel - Book4
Billing_Query_AK_3
Sales Organization
Material group
Material type
Bill-to party
Billing category
Calendar Year/Month
Key Figures
Material
Sold-to party
Select filter value ...
Drilldown
Properties ...
Select this menu item
Business Explorer

Copyright SAP AG

Notice that the Context Menu items displayed on Figure 94 (activated from the *Slice and Dice* area) are different compared to the Context Menu items displayed on Figure 88 (activated from the *Results Area*).

- Select the menu item *Select filter value*

This will cause the next window to pop-up, Figure 95, where the filter can be specified.

Figure 95

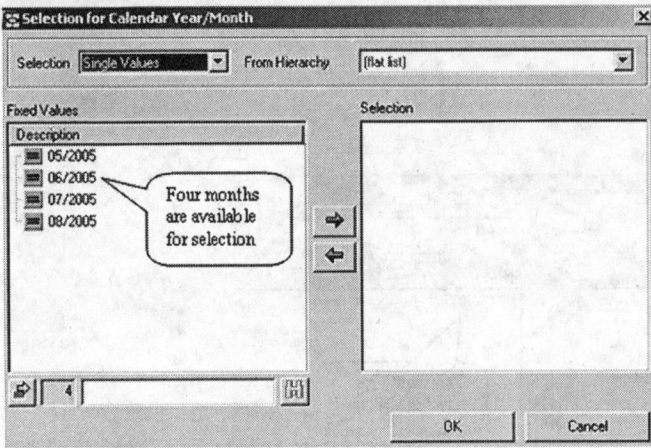

Copyright SAP AG

Notice that there are four values (months) listed in the left-hand window. Since we want to apply a filter for 06/2006:

- Click the desired month, as shown on Figure 96

Figure 96

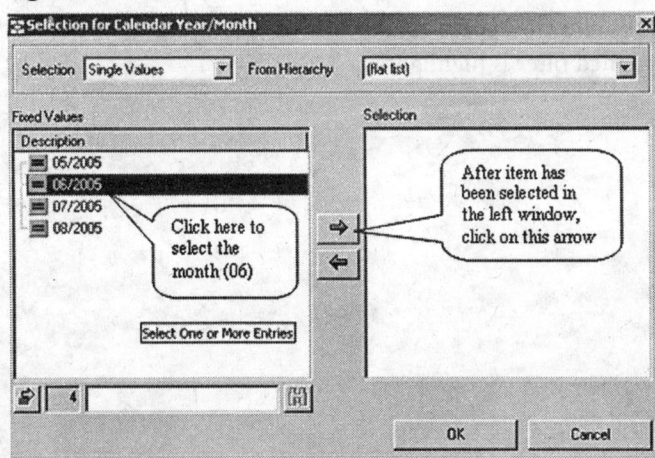

Copyright SAP AG

After the desired month has been selected in the left-hand window:

- Click the right arrow located between the two windows, as shown on Figure 96

This will cause the selected value to be moved into the right-hand window, as shown on Figure 97.

Figure 97

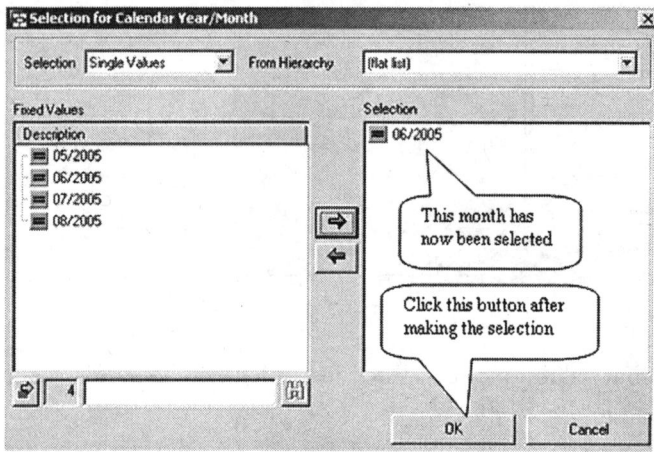

Copyright SAP AG

- Click the *OK* button

This will apply the filter and the report results will be displayed, as shown on Figure 98, where the applied filter is highlighted.

Figure 98

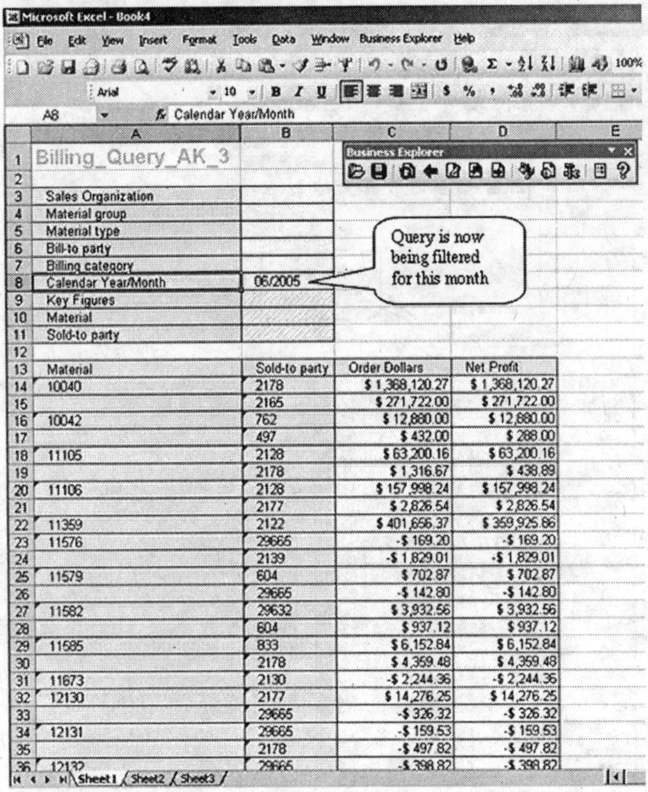

[Screenshot of Microsoft Excel - Book4 showing Billing_Query_AK_3 with Calendar Year/Month filtered to 06/2005, with callout "Query is now being filtered for this month"]

Remove filter value

We will now remove the filter that was applied on Figure 98.

- Right-click on the characteristic (*Calendar Year/Month*)

This will cause the Context Menu to pop-up, which is displayed on Figure 99.

94 • SAP® BEx Simplified

Figure 99

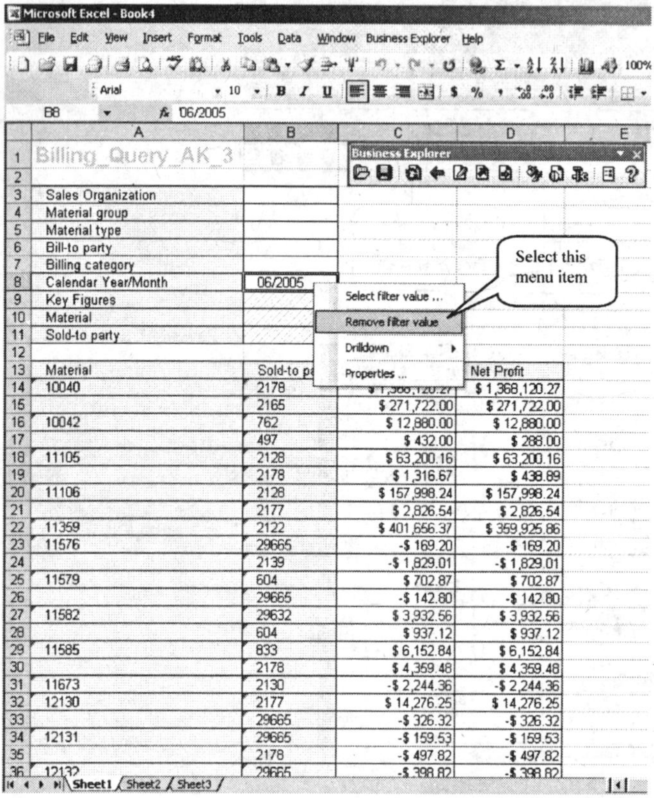

Copyright SAP AG

- Select the menu item *Remove filter value*

This will cause the filter to be removed and the original results will be displayed, as shown on Figure 100 (which is the same as Figure 93, the starting point before the filter was applied).

Figure 100

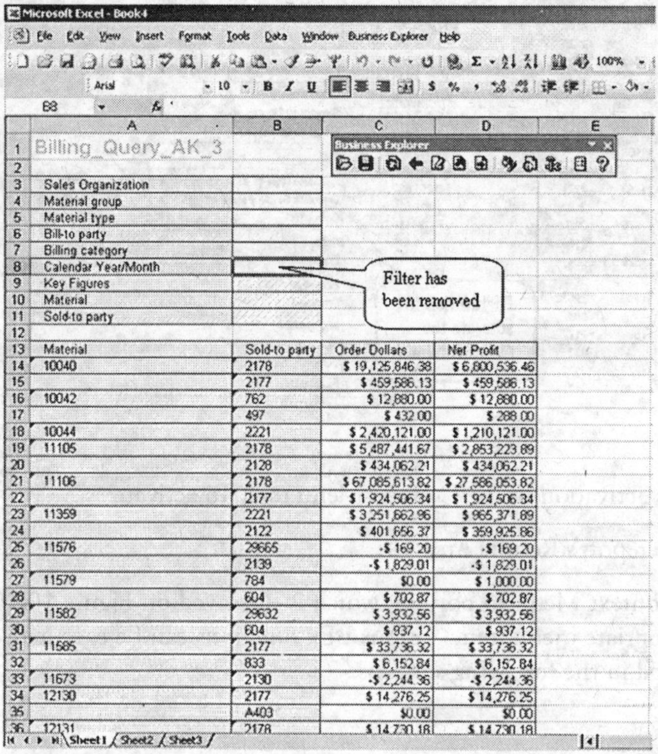

	A	B	C	D	E
1	Billing_Query_AK_3				
2					
3	Sales Organization				
4	Material group				
5	Material type				
6	Bill-to party				
7	Billing category				
8	Calendar Year/Month				
9	Key Figures				
10	Material				
11	Sold-to party				
12					
13	Material		Sold-to party	Order Dollars	Net Profit
14	10040		2178	$ 19,125,846.38	$ 6,800,536.46
15			2177	$ 459,586.13	$ 459,586.13
16	10042		762	$ 12,880.00	$ 12,880.00
17			497	$ 432.00	$ 288.00
18	10044		2221	$ 2,420,121.00	$ 1,210,121.00
19	11105		2178	$ 5,487,441.67	$ 2,853,223.89
20			2128	$ 434,062.21	$ 434,062.21
21	11106		2178	$ 67,085,613.82	$ 27,586,053.82
22			2177	$ 1,924,506.34	$ 1,924,506.34
23	11359		2221	$ 3,251,662.86	$ 965,371.89
24			2122	$ 401,656.37	$ 359,925.86
25	11576		29665	-$ 169.20	-$ 169.20
26			2139	-$ 1,829.01	-$ 1,829.01
27	11579		784	$0.00	$ 1,000.00
28			604	$ 702.87	$ 702.87
29	11582		29632	$ 3,932.56	$ 3,932.56
30			604	$ 937.12	$ 937.12
31	11585		2177	$ 33,736.32	$ 33,736.32
32			833	$ 6,152.84	$ 6,152.84
33	11673		2130	-$ 2,244.36	-$ 2,244.36
34	12130		2177	$ 14,276.25	$ 14,276.25
35			A403	$0.00	$0.00
36	12131		2178	$ 14,730.18	$ 14,730.18

Filter has been removed

Using common functions on the web

Most of the functions executed in Excel can also be performed on the web using the Context Menu. We will use the following report, Figure 101, as the starting point for demonstrating various functions on the web.

Figure 101

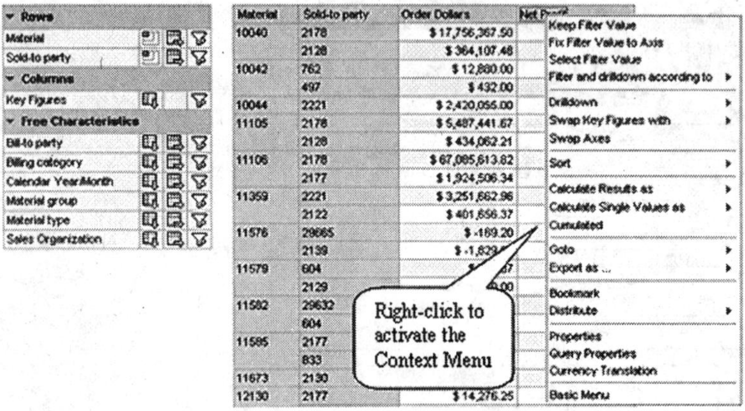

Copyright SAP AG

The first step requires activation of the Context Menu tool. To activate:

- Right-click in the report's Results Area

This will cause the Context Menu to pop-up, which is displayed on Figure 101. By selecting the appropriate menu item, various BEx functions can be executed, as will be demonstrated in the following sections.

Back

To execute this function:

- Right-click in the Results Area

This will cause the Context Menu to pop-up, which is displayed on Figure 102.

Figure 102

Material	Sold-to party	Order Dollars		Net Profit
10040	Back		38	$ 6,800,536.46
	Back to Start		13	$ 459,586.13
10042	Keep Filter Value			
	Select Filter Value			
10044	Filter and drilldown according to ▶			
11105			67	$ 2,853,223.89
	Drilldown ▶		21	$ 434,062.21
	Remove Drilldown			
11106			82	$ 27,586,053.82
	Sort Sold-to party ▶		34	$ 1,924,506.34
11359	Goto ▶		96	$ 965,371.89
			37	$ 359,925.86
11576	Bookmark		20	$ -169.20
	Distribute ▶		01	$ -1,829.01
11579	Enhanced Menu		00	$ 1,000.00
	604	$ 702.87		$ 702.87
11582	29632	$ 3,932.56		$ 3,932.56
	604	$ 937.12		$ 937.12

(Rows: Material, Sold-to party; Columns: Key Figures; Free Characteristics: Bill-to party, Billing category, Calendar Year/Month, Material group, Material type, Sales Organization — Right-click to activate the Context Menu; Select this menu item)

Copyright SAP AG

- Select the menu item *Back*, which has been highlighted on Figure 102

This will reverse the last step, navigation or analysis, which was executed.

Back to Start

To execute this function:

- Right-click in the Results Area

This will cause the Context Menu to pop-up, which is displayed on Figure 103.

Figure 103

Material	Sold-to party	Order Dollars		Net Profit
10040	Back		38	$ 6,800,536.46
	Back to Start		13	$ 459,586.13
10042	Keep Filter Value			$ 12,880.00
	Select Filter Value			
10044	Filter and drilldown according to ▶			
11105	Drilldown ▶		21	
	Remove Drilldown			
11106			82	$ 27,586,053.82
	Sort Sold-to party ▶		34	$ 1,924,506.34
11359	Goto ▶		96	$ 965,371.89
			37	$ 359,925.86
11576	Bookmark		20	$ -169.20
	Distribute ▶		01	$ -1,829.01
11579	Enhanced Menu		00	$ 1,000.00
	604	$ 702.87		$ 702.87
11582	29632	$ 3,932.56		$ 3,932.56

(Right-click to activate the Context Menu; Select this menu item)

Copyright SAP AG

- Select the menu item *Back to Start*, which has been highlighted on Figure 103

This will reverse all the steps executed since the report was first run and display the initial report results.

Keep filter value

To execute this function:

- Right-click on *Material 11105*

This will cause the Context Menu to pop-up, which is displayed on Figure 104.

Figure 104

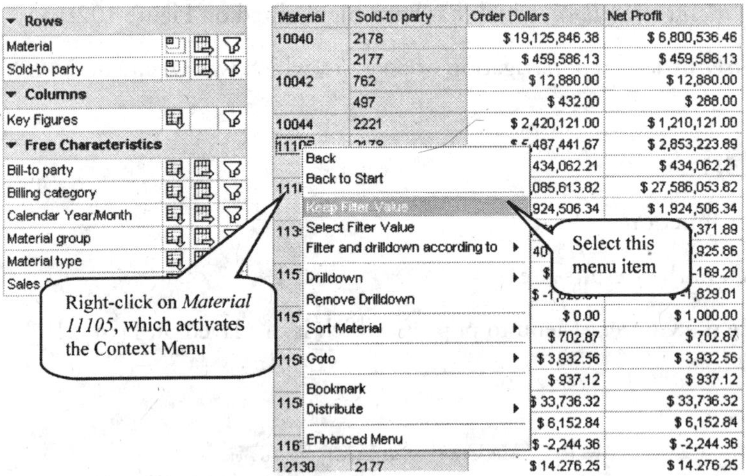

Copyright SAP AG

- Select the menu item *Keep Filter Value*, which has been highlighted on Figure 104

This will execute the function and the report results will be displayed, as shown on Figure 105, where the applied filter for *Material 11105* is highlighted.

Figure 105

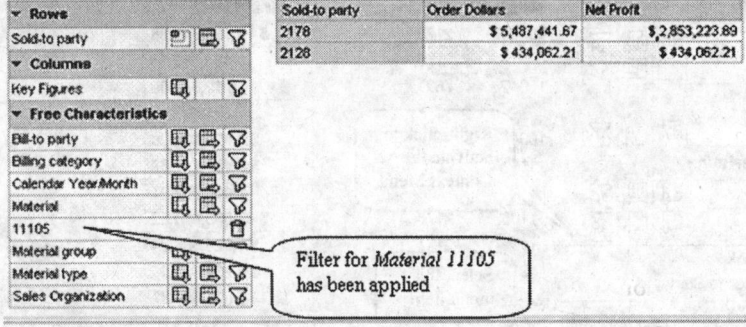

Copyright SAP AG

Select filter value

There are two methods that can be used to execute this function:

- Context Menu
- Filter icon

<u>Using the Context Menu</u>

To select a filter value using the Context Menu:

- Right-click on the characteristic *Calendar Year/Month*, as shown on Figure 106

This will cause the Context Menu to pop-up, which is displayed on Figure 106.

Figure 106

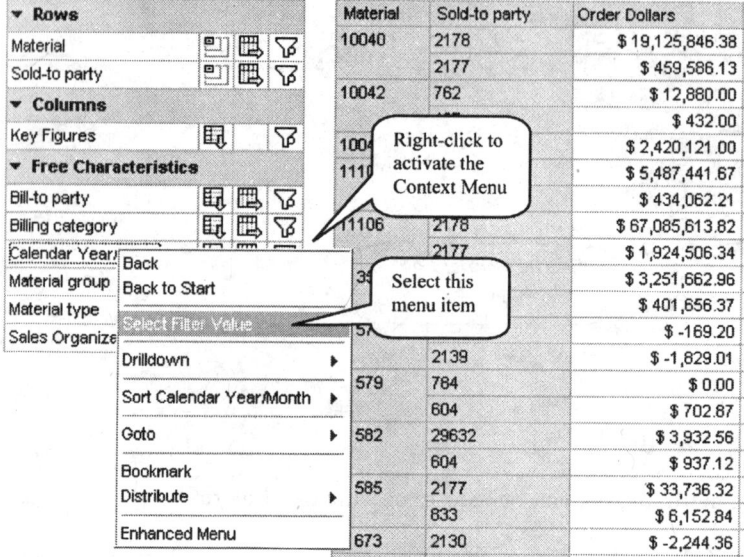

Copyright SAP AG

- Select the menu item *Select Filter Value*

This will cause the next window to pop-up, Figure 107, where the appropriate selections and/or entries can be made for specifying the filter. This procedure is explained in greater detail in the next section (*Using the filter icon*).

Figure 107

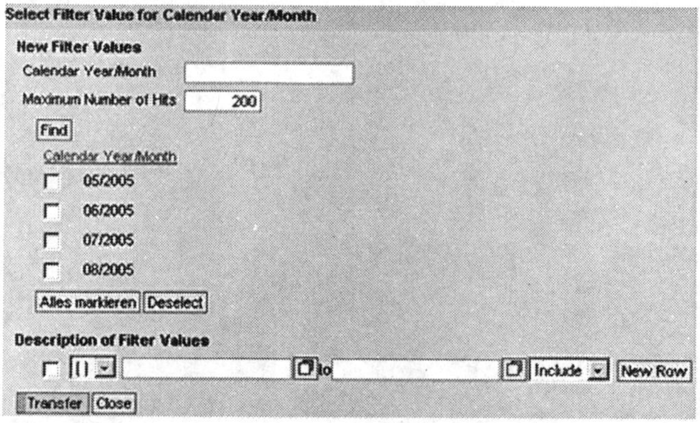

Copyright SAP AG

Using the filter icon

To select a filter value using the filter icon:

- Click the filter icon, which is highlighted on Figure 108

Figure 108

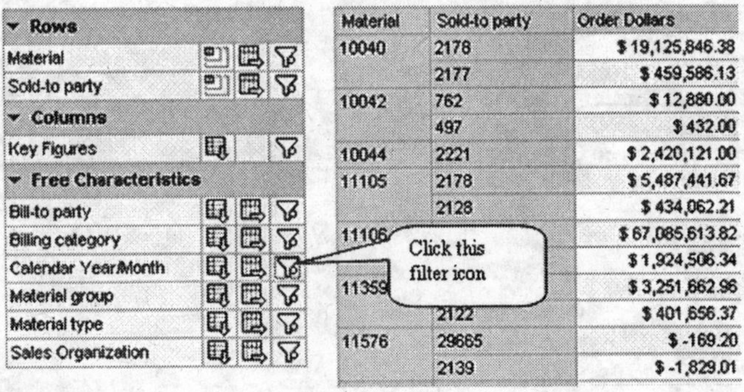

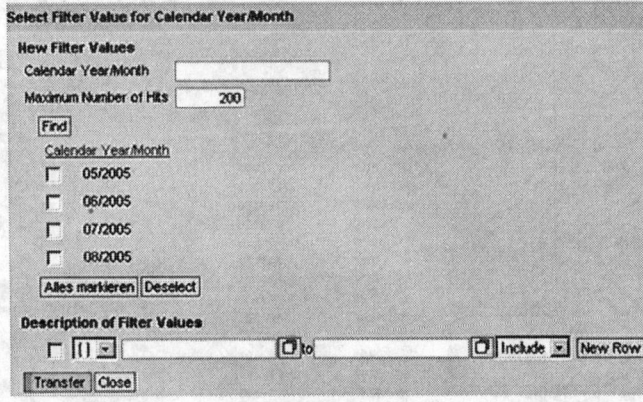

Copyright SAP AG

This will cause the following window to pop-up (Figure 109).

Figure 109

Copyright SAP AG

Notice that this is the same window as Figure 107, which popped-up when the Context Menu was used in the previous section (*Using the Context Menu*). On

Figure 109, four values (months) are available for selection (May through August 2005). To select the June filter value:

- Click the checkbox next to the desired item, 06/2005, as shown on Figure 110

Figure 110

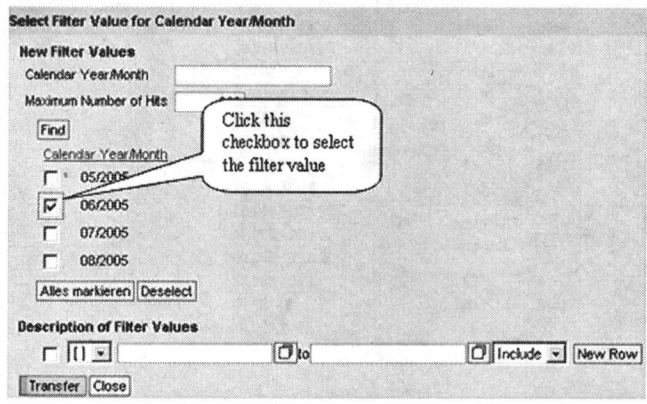

Copyright SAP AG

- Click the *Transfer* button

This action will apply the filter and the report results will be displayed. Figure 111 highlights the applied filter (06/2005).

Figure 111

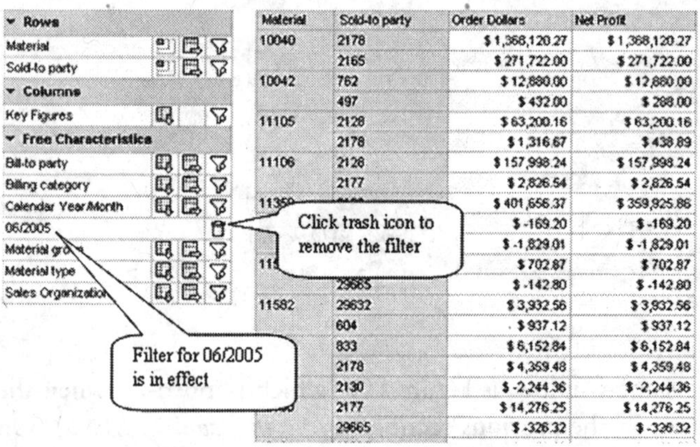

Copyright SAP AG

Remove filter value

We will now remove the filter that was applied on Figure 111:

- Click the *Trash* icon, which is highlighted on Figure 111

This will remove the filter and the original results (Figure 108), before the filter was applied, will be displayed.

A filter can also be removed using the Context Menu. To remove a filter using this method:

- Right-click on the characteristic (*Calendar Year/Month*)

This will activate the Context Menu, which is displayed on Figure 112.

Figure 112

Rows		Material	Sold-to party	Order Dollars	Net Profit
Material		10040	2178	$ 1,368,120.27	$ 1,368,120.27
Sold-to party			2165	$ 271,722.00	$ 271,722.00
Columns		10042	762	$ 12,880.00	$ 12,880.00
Key Figures			497	$ 432.00	$ 288.00
Free Characteristics		11105	2128	$ 63,200.16	$ 63,200.16
Bill-to party			2178	$ 1,316.67	$ 438.89
Billing category		11106	2128	$ 157,998.24	$ 157,998.24
Calendar	Back		2177	$ 2,826.54	$ 2,826.54
06/2005	Back to Start			$ 401,656.37	$ 359,925.86
Material	Select Filter Value			$ -169.20	$ -169.20
Material	Remove Filter			$ -1,829.01	$ -1,829.01
Sales Or				$ 702.87	$ 702.87
	Drilldown		29665	$ -142.80	$ -142.80
	Sort Calendar Year/Month	11582		$ 3,932.56	$ 3,932.56
				$ 937.12	$ 937.12
	Goto	11585		$ 6,152.84	$ 6,152.84
	Bookmark			$ 4,359.48	$ 4,359.48
	Distribute	11673		$ -2,244.36	$ -2,244.36
	Enhanced Menu	12130	2177	$ 14,276.25	$ 14,276.25
			29665	$ -326.32	$ -326.32
		12131	29665	$ -159.53	$ -159.53

(Select this menu item — Remove Filter)
(Right-click to activate the Context Menu)

Copyright SAP AG

- Select the menu item *Remove filter*

This will cause the filter to be removed.

Chapter 10: Slicing, Dicing, and Drilling

What is slicing and dicing

This is a widely used technique for analyzing data comprehensively. It provides the ability to analyze data using different scenarios such as sales by products, region, channel, and period. The slicing and dicing technique leads to a re-arrangement of data so that it can be viewed from different perspectives (such as by period and cost center).

Slicing and dicing enables the data returned by a query to be displayed in different ways by manipulating the initially displayed results. For example, the initial query results can display the total sales for each region. Using the slice and dice technique, the displayed results can be manipulated so that the sales for each state are displayed. Further slicing and dicing can lead to the display of sales by product line and by store. Figure 113 provides an example of how data can be viewed from three different angles.

Figure 113

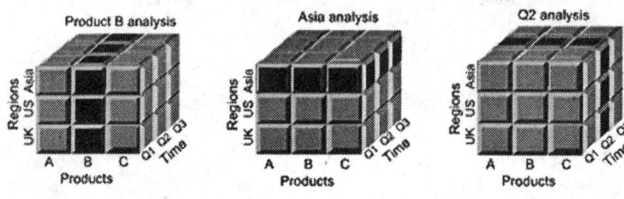

What is drill-down

Drilling provides the ability to navigate between hierarchy levels when viewing data. The drill-down technique enables navigation from the summary results to the underlying detailed data. It displays detailed data that was used in creating the summary level of data. For example, a regional store manager can execute a report that, initially, displays the total expenses for the fiscal year for all stores. Using drill-down, the manager can view the expenses for each individual store. For more comprehensive analysis, additional drill-down can be performed to view the expenses by period, expense type, etc.

The effect of drill-down is to insert an additional row(s) in the results table, thus providing more detailed data. Drill-down can be performed in two ways:

- Drill-down by rows
- Drill-down by columns

These techniques enable the information displayed to be expanded further—by the row or column stipulated in the drill-down.

Example of drill-down

The next window, Figure 114, displays the initial results after an Excel report is executed.

Figure 114

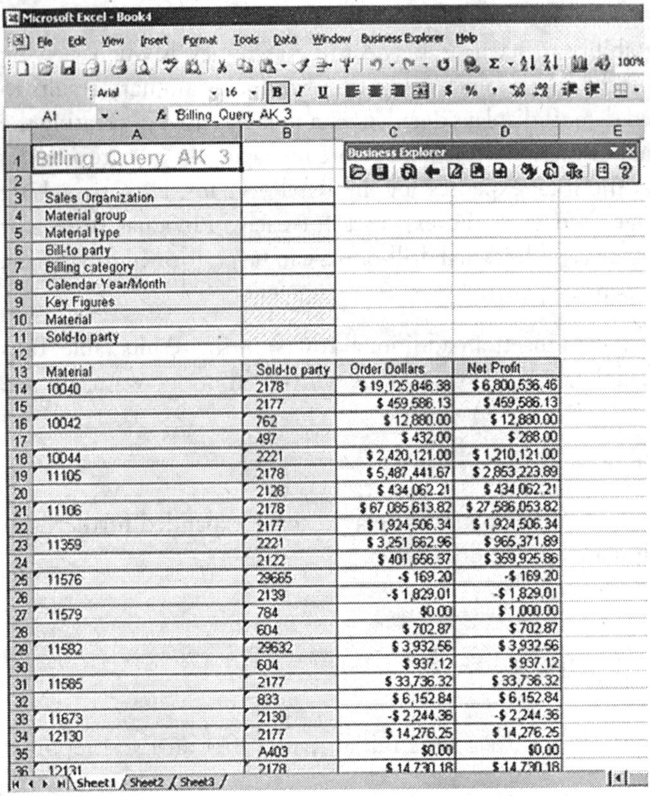

	A	B	C	D	E
1	Billing Query AK_3		Business Explorer		▼ X
2					
3	Sales Organization				
4	Material group				
5	Material type				
6	Bill-to party				
7	Billing category				
8	Calendar Year/Month				
9	Key Figures				
10	Material				
11	Sold-to party				
12					
13	Material		Sold-to party	Order Dollars	Net Profit
14	10040		2178	$ 19,125,846.38	$ 6,800,536.46
15			2177	$ 459,586.13	$ 459,586.13
16	10042		762	$ 12,880.00	$ 12,880.00
17			497	$ 432.00	$ 288.00
18	10044		2221	$ 2,420,121.00	$ 1,210,121.00
19	11105		2178	$ 5,487,441.67	$ 2,853,223.89
20			2128	$ 434,062.21	$ 434,062.21
21	11106		2178	$ 67,085,613.82	$ 27,586,053.82
22			2177	$ 1,924,506.34	$ 1,924,506.34
23	11359		2221	$ 3,251,662.96	$ 965,371.89
24			2122	$ 401,656.37	$ 369,925.86
25	11576		29665	-$ 169.20	-$ 169.20
26			2139	-$ 1,829.01	-$ 1,829.01
27	11579		784	$0.00	$ 1,000.00
28			604	$ 702.87	$ 702.87
29	11582		29632	$ 3,932.56	$ 3,932.56
30			604	$ 937.12	$ 937.12
31	11585		2177	$ 33,736.32	$ 33,736.32
32			833	$ 6,152.84	$ 6,152.84
33	11673		2130	-$ 2,244.36	-$ 2,244.36
34	12130		2177	$ 14,276.25	$ 14,276.25
35			A403	$0.00	$0.00
36	12131		2178	$ 14,730.18	$ 14,730.18

The next window, Figure 115, displays the results after a drill-down by *Calendar Year/Month* was performed on the report displayed on Figure 114.

Figure 115

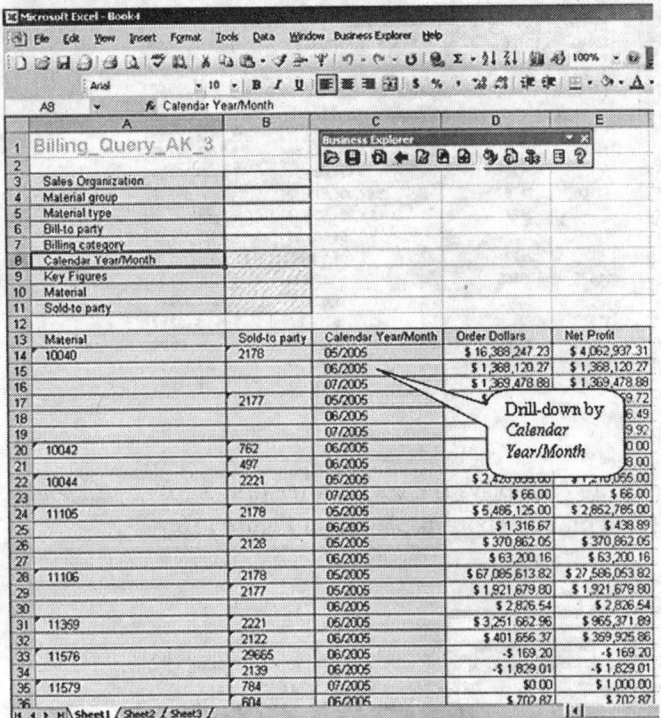

What is drill-across

The drill-across technique is similar to drill-down with the difference being that the drilling is done horizontally, rather than vertically. For example, after initially displaying the annual sales results, drill-across can be used to display the sales for each month. The effect of drill-across is that an additional column is added to the report, thus providing more detailed data.

Example of drill-across

The next window, Figure 116, displays the initial results after a web report is executed.

Figure 116

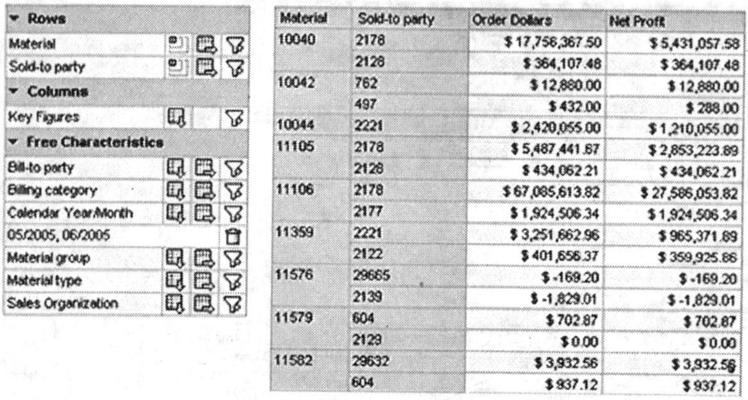

Material	Sold-to party	Order Dollars	Net Profit
10040	2178	$ 17,756,367.50	$ 5,431,057.58
	2128	$ 364,107.48	$ 364,107.48
10042	762	$ 12,880.00	$ 12,880.00
	497	$ 432.00	$ 288.00
10044	2221	$ 2,420,055.00	$ 1,210,055.00
11105	2178	$ 5,487,441.67	$ 2,853,223.89
	2128	$ 434,062.21	$ 434,062.21
11106	2178	$ 67,085,613.82	$ 27,586,053.82
	2177	$ 1,924,506.34	$ 1,924,506.34
11359	2221	$ 3,251,662.96	$ 965,371.89
	2122	$ 401,656.37	$ 359,925.86
11576	29665	$ -169.20	$ -169.20
	2139	$ -1,829.01	$ -1,829.01
11579	604	$ 702.87	$ 702.87
	2129	$ 0.00	$ 0.00
11582	29632	$ 3,932.56	$ 3,932.56
	604	$ 937.12	$ 937.12

Copyright SAP AG

The next window, Figure 117, displays the results after drill-across by *Calendar Year/Month* was performed on the report displayed on Figure 116.

Figure 117

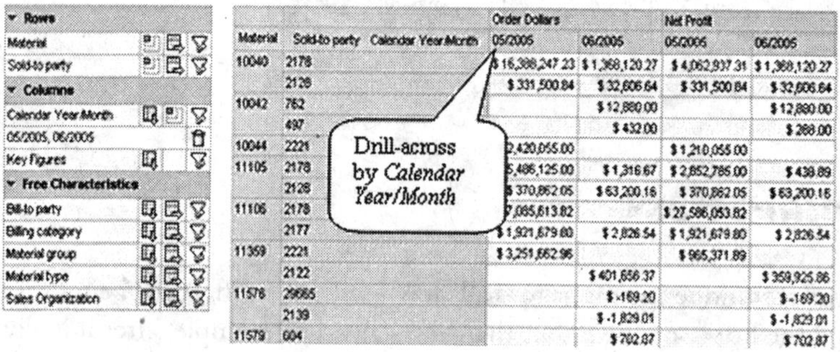

Material	Sold-to party	Calendar Year/Month	Order Dollars 05/2005	Order Dollars 06/2005	Net Profit 05/2005	Net Profit 06/2005
10040	2178		$ 16,388,247.23	$ 1,368,120.27	$ 4,062,937.31	$ 1,368,120.27
	2128		$ 331,500.84	$ 32,606.64	$ 331,500.84	$ 32,606.64
10042	762			$ 12,880.00		$ 12,880.00
	497			$ 432.00		$ 288.00
10044	2221		2,420,055.00		$ 1,210,055.00	
11105	2178		5,486,125.00	$ 1,316.67	$ 2,852,785.00	$ 438.89
	2128		$ 370,862.05	$ 63,200.16	$ 370,862.05	$ 63,200.16
11106	2178		7,085,613.82		$ 27,586,053.82	
	2177		$ 1,921,679.80	$ 2,826.54	$ 1,921,679.80	$ 2,826.54
11359	2221		$ 3,251,662.96		$ 965,371.89	
	2122			$ 401,656.37		$ 359,925.86
11576	29665			$ -169.20		$ -169.20
	2139			$ -1,829.01		$ -1,829.01
11579	604			$ 702.87		$ 702.87

Copyright SAP AG

Chapter 11: Analysis using the Analyzer

After a report is executed, it needs to be analyzed from different perspectives, using a number of analytical techniques. Two of the most commonly-used techniques are drill-down and drill-across, whose execution is demonstrated in this chapter.

Drill-down and drill-across

How to drill-down using the Context Menu

After a report has been executed and the results are displayed (Figure 118), activate the Context Menu:

- Right-click on the characteristic *Calendar Year/Month*

This will cause the Context Menu to pop-up, which is displayed on Figure 118.

Figure 118

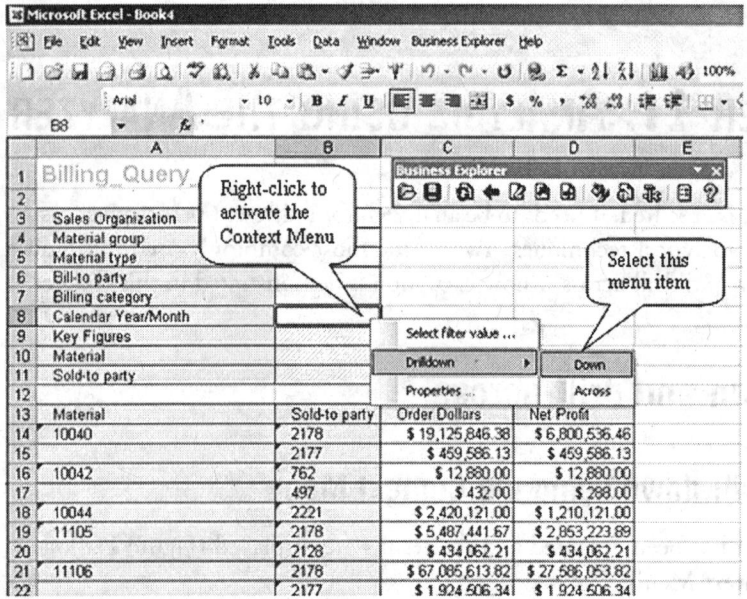

Copyright SAP AG

- Navigate via the menu path *Drilldown > Down*, as shown on Figure 118

This will cause the drill-down to be executed and the report results will be displayed, as shown on Figure 119, where the drill-down has been performed by *Calendar Year/Month*.

Figure 119

	A	B	C	D	E
1	Billing_Query_AK_3				
2					
3	Sales Organization				
4	Material group				
5	Material type				
6	Bill-to party				
7	Billing category				
8	Calendar Year/Month				
9	Key Figures				
10	Material				
11	Sold-to party				
12					
13	Material	Sold-to party	Calendar Year/Month	Order Dollars	Net Profit
14	10040	2178	05/2005	$16,388,247.23	$4,062,937.31
15			06/2005	$1,368,120.27	$1,368,120.27
16			07/2005	$1,369,478.88	$1,369,478.88
17		2177	05/2005	$342,369.72	$342,369.72
18			06/2005	$19,396.49	$19,396.49
19			07/2005	$97,819.92	$97,819.92
20	10042	762	06/2005	$12,880.00	$12,880.00
21		497	06/2005	$432.00	$288.00
22	10044	2221	05/2005	$2,420,055.00	$1,210,055.00
23			07/2005	$66.00	$66.00
24	11105	2178	05/2005	$5,486,125.00	$2,852,785.00
25			06/2005	$1,316.67	$438.89
26		2128	05/2005	$370,862.05	$370,862.05
27			06/2005	$63,200.16	$63,200.16
28	11106	2178	05/2005	$67,085,613.82	$27,586,053.82
29		2177	05/2005	$1,921,679.80	$1,921,679.80
30			06/2005	$2,826.54	$2,826.54
31	11359	2221	05/2005	$3,251,662.96	$965,371.89
32		2122	06/2005	$401,656.37	$359,925.86
33	11576	29665	06/2005	-$169.20	-$169.20
34		2139	06/2005	-$1,829.01	-$1,829.01
35	11579	784	07/2005	$0.00	$1,000.00
36		604	06/2005	$702.82	$702.87

Drill-down by Calendar Year/Month

How to drill-across using the Context Menu

To perform a drill-across, instead of drill-down, proceed as follows after the report results are displayed (Figure 120):

- Right-click on the characteristic *Calendar Year/Month*

This will cause the Context Menu to pop-up, which is displayed on Figure 120.

Figure 120

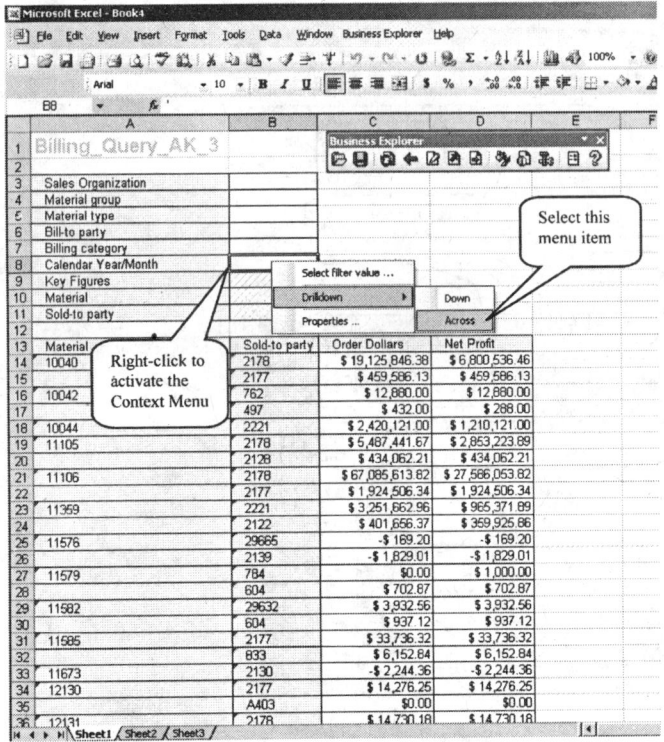

Copyright SAP AG

- Navigate via the menu path *Drilldown > Across*, as shown on Figure 120

This will cause the drill-across to be executed and the report results will be displayed, as shown on Figure 121, where the drill-across has been performed by *Calendar Year/Month*.

Figure 121

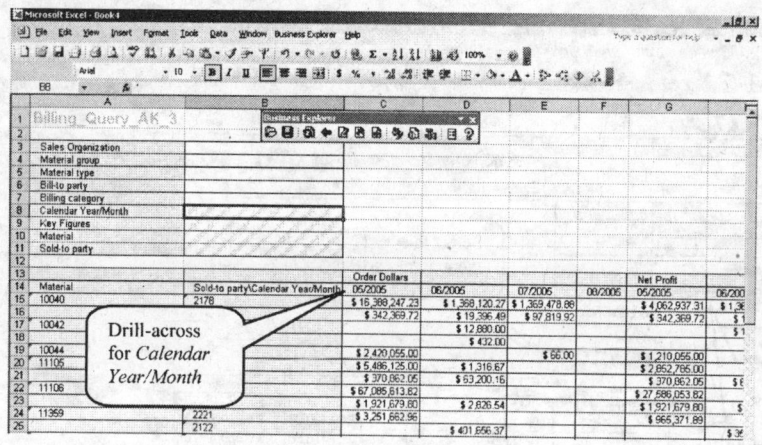

How to remove drill-down

After a drill-down has been performed, it can be easily reversed using the Context Menu. To execute this function on the report displayed on Figure 119, where a drill-down is in effect:

- Right-click on the characteristic *Calendar Year/Month*

This will cause the Context Menu to pop-up, which is displayed on Figure 122.

114 • SAP® BEx Simplified

Figure 122

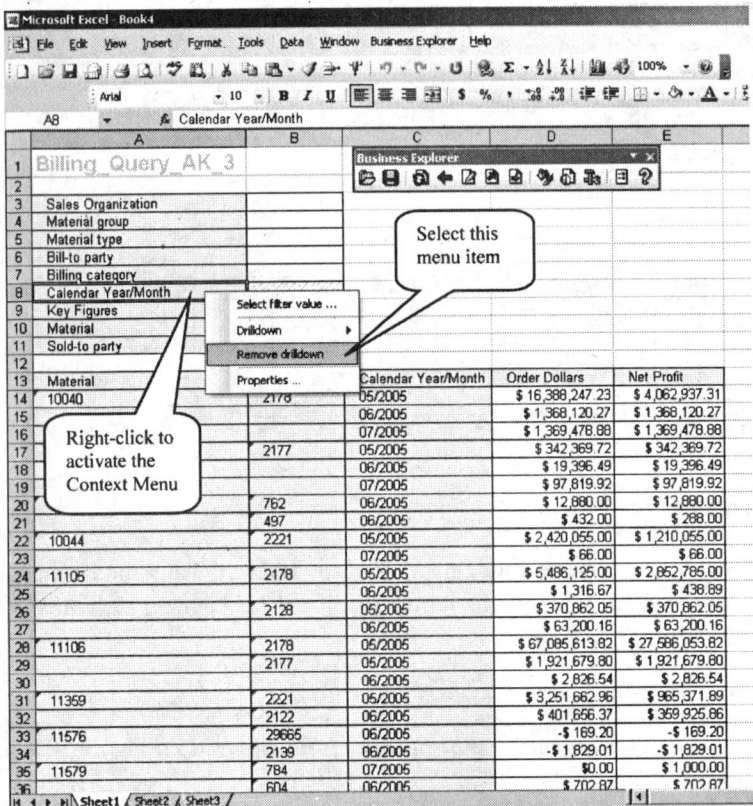

Copyright SAP AG

- Select the menu item *Remove drilldown*

This will remove the drill-down and the report results will be displayed, as shown on Figure 123 (which is the same as the starting point before the drill-down—Figure 118).

Figure 123

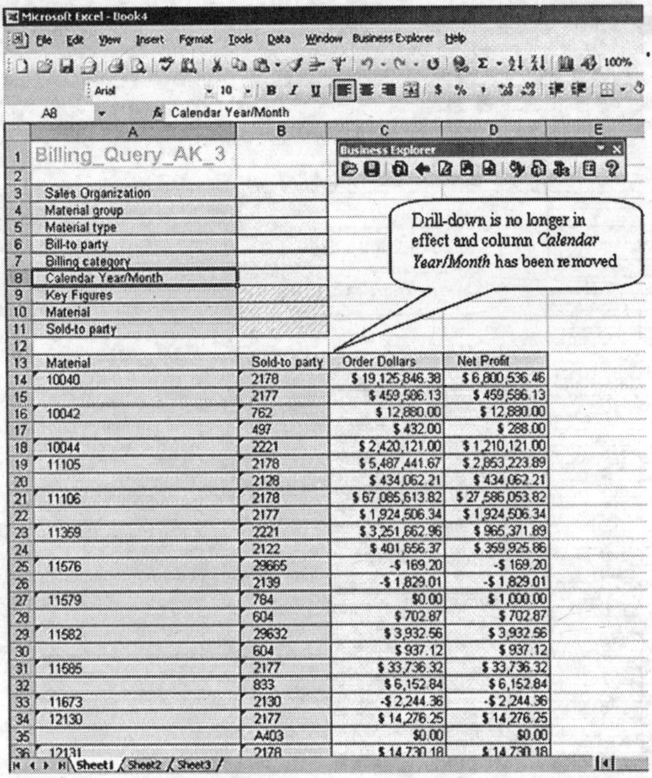

	A	B	C	D	E
1	Billing_Query_AK_3				
2					
3	Sales Organization				
4	Material group				
5	Material type				
6	Bill-to party				
7	Billing category				
8	Calendar Year/Month				
9	Key Figures				
10	Material				
11	Sold-to party				
12					
13	Material		Sold-to party	Order Dollars	Net Profit
14	10040		2178	$ 19,125,846.38	$ 6,800,536.46
15			2177	$ 459,586.13	$ 459,586.13
16	10042		762	$ 12,880.00	$ 12,880.00
17			497	$ 432.00	$ 288.00
18	10044		2221	$ 2,420,121.00	$ 1,210,121.00
19	11105		2178	$ 5,487,441.67	$ 2,853,223.89
20			2128	$ 434,062.21	$ 434,062.21
21	11106		2178	$ 67,085,613.82	$ 27,586,053.82
22			2177	$ 1,924,506.34	$ 1,924,506.34
23	11359		2221	$ 3,251,662.96	$ 965,371.89
24			2122	$ 401,656.37	$ 359,925.86
25	11576		29665	-$ 169.20	-$ 169.20
26			2139	-$ 1,829.01	-$ 1,829.01
27	11579		784	$0.00	$ 1,000.00
28			604	$ 702.87	$ 702.87
29	11582		29632	$ 3,932.56	$ 3,932.56
30			604	$ 937.12	$ 937.12
31	11585		2177	$ 33,736.32	$ 33,736.32
32			833	$ 6,152.84	$ 6,152.84
33	11673		2130	-$ 2,244.36	-$ 2,244.36
34	12130		2177	$ 14,276.25	$ 14,276.25
35			A403	$0.00	$0.00
36	12131		2178	$ 14,730.18	$ 14,730.18

Drill-down is no longer in effect and column Calendar Year/Month has been removed

Drill-down by double-clicking

Drill-down can also be performed by double-clicking on a characteristic in the slice and dice area. To demonstrate this feature, we will start with the following report (Figure 124):

Figure 124

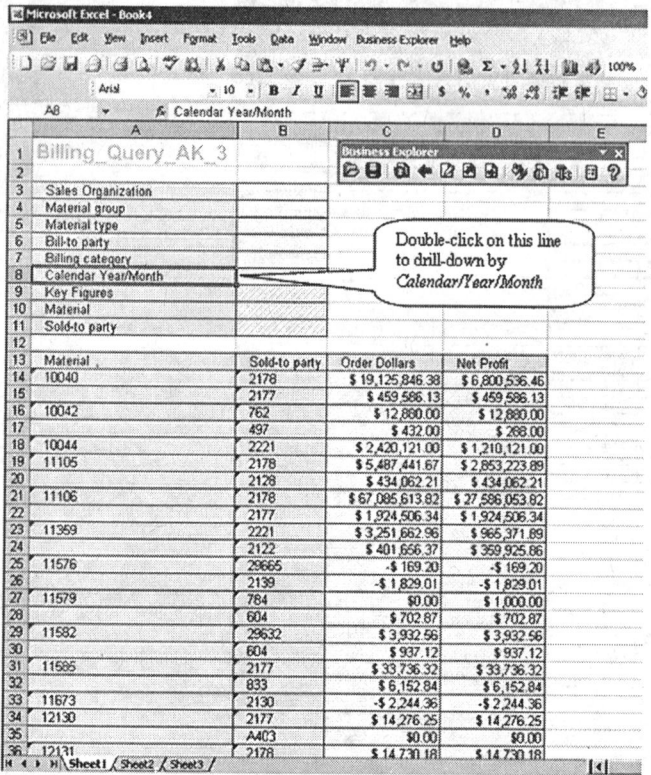

- Double-click on the characteristic *Calendar Month/Year*, which is highlighted on Figure 124

This will execute the drill-down and lead to the results displayed on Figure 125.

Figure 125

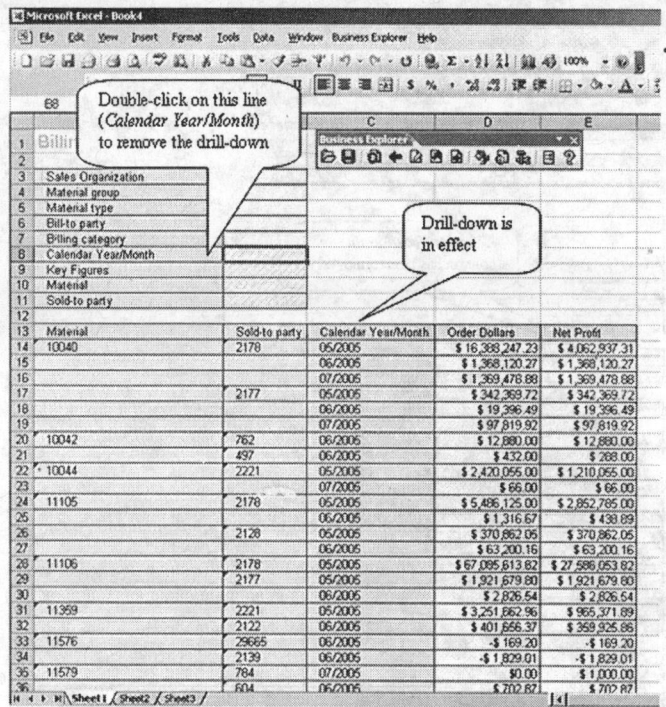

Reversing a drill-down by double-clicking

A drill-down can be reversed by double-clicking on the appropriate characteristic. To reverse the drill-down that is in effect on Figure 125:

- Double-click on the characteristic *Calendar Year/Month*, which is highlighted on Figure 125

This will reverse the drill-down and display the report, as shown on Figure 126, which is the same as the original report (Figure 124).

Figure 126

	A	B	C	D	E
1	Billing_Query_AK_3				
2					
3	Sales Organization				
4	Material group				
5	Material type				
6	Bill-to party				
7	Billing category				
8	Calendar Year/Month				
9	Key Figures				
10	Material				
11	Sold-to party				
12					
13	Material	Sold-to party	Order Dollars	Net Profit	
14	10040	2178	$ 19,125,846.38	$ 6,800,536.46	
15		2177	$ 459,586.13	$ 459,586.13	
16	10042	762	$ 12,880.00	$ 12,880.00	
17		497	$ 432.00	$ 288.00	
18	10044	2221	$ 2,420,121.00	$ 1,210,121.00	
19	11105	2178	$ 5,487,441.67	$ 2,853,223.89	
20		2128	$ 434,062.21	$ 434,062.21	
21	11106	2178	$ 67,085,613.82	$ 27,586,053.82	
22		2177	$ 1,924,506.34	$ 1,924,506.34	
23	11359	2221	$ 3,251,662.96	$ 965,371.89	
24		2122	$ 401,656.37	$ 359,925.86	
25	11576	29665	-$ 169.20	-$ 169.20	
26		2139	-$ 1,829.01	-$ 1,829.01	
27	11579	784	$0.00	$ 1,000.00	
28		604	$ 702.87	$ 702.87	
29	11582	29632	$ 3,932.56	$ 3,932.56	
30		604	$ 937.12	$ 937.12	
31	11585	2177	$ 33,736.32	$ 33,736.32	
32		833	$ 6,152.84	$ 6,152.84	
33	11673	2130	-$ 2,244.36	-$ 2,244.36	
34	12130	2177	$ 14,276.25	$ 14,276.25	
35		A403	$0.00	$0.00	
36	12131	2178	$ 14,730.18	$ 14,730.18	

Calendar Year/Month column has been removed

Filter and drilldown according to

This function can be used when it is desired to fix a characteristic to a value in one step (filter it) and then drill-down according to another characteristic on the same axis (row axis or column axis). For example, this function can be used to choose *Region* for the characteristic value *France*, which will filter the data for *France*. It will also cause the characteristic value *France* to disappear from the drill-down. Simultaneously, the *Region* characteristic will be drilled-down.

To demonstrate this functionality, we will start with the report displayed on Figure 127.

Figure 127

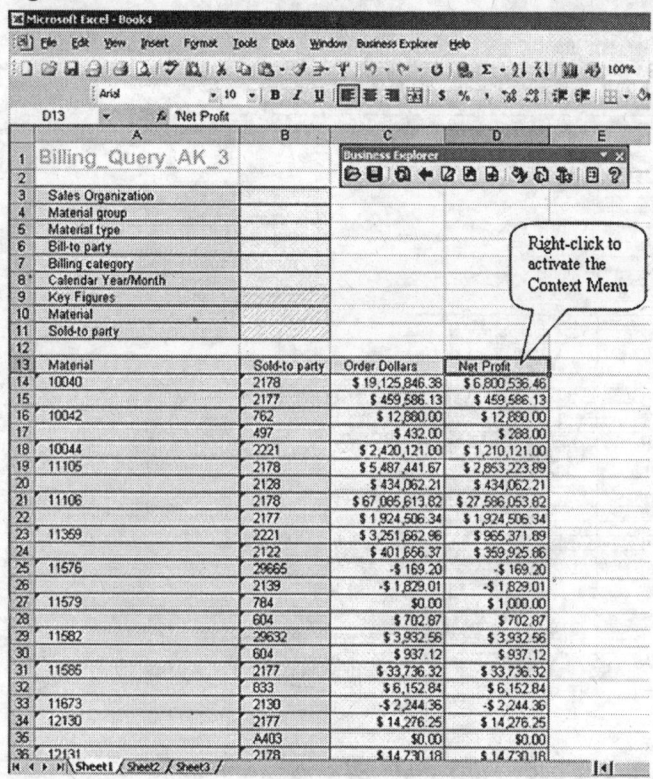

To execute the *Filter and drill-down according to* function:

- Right-click on *Net Profit*, as shown on Figure 127

This will cause the Context Menu to pop-up, which is displayed on Figure 128.

Figure 128

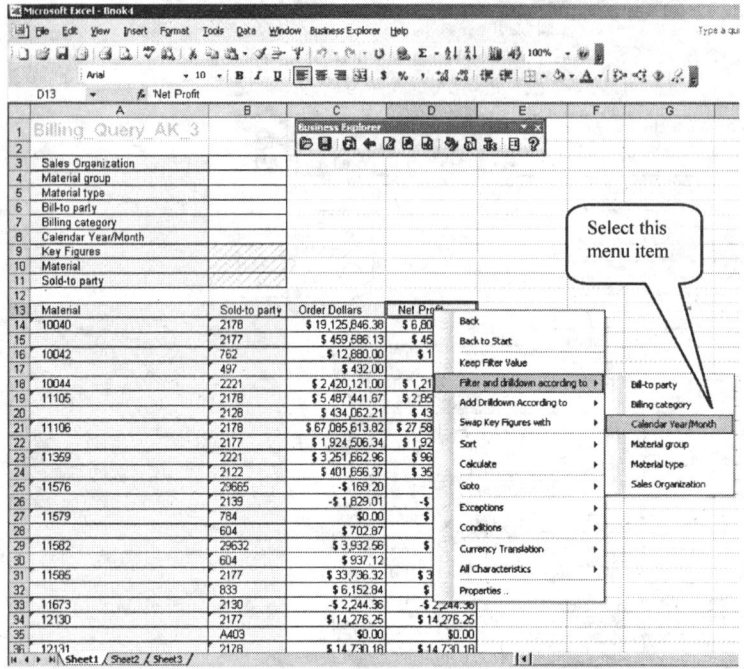

Copyright SAP AG

- Navigate via the menu path *Filter and drilldown according to > Calendar Year/Month*, as shown on Figure 128

This will execute the *Filter and drilldown according to* function and lead to the results displayed on Figure 129.

Figure 129

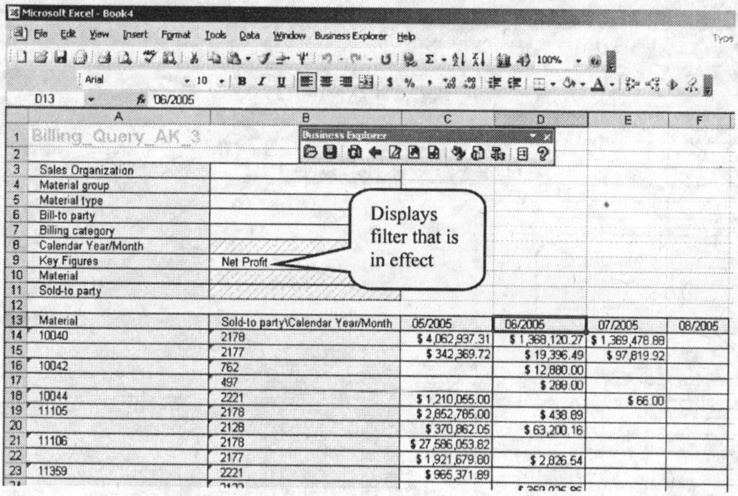

	A	B	C	D	E	F
1	Billing Query AK_3					
2		Business Explorer				
3	Sales Organization					
4	Material group					
5	Material type					
6	Bill-to party					
7	Billing category		Displays filter that is in effect			
8	Calendar Year/Month					
9	Key Figures	Net Profit				
10	Material					
11	Sold-to party					
12						
13	Material	Sold-to party\Calendar Year/Month	05/2005	06/2005	07/2005	08/2005
14	10040	2178	$ 4,062,937.31	$ 1,368,120.27	$ 1,369,478.88	
15		2177	$ 342,369.72	$ 19,396.49	$ 97,819.92	
16	10042	762		$ 12,880.00		
17		497		$ 288.00		
18	10044	2221	$ 1,210,055.00		$ 66.00	
19	11105	2178	$ 2,852,785.00	$ 438.89		
20		2128	$ 370,862.05	$ 63,200.16		
21	11106	2178	$ 27,586,053.82			
22		2177	$ 1,921,679.80	$ 2,826.54		
23	11359	2221	$ 965,371.89			

How to swap axes

What is swapping

The swap function enables a report layout to be changed by switching rows with columns. For example, if the characteristics are displayed in the rows and key figures in the columns, executing the swap function will cause the characteristics to be displayed in the columns and the key figures in the rows. Like a pivot table in Excel, this function enables analysis from different angles. The swap function, which can be executed via the Context Menu, can also be reversed.

How to swap

To demonstrate this function, we will start with the report displayed on Figure 130:

Figure 130

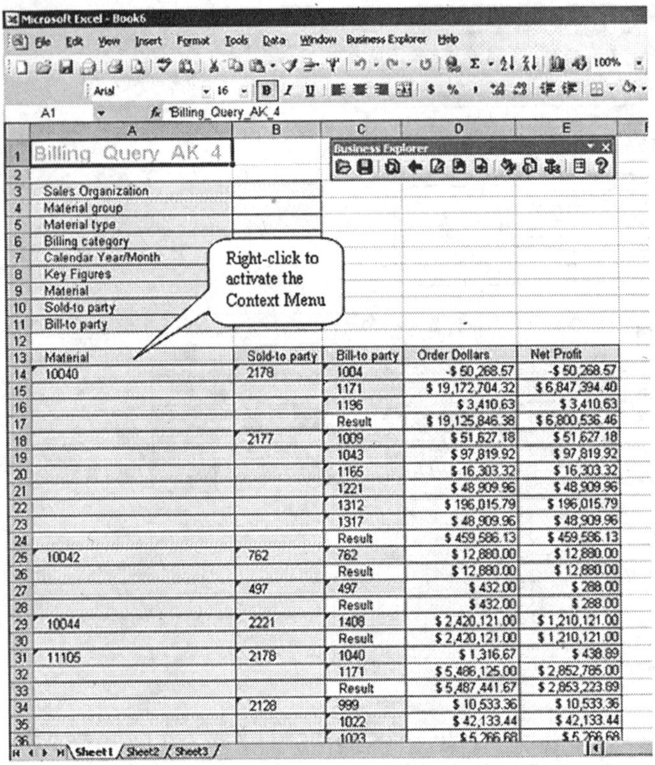

	A	B	C	D	E
1	Billing Query AK 4		Business Explorer		
2					
3	Sales Organization				
4	Material group				
5	Material type				
6	Billing category				
7	Calendar Year/Month				
8	Key Figures		*Right-click to activate the Context Menu*		
9	Material				
10	Sold-to party				
11	Bill-to party				
12					
13	Material	Sold-to party	Bill-to party	Order Dollars	Net Profit
14	10040	2178	1004	-$ 50,268.57	-$ 50,268.57
15			1171	$ 19,172,704.32	$ 6,847,394.40
16			1196	$ 3,410.63	$ 3,410.63
17			Result	$ 19,125,846.38	$ 6,800,536.46
18		2177	1009	$ 51,627.18	$ 51,627.18
19			1043	$ 97,819.92	$ 97,819.92
20			1165	$ 16,303.32	$ 16,303.32
21			1221	$ 48,909.96	$ 48,909.96
22			1312	$ 196,015.79	$ 196,015.79
23			1317	$ 48,909.96	$ 48,909.96
24			Result	$ 459,586.13	$ 459,586.13
25	10042	762	762	$ 12,880.00	$ 12,880.00
26			Result	$ 12,880.00	$ 12,880.00
27		497	497	$ 432.00	$ 288.00
28			Result	$ 432.00	$ 288.00
29	10044	2221	1408	$ 2,420,121.00	$ 1,210,121.00
30			Result	$ 2,420,121.00	$ 1,210,121.00
31	11105	2178	1040	$ 1,316.67	$ 438.89
32			1171	$ 5,486,125.00	$ 2,852,785.00
33			Result	$ 5,487,441.67	$ 2,853,223.89
34		2128	999	$ 10,533.36	$ 10,533.36
35			1022	$ 42,133.44	$ 42,133.44
36			1023	$ 5,266.68	$ 5,266.68

To perform a swap for the characteristic *Material*:

- Right-click on the characteristic (*Material*), as shown on Figure 130

This will cause the Context Menu to pop-up, which is displayed on Figure 131.

Figure 131

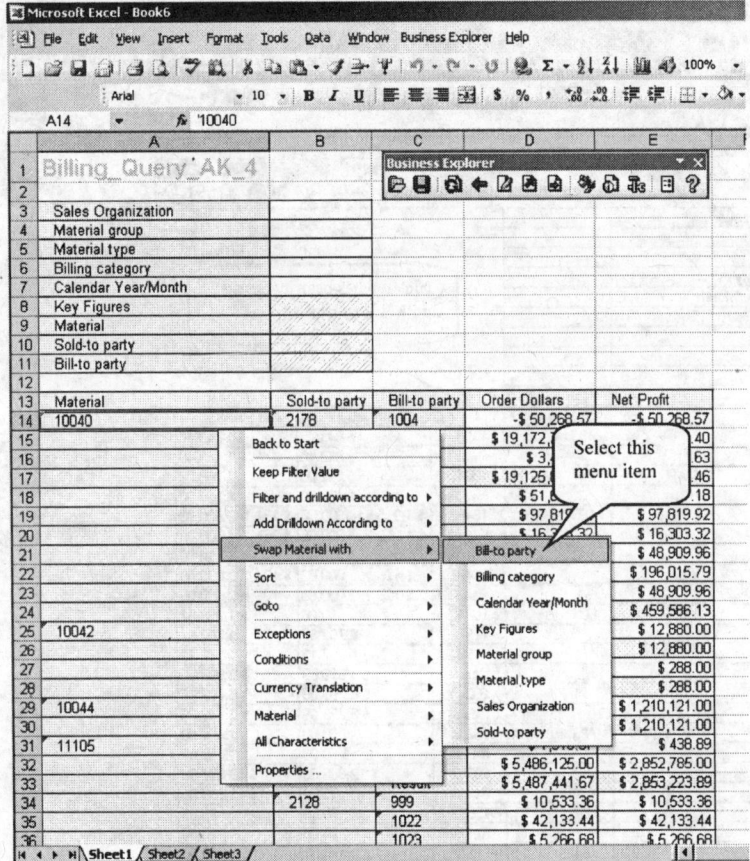

Copyright SAP AG

- Navigate via the menu path *Swap Material with > Bill-to-party*, as shown on Figure 131

This will execute the swap function and lead to the results displayed on Figure 132.

Figure 132

	A	B	C	D	E
1	Billing_Query_AK_4		Business Explorer		
2					
3	Sales Organization				
4	Material group				
5	Material type				
6	Billing category				
7	Calendar Year/Month				
8	Key Figures				
9	Material				
10	Sold-to party				
11	Bill-to party				
12					
13	Bill-to party		Sold-to party	Material	Order Dollars	Net Profit
14	493		493	11585	$843.40	$843.40
15				Result	$843.40	$843.40
16	497		497	10042	$432.00	$288.00
17				Result	$432.00	$288.00
18	498		498	16482	$1,255,914,000.00	$251,182,800.00
19				Result	$1,255,914,000.00	$251,182,800.00
20	500		500	11105	$0.00	$0.00
21				16482	$126,192,000.00	$126,192,000.00
22				Result	$126,192,000.00	$126,192,000.00
23	604		604	10040	$0.00	$1,358.61
24				11579	$702.87	$702.87
25				11582	$937.12	$937.12
26				Result	$1,639.99	$2,998.60
27	611		611	10040	$6,793.05	$6,793.05
28				Result	$6,793.05	$6,793.05
29	723		723	15734	-$50.00	-$50.00
30				Result	-$50.00	-$50.00
31	762		762	10042	$12,880.00	$12,880.00
32				Result	$12,880.00	$12,880.00
33	782		782	12582	$0.00	$0.00
34				Result	$0.00	$0.00
35	784		784	11579	$0.00	$1,000.00
36				Result	$0.00	$1,000.00

Material has been swapped with Bill-to-party

How to sort

The sort function enables sorting of values in ascending or descending order, which can help organize data and aid in its analysis. Sorting can be performed on a key figure or a characteristic. A key figure can be sorted in ascending or descending order. A characteristic can be sorted by its key or description, either in ascending or descending order.

To sort a characteristic in descending order (Figure 133):

- Right-click the column heading of the *Order Dollars* characteristic

This will cause the Context Menu to pop-up, which is displayed on Figure 133.

Figure 133

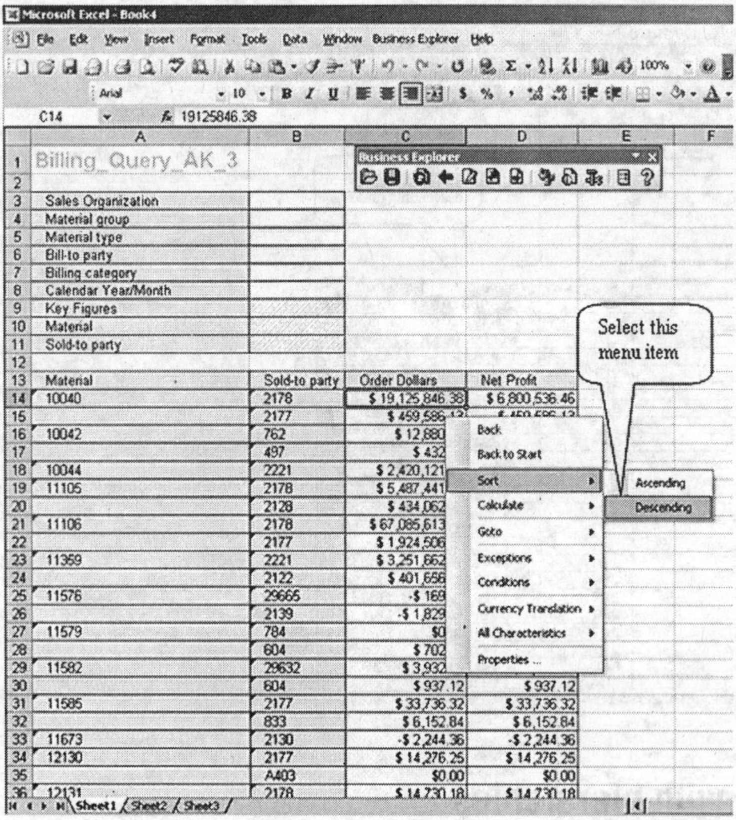

Copyright SAP AG

- Navigate via the menu path *Sort > Descending*, as shown on Figure 133

This will execute the sort function and lead to the results displayed on Figure 134.

Figure 134

	A	B	C	D	E
1	Billing_Query_AK_3				
2					
3	Sales Organization				
4	Material group				
5	Material type				
6	Bill-to party				
7	Billing category				
8	Calendar Year/Month				
9	Key Figures				
10	Material				
11	Sold-to party				
12					
13	Material	Sold-to party	Order Dollars	Net Profit	
14	16482	498	$ 1,255,914,000.00	$ 251,182,800.00	
15	16482	500	$ 126,192,000.00	$ 126,192,000.00	
16	11106	2178	$ 67,085,613.82	$ 27,586,053.82	
17	12582	2178	$ 49,363,269.12	$ 14,353,569.12	
18	16502	2178	$ 34,484,000.00	$ 11,184,000.00	
19	8527	2178	$ 27,927,120.89	$ 14,308,020.89	
20	10040	2178	$ 19,125,846.38	$ 6,800,536.46	
21	16501	2178	$ 17,118,600.00	$ 8,878,600.00	
22	15734	2178	$ 8,043,750.00	$ 6,063,750.00	
23	15534	2178	$ 7,519,049.99	$ 7,504,991.33	
24	13013	2178	$ 5,592,649.65	$ 2,864,749.65	
25	11105	2178	$ 5,487,441.67	$ 2,853,223.89	
26	16500	2178	$ 5,325,000.00	$ 2,325,000.00	
27	15734	2177	$ 3,762,000.00	$ 2,046,000.00	
28	11359	2221	$ 3,251,662.96	$ 965,371.89	
29	10044	2221	$ 2,420,121.00	$ 1,210,121.00	
30	11106	2177	$ 1,924,506.34	$ 1,924,506.34	
31	4413	2178	$ 1,092,251.82	$ 656,440.62	
32	15534	2177	$ 811,925.01	$ 811,925.01	
33	16502	2177	$ 643,385.93	$ 643,385.93	
34	10040	2177	$ 459,586.13	$ 459,586.13	
35	15620	940	$ 449,082.00	$ 299,304.00	
36	11105	2128	$ 434,062.21	$ 434,062.21	

Sorted results in descending order

Working with hierarchies

What is a hierarchy

A hierarchy provides a structured and grouped method for displaying characteristics based on individual analysis needs. A hierarchy structure contains different levels, where inter-dependency exists among elements at various levels. Hierarchies, which are used as the basis for aggregation and drill-down within reports, enable data analysis at different levels of the hierarchy. BW supports the modeling of hierarchical structures, such as profit centers that are grouped in profit center groups.

BW reports use hierarchies extensively. When a report is run, the results are displayed in collapsed or expanded mode, depending on the selection variables and query structure. A collapsed hierarchy can be expanded, while an expanded hierarchy can be collapsed. This enables the results to be viewed and/or analyzed at the desired hierarchy level(s).

The hierarchy function can be accessed via the Context Menu, which provides the ability to expand a hierarchy (at different levels), collapse a hierarchy, and deactivate a hierarchy. A reporting hierarchy can be deactivated for removing rollup values, which enables the lowest level values to be displayed instead of the aggregate level values.

Expanding a hierarchy

We will start with the hierarchy shown in the report on Figure 135, which will be expanded to display lower levels.

Figure 135

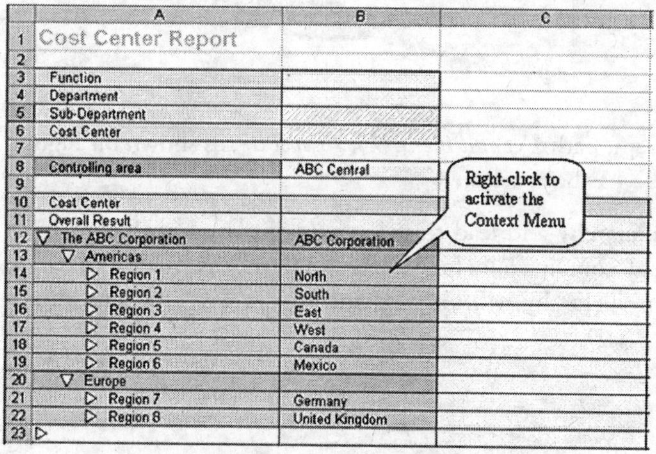

	A	B	C
1	Cost Center Report		
2			
3	Function		
4	Department		
5	Sub-Department		
6	Cost Center		
7			
8	Controlling area	ABC Central	
9			Right-click to activate the Context Menu
10	Cost Center		
11	Overall Result		
12	▽ The ABC Corporation	ABC Corporation	
13	▽ Americas		
14	▷ Region 1	North	
15	▷ Region 2	South	
16	▷ Region 3	East	
17	▷ Region 4	West	
18	▷ Region 5	Canada	
19	▷ Region 6	Mexico	
20	▽ Europe		
21	▷ Region 7	Germany	
22	▷ Region 8	United Kingdom	
23	▷		

- Right-click in the Results Area

This will cause the Context Menu to pop-up, which is displayed on Figure 136.

Figure 136

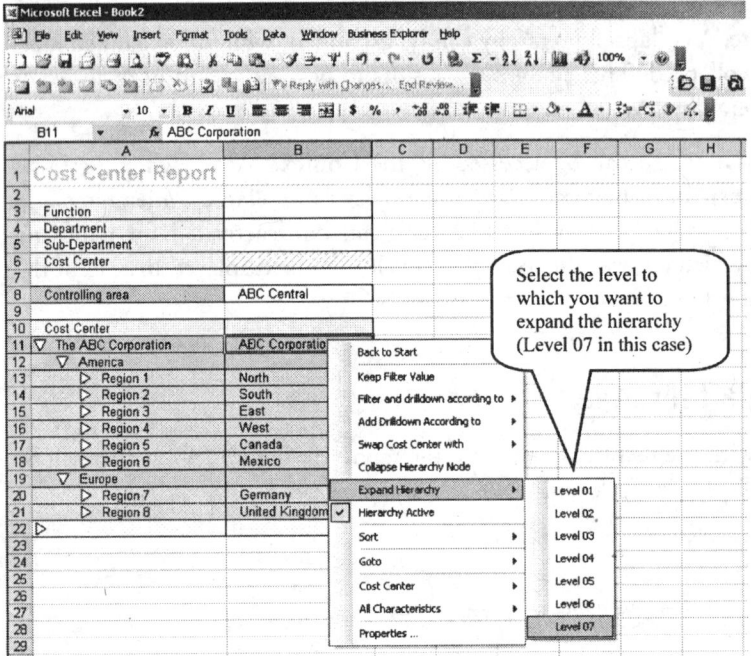

Copyright SAP AG

- Navigate via the menu path *Expand hierarchy > Level 07*, as shown on Figure 136, where Level 07 has been selected

This will expand the hierarchy and lead to the results displayed on Figure 137. Note that if the hierarchy contains only four levels and Level 7 is selected through the Context Menu, the hierarchy will only expand to Level 4—the maximum possible.

Figure 137

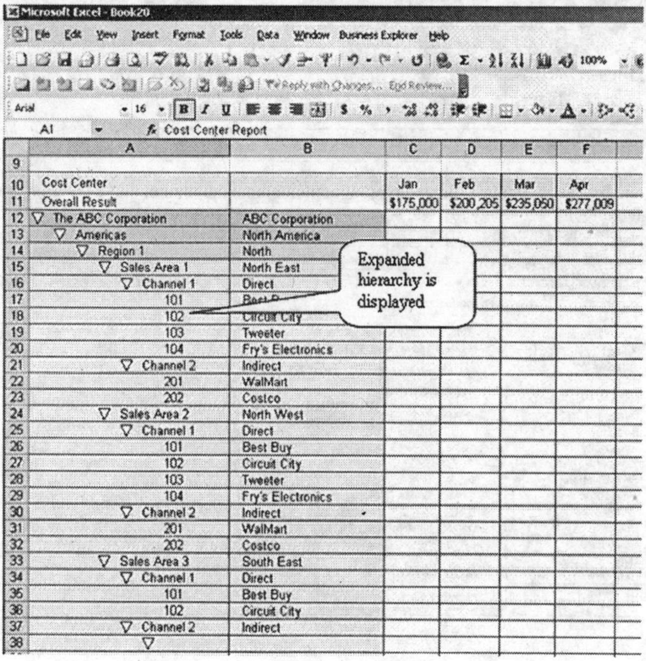

	A	B	C	D	E	F
	A1	Cost Center Report				
9						
10	Cost Center		Jan	Feb	Mar	Apr
11	Overall Result		$175,000	$200,205	$235,050	$277,009
12	▽ The ABC Corporation	ABC Corporation				
13	▽ Americas	North America				
14	▽ Region 1	North				
15	▽ Sales Area 1	North East				
16	▽ Channel 1	Direct				
17	101	Best Buy				
18	102	Circuit City				
19	103	Tweeter				
20	104	Fry's Electronics				
21	▽ Channel 2	Indirect				
22	201	WalMart				
23	202	Costco				
24	▽ Sales Area 2	North West				
25	▽ Channel 1	Direct				
26	101	Best Buy				
27	102	Circuit City				
28	103	Tweeter				
29	104	Fry's Electronics				
30	▽ Channel 2	Indirect				
31	201	WalMart				
32	202	Costco				
33	▽ Sales Area 3	South East				
34	▽ Channel 1	Direct				
35	101	Best Buy				
36	102	Circuit City				
37	▽ Channel 2	Indirect				
38	▽					

Expanded hierarchy is displayed

Collapsing a hierarchy node

In the next step, we will collapse a hierarchy node.

To start the procedure:

- Right-click in the Results Area

This will cause the Context Menu to pop-up, which is displayed on Figure 138.

Figure 138

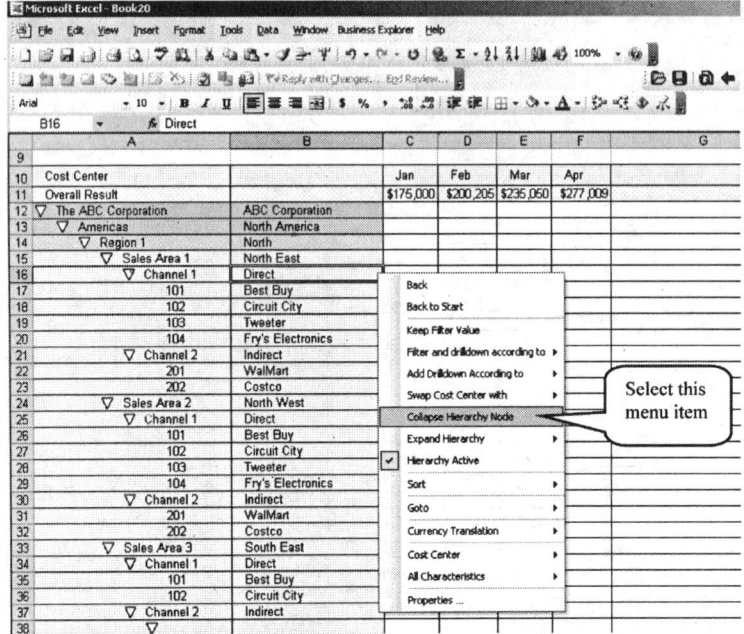

Copyright SAP AG

- Select the menu item *Collapse Hierarchy Node*, which has been highlighted on Figure 138

This will collapse the hierarchy node and lead to the results displayed on Figure 139.

Figure 139

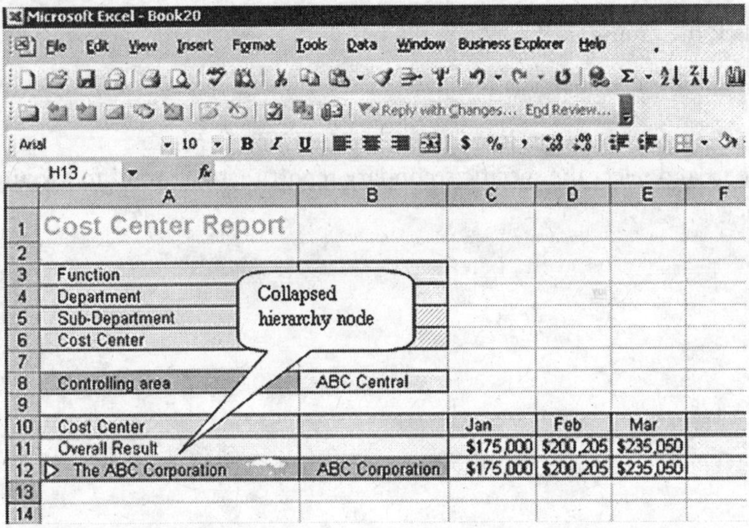

	A	B	C	D	E	F
1	Cost Center Report					
2						
3	Function					
4	Department					
5	Sub-Department	(Collapsed hierarchy node)				
6	Cost Center					
7						
8	Controlling area	ABC Central				
9						
10	Cost Center		Jan	Feb	Mar	
11	Overall Result		$175,000	$200,205	$235,050	
12	▷ The ABC Corporation	ABC Corporation	$175,000	$200,205	$235,050	
13						
14						

Deactivating a hierarchy

In the next step, we will deactivate a hierarchy. To start the procedure:

- Right-click to activate the Context Menu
- Select the menu item *Deactivate Hierarchy*

Note that it is only possible to deactivate a hierarchy when the *Deactivate Hierarchy* menu item is displayed on the Context Menu.

How to jump

The review of report results can establish the need to perform further analysis of the source data. This may require a user to execute another (secondary) report or navigate to the source data. For this purpose, BW provides a useful feature, called the jump function. This function can be accessed through the Context Menu. It enables a user to navigate away from the currently displayed report to another report (which can display the source data). For example, if you are reviewing a P&L report and observe a deviation, you can jump directly to the report(s) that can display the underlying data contributing to the P&L report.

To activate the jump feature after a report has been displayed:

- Right-click the mouse

This will activate the Context Menu.

- Select the appropriate menu item, *Jump*, on the Context Menu
- Navigate to and select the specific secondary report that you want to execute and review

CHAPTER 12: MISCELLANEOUS FUNCTIONS USING THE ANALYZER

In this chapter, some additional BEx Analyzer functions will be demonstrated. These include the exporting of results to Excel, printing, e-mailing, and deleting reports from the favorites.

How to export report results to Excel

Report results can be exported to MS-Excel, where they can be further analyzed, manipulated, or reformatted using standard MS-Excel functionality. BW functions can continue to be used on the report provided the BW system is not disconnected. The exported Excel file can be saved to the local drive or a shared drive.

To export report results:

- Click the *Save* icon on the MS-Excel Toolbar

This will cause the *Save As* window to pop-up (Figure 140):

Figure 140

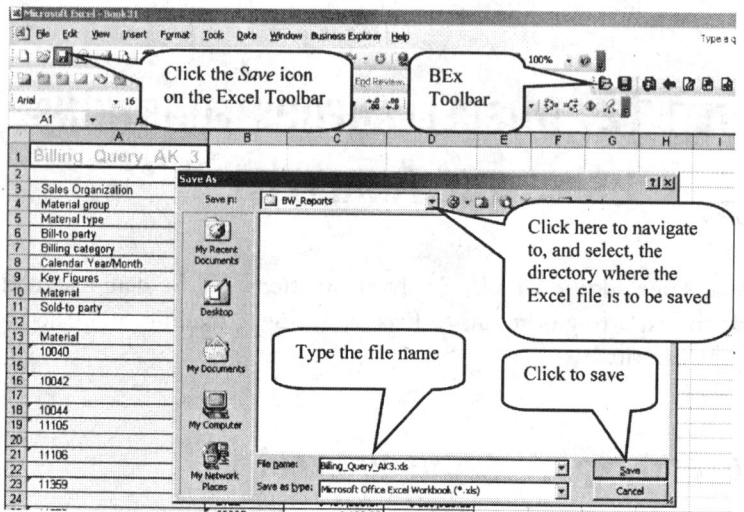

- Select the directory where the Excel file is to be saved, as shown on Figure 140
- Type the name of the file that you want to save (or accept the default file name proposed by the system)
- Click the *Save* button

The saved Excel file can be e-mailed to other BW and non-BW users as an attachment. A non-BW user can modify such a file but cannot refresh it. However, a BW user can modify such a file, refresh it, or add it to his favorites.

How to add a report to the favorites

A BW favorite is just like an Internet browser bookmark, which is a saved reference in the form of a link. In this case, the link provides direct access to a BW report, eliminating the need to navigate to it or find it.

To add a query to your favorites:

- Navigate to the folder where the query, to be added to the favorites, is located

Note: You can also use the *Find* function to quickly locate the desired query.

Figure 141

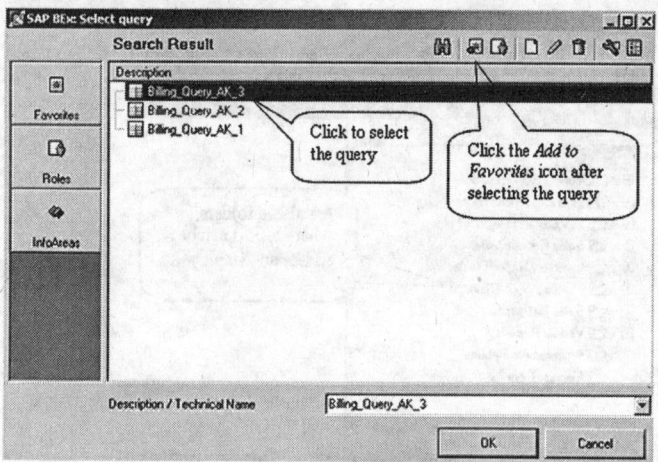

Copyright SAP AG

After the desired query name is displayed, as shown on Figure 141:

- Click the query that is to be added to the favorites

This will highlight and select the query. On Figure 141, *Billing_Query_AK_3* has been selected:

- Click the *Add to Favorites* icon

This will cause the *Add Favorite* window to pop-up (Figure 142):

Figure 142

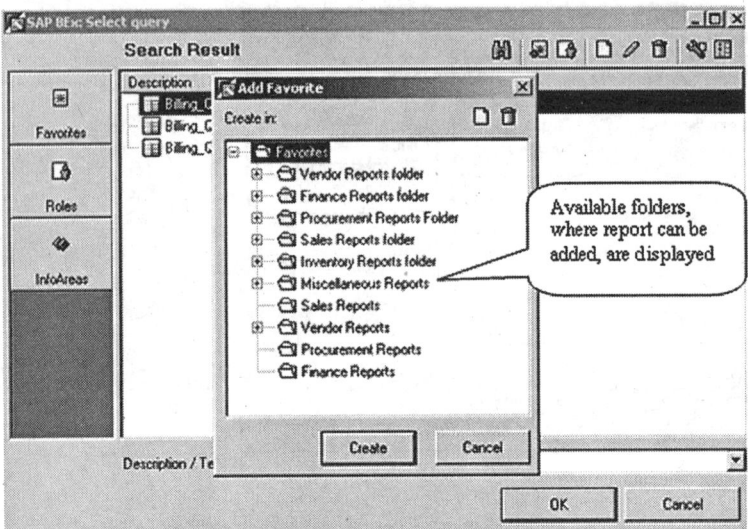

Copyright SAP AG

- Click the *Miscellaneous Reports* folder, where the favorite is to be added, as shown on Figure 143

Figure 143

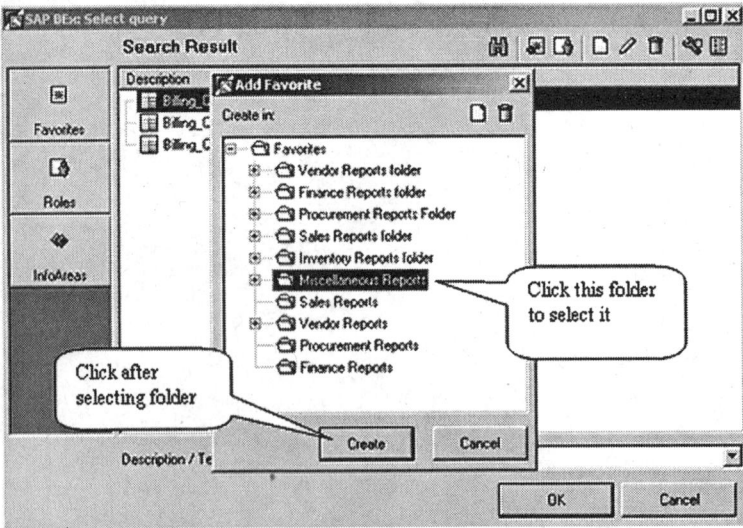

Copyright SAP AG

- Click the *Create* button

This will add the report to the favorites. To confirm that the report has been added to the favorites, drill-down into the *Miscellaneous Reports* folder, as shown on Figure 144.

Figure 144

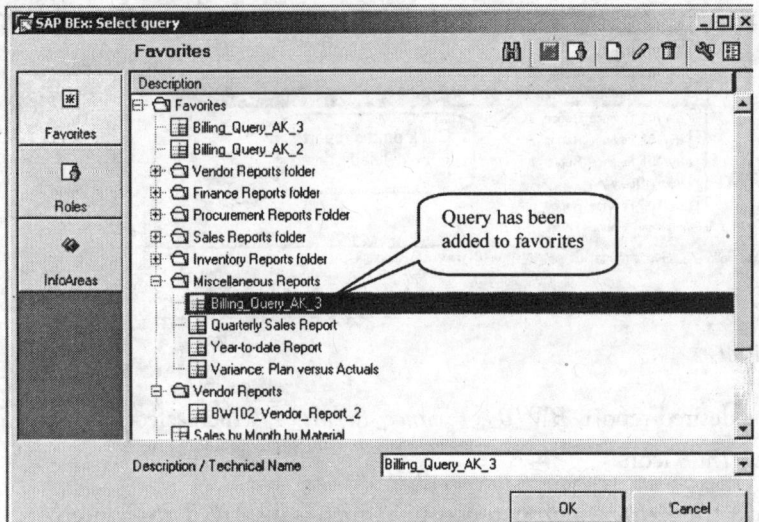

Copyright SAP AG

How to delete a report from the favorites folder

A report can be easily deleted from the favorites. To delete a favorite:

- Navigate to the folder where the report is located, as shown on Figure 145

Figure 145

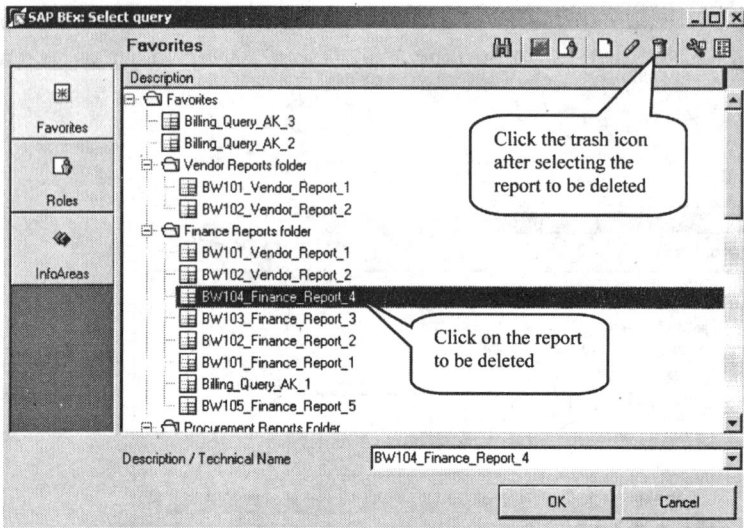

Copyright SAP AG

- Click the desired report, *BW104_Finance_Report_4*, which selects it
- Click the *Trash* icon

This will cause the *Delete* window to pop-up, which is displayed on Figure 146.

Figure 146

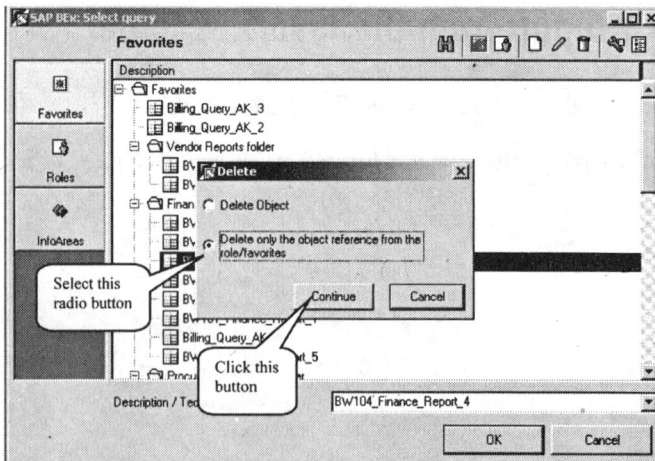

Copyright SAP AG

- Select the *Delete only the object reference from the role/favorites* radio button
- Click the *Continue* button

This will delete the report from the favorites. On Figure 147, it can now be observed that the deleted favorite, *BW104_Finance_Report_4*, is no longer displayed in the list of reports.

Figure 147

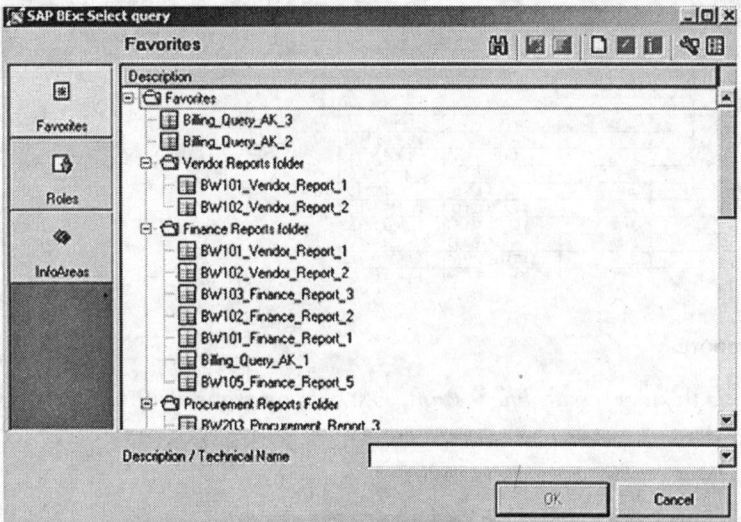

Copyright SAP AG

How to print a report

BW Analyzer reports can be printed using standard MS-Excel printing functionality. Care should be taken when printing a BW report as it can contain thousands of pages and, therefore, an incorrect print request can waste hundreds of pages.

To set the print area:

- Navigate via the menu path *File > Print Area > Set Print Area*, as shown on Figure 148

Figure 148

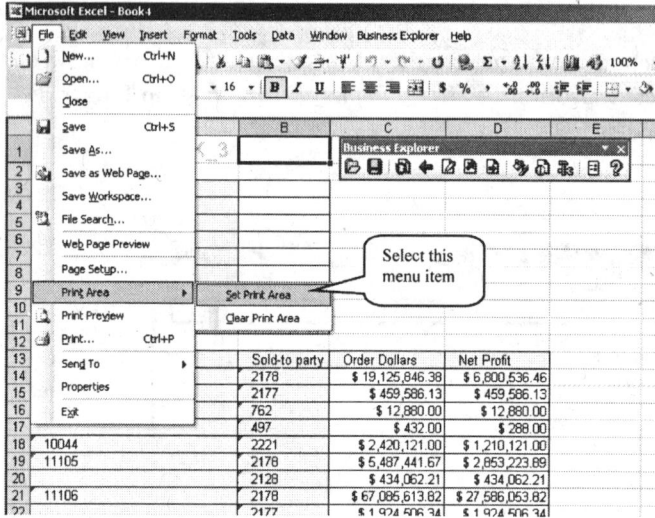

To print the report:

- Navigate via the menu path *File > Print*, as shown on Figure 149

Figure 149

How to e-mail a report

A BW report can be e-mailed to BW users, as well as non-BW users, as a file attachment. The steps involved in sending a report are:
- Save the report to the local/hard drive as an Excel spreadsheet file
- Compose a routine e-mail, as shown on Figure 150

Figure 150

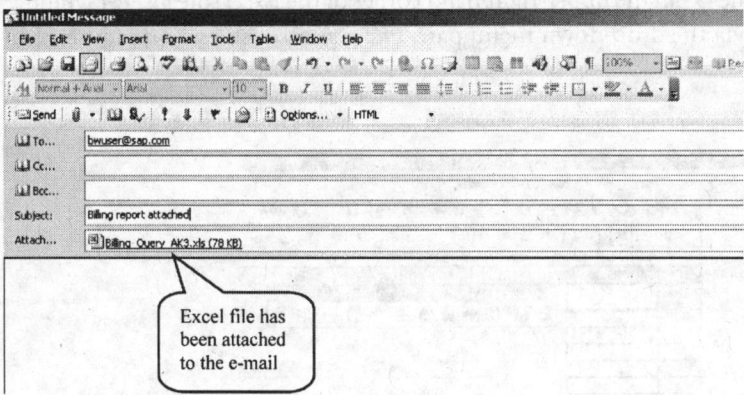

Excel file has been attached to the e-mail

- Attach the saved Excel file

Figure 150 shows that the file has been attached to the e-mail.

- Click the *Send* button to send the e-mail

How to receive a report via e-mail

To open a BW report that has been received via an e-mail:
- Launch the BEx Analyzer
- Open the e-mail attachment
- Click the *Enable Macros* button

After the file (report) has been opened:
- Click the *Refresh* icon

A non-BW user can open the e-mail attachment without launching the BEx Analyzer. In such a case, the user will be receiving a spreadsheet file that cannot be refreshed due to the unavailability of BEx functionality.

How to logoff

A couple of methods can be used to exit the Analyzer:

- Click on the "x" in the upper-right hand corner of the Excel spreadsheet window
- Navigate via the drop-down menu path *File > Exit*, as shown on Figure 151

Figure 151

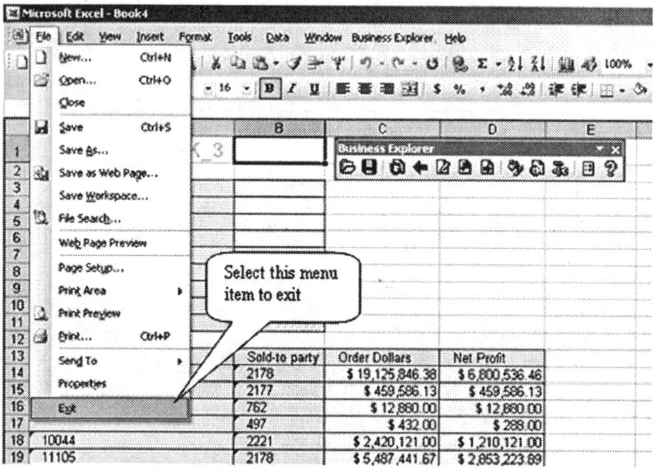

To disconnect from the BW system using the BEx Toolbar:

- Click the *Settings* icon on the BEx Toolbar, as shown on Figure 152

This will display the drop-down menu shown on Figure 152.

Figure 152

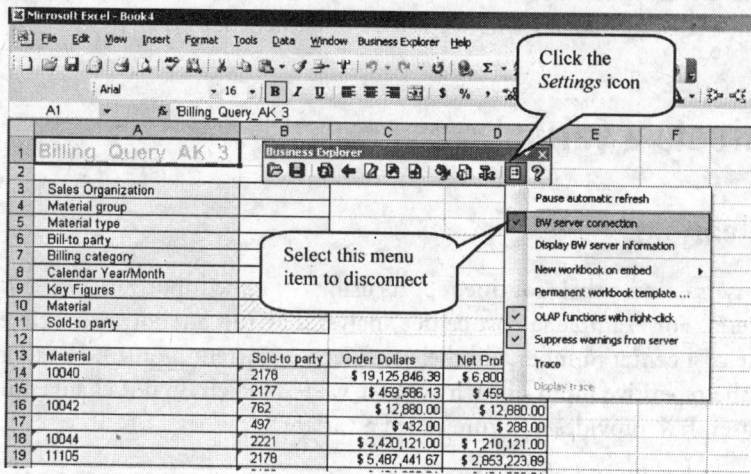

Copyright SAP AG

- Click the menu item *BW server connection*

This will cause a window to pop-up, which is displayed on Figure 153.

Figure 153

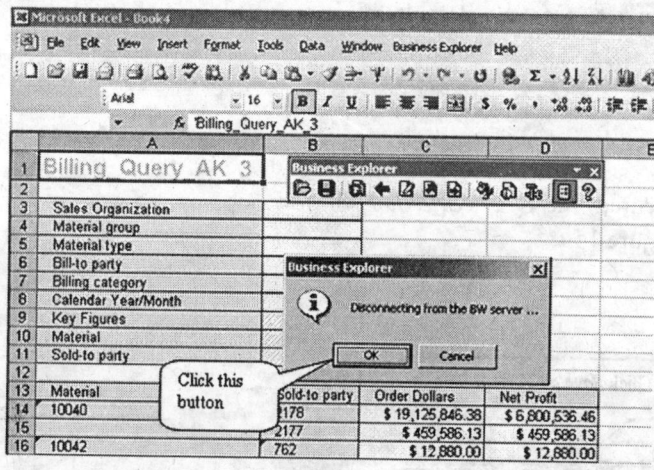

Copyright SAP AG

- Click the *OK* button

This will close the connection to the BW system. To refresh a report after such a disconnection, the BEx Analyzer will need to be re-launched.

How to create a variant

What is a variant

Most report users execute their routine reports using the same input variables and selection criteria. For example, a cost center analyst may run a report every time with the same cost center number and the same period (current month). In order to eliminate the repetitive input of such variable values, which do not change for a particular user, BW provides a feature called a variant.

A variant saves the field values in a *Query Selection* window, eliminating the need to enter such values every time the report is run. When a variant is executed, the field values for a variable are not required to be entered, as they have been previously saved (when the variant was created).

A variant can be retrieved and executed, as needed. It can also be modified or deleted. A query can contain more than one variant. At run time, the desired variant can be selected from the list of saved variants. After a variant has been selected, it remains in effect as the default selection until it is manually de-selected by the user.

Creating a variant

When a report is executed, the *Query Selection* window pops-up, an example of which is shown on Figure 154:

Figure 154

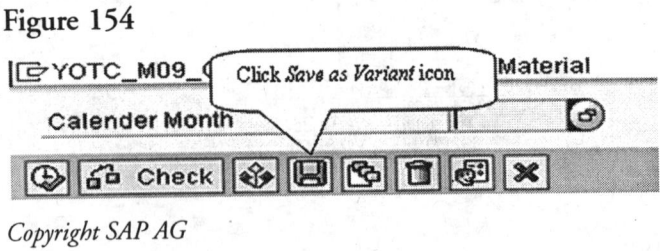

Copyright SAP AG

In order to be able to use the same value for the *Calendar Month* field every time the report is run during the current month, we will create a variant.

To create the variant:

- Click the *Save as Variant* icon, as shown on Figure 154

This will lead to the *Variant Attributes* window (Figure 155):

Figure 155

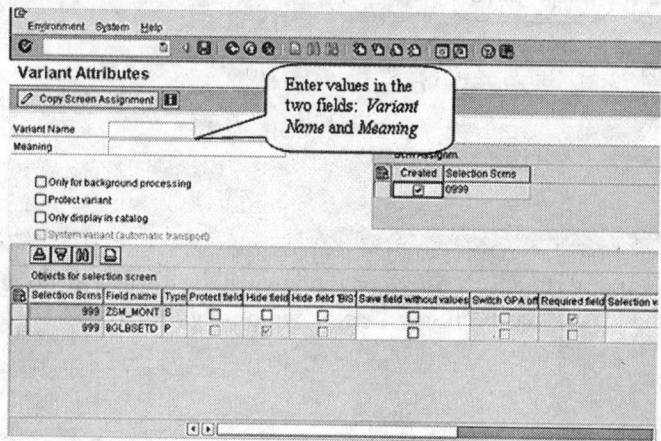

Copyright SAP AG

- Enter the *Variant Name* (*Arshad_1*)
- Enter the *Meaning* (Description of the variant: *Monthly Sales—Variant #1*)

Figure 156 displays the window after the two fields, *Variant Name* and *Meaning*, have been populated:

Figure 156

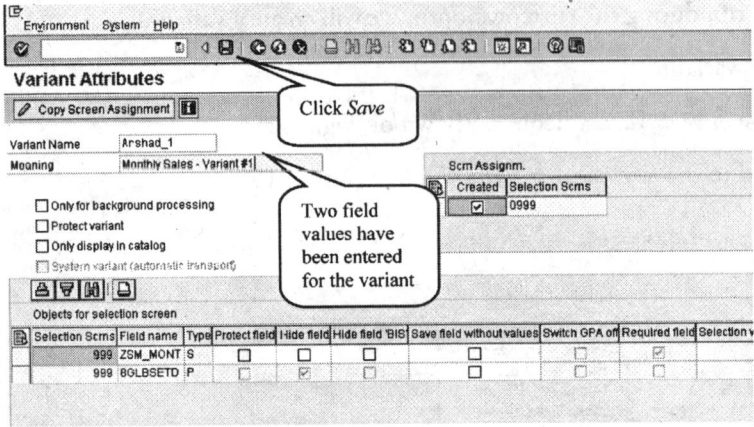

Copyright SAP AG

- Click the *Save* icon

This will save the variant and the *Query Selection* window will be displayed, along with a message that the variant has been saved, as shown on Figure 157.

Figure 157

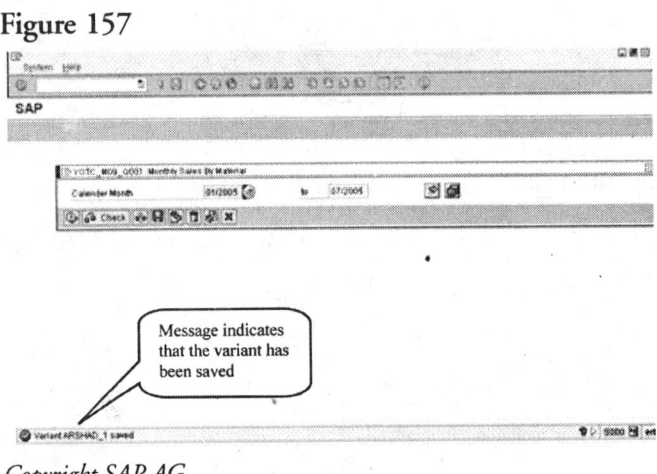

Copyright SAP AG

How to retrieve a variant

When a report is executed, it causes the *Query Selection* window to pop-up, as shown on Figure 158.

Figure 158

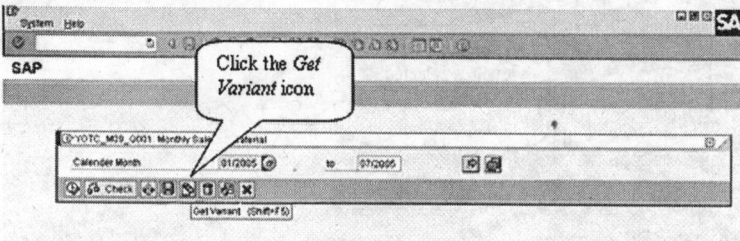

Copyright SAP AG

- Click the *Get Variant* icon, as shown on Figure 158

This will cause a window to pop-up, Figure 159, where the available variants for the query being executed are listed.

Figure 159

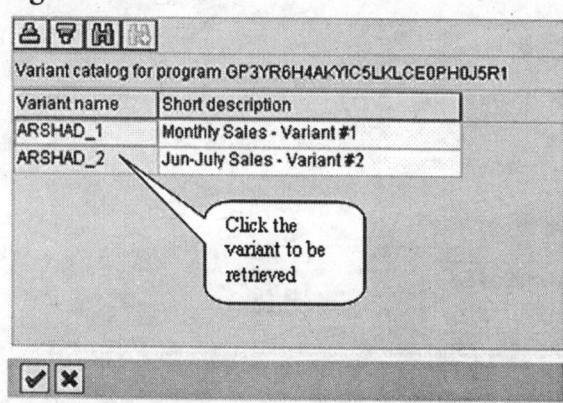

Copyright SAP AG

- Click the second variant, *Arshad_2*, to select it

Figure 160 shows that highlighted variant *Arshad_2 (Jun-July Sales)* has been selected:

Figure 160

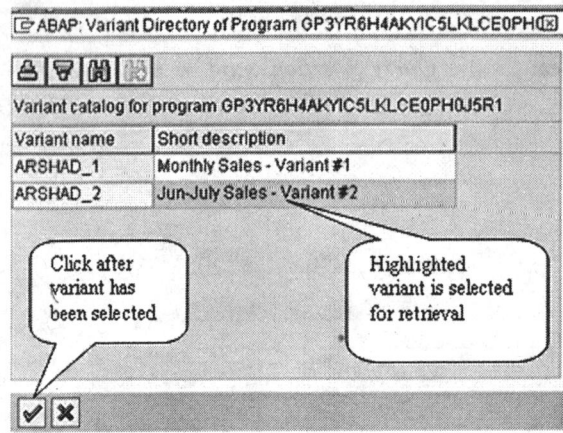

Copyright SAP AG

- Click the checkmark, which is highlighted on Figure 160

This will complete the retrieval procedure and the selected variant, *Arshad_2*, will be activated.

How to delete a variant

To delete a variant:

- Execute the query, which will cause the *Query Selection* window to pop-up (Figure 161)

Figure 161

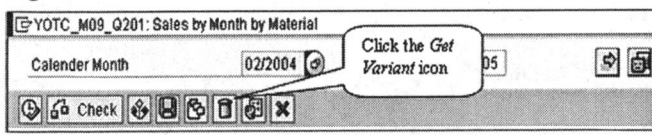

Copyright SAP AG

- Click the *Get Variant* icon, as shown on Figure 161

This will cause the *Delete variants* window, where the query's available variants are listed, to pop-up (Figure 162).

Figure 162

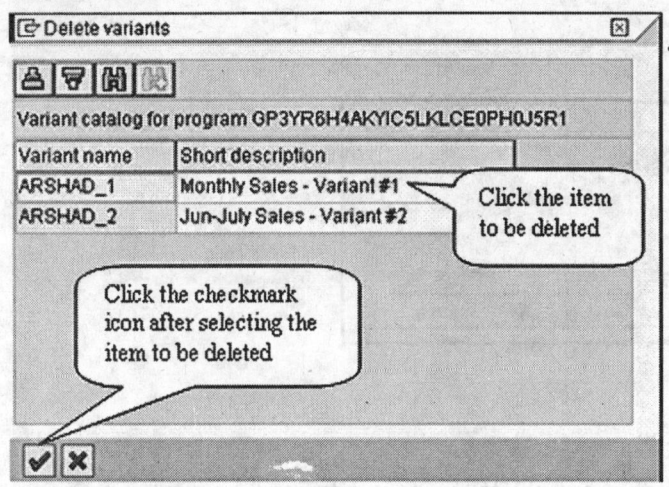

Copyright SAP AG

- Click the variant to be deleted (*Arshad_1*)
- Click the checkmark, which is highlighted on Figure 162

This will cause the next window, *ABAP: Delete Variants*, to pop-up (Figure 163):

Figure 163

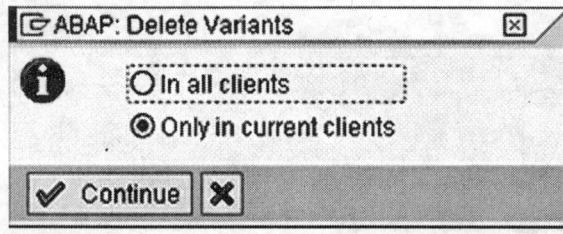

Copyright SAP AG

- Click the radio button *Only in current clients*
- Click the *Continue* button

This will cause the next window to pop-up (Figure 164):

Figure 164

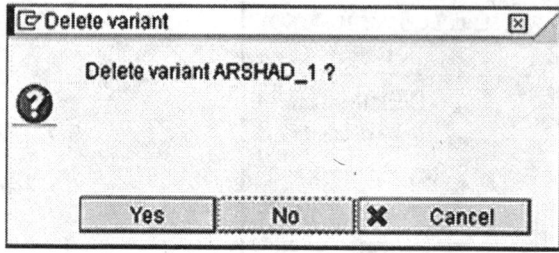

Copyright SAP AG

- Click the *Yes* button

This will delete the variant and the following window will be displayed, Figure 165, where the deletion is confirmed by the displayed message.

Figure 165

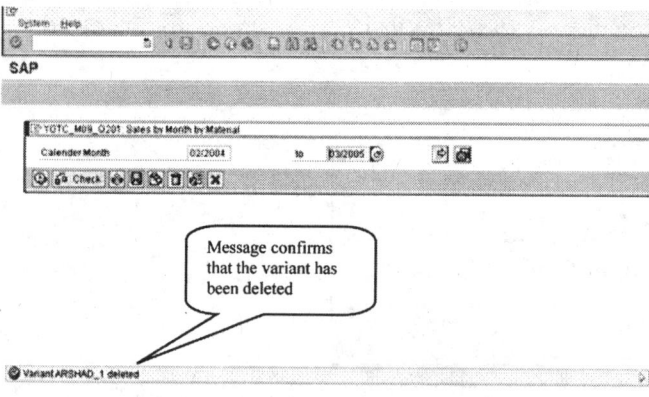

Copyright SAP AG

CHAPTER 13: ANALYSIS ON THE WEB

Drill-down and drill-across

The basic principles for drill-down and drill-across are the same for Excel and web-based reports, though the techniques for executing them are slightly different due to the differences in the tools being used. In web reports, drill-down or drill-across can be executed, or removed, by using the Generic Navigation Block (icon-driven) or the Context Menu (menu-driven).

A simple method for executing a drill-down is to click on the vertical drill-down icon on the Navigation Block, highlighted on Figure 166, which causes a vertical expansion. The horizontal drill-across icon, also highlighted on Figure 166, leads to expansion in the horizontal direction. When a drill-down (or drill-across) is in effect, the relevant icon (pointing right or down) is replaced by a depressed icon. For example, as shown on Figure 166, the depressed *Cost Center* icon indicates that a drill-down is in effect for *Cost Center*. Clicking on a depressed icon removes the drill-down or drill-across in effect.

Figure 166

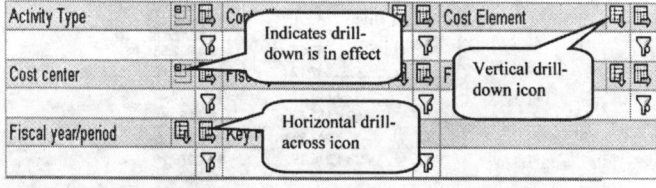

Copyright SAP AG

To perform a drill-down on *Cost Element*:

- Click the drill-down icon next to *Cost Element*, which is highlighted on Figure 166

To perform a drill-across on *Fiscal year/period*:

- Click the drill-across icon next to *Fiscal year/period*, which is highlighted on Figure 166

Two methods are commonly used to perform a drill-down. They are initiated from the Navigation Area or the Results Area.

How to drill-down from the Navigation Area

To drill-down from the Navigation Area, click the cell (characteristic or key figure) that you want to drill-down on, i.e., add to the report.

To drill-down by *Calendar Year/Month* (Figure 167):

- Right-click the characteristic *Calendar Year/Month* in the Navigation Area

This will cause the Context Menu to pop-up, which is displayed on Figure 167.

Figure 167

▼ Rows			Material	Sold-to party	Order Dollars	Net Profit
Material			10040	2178	$ 19,125,846.38	$ 6,800,536.46
Sold-to party				2177	$ 459,586.13	$ 459,586.13
▼ Columns			10042	762	$ 12,880.00	$ 12,880.00
Key Figures					$ 432.00	$ 268.00
▼ Free Characteristics			Right-click the item that is to be drilled down		$ 2,420,121.00	$ 1,210,121.00
Bill-to party					$ 5,487,441.67	$ 2,853,223.89
Billing category					$ 434,062.21	$ 434,062.21
Calendar Year/Month					$ 67,085,613.82	$ 27,586,053.82
Material group	Back		9	2177	$ 1,924,506.34	$ 1,924,506.34
Material type	Back to Start			2221	$ 3,251,662.96	$ 965,371.89
Sales Organization	Select Filter Value		6	2122	$ 401,656.37	$ 359,925.86
	Drilldown	▶	Vertical	29665	$ -169.20	$ -169.20
	Sort Calendar Year/Month	▶	Horizontal		$ -1,829.01	$ -1,829.01
	Goto	▶	2	29632	Select this menu item	$ 1,000.00
				604		$ 702.87
	Bookmark			2177		$ 3,932.56
	Distribute	▶	5	833	$ 33,736.32	$ 937.12
	Enhanced Menu		3	2130	$ 6,152.84	$ 33,736.32
			12130	2177	$ -2,244.36	$ 6,152.84
					$ 14,276.25	$ -2,244.36
						$ 14,276.25

Copyright SAP AG

- Navigate via the menu path *Drilldown > Vertical*, as shown on Figure 167

This will perform the drill-down, by *Calendar Year/Month*, and the selected characteristic will be added to the report, as shown on Figure 168.

Figure 168

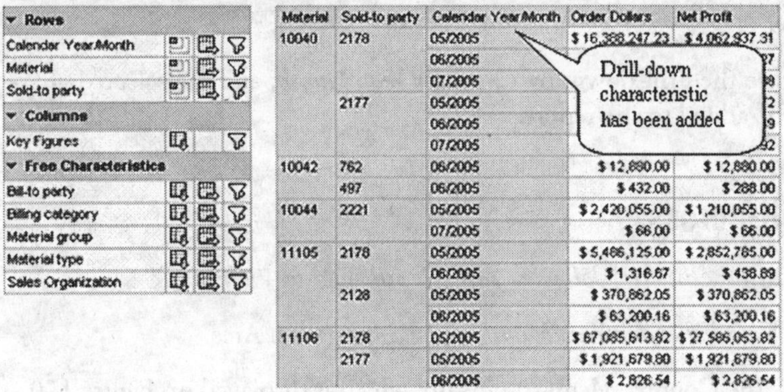

Copyright SAP AG

How to drill-down from the Results Area

To drill-down from the Results Area (Figure 169):

- Right-click in the Results Area

This will cause the Context Menu to pop-up, which is displayed on Figure 169. Note that this Context Menu is different compared to the one launched from the Navigation Area (Figure 167).

Figure 169

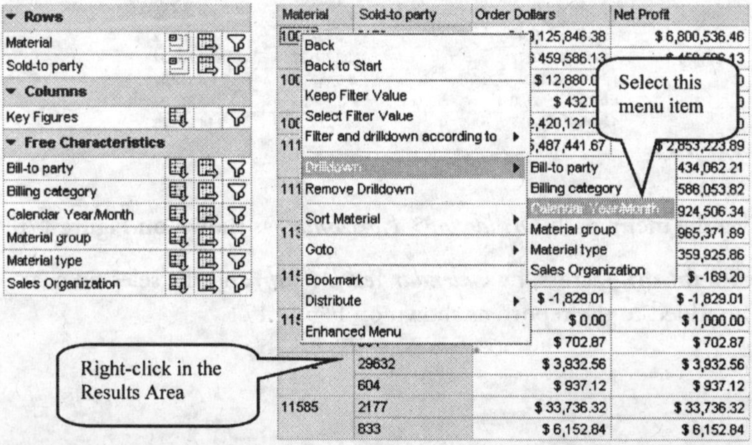

Copyright SAP AG

- Navigate via the menu path *Drilldown > Calendar Year/Month*, as shown on Figure 169

This will execute the drill-down, by *Calendar Year/Month*, and the selected characteristic will be added to the report.

How to drill-across

To perform a drill-across by *Calendar Year/Month* (Figure 170):

- Right-click on *Calendar Year/Month* in the Navigation Area

This will cause the Context Menu to pop-up, which is displayed on Figure 170.

Figure 170

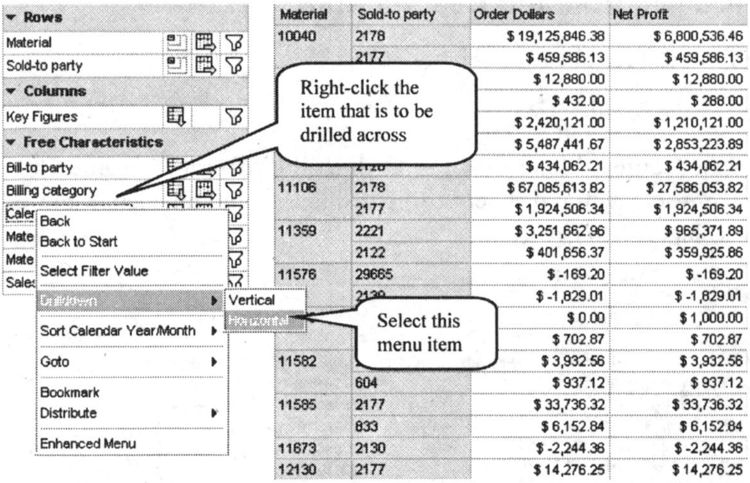

Copyright SAP AG

- Navigate via the menu path *Drilldown > Horizontal*, as shown on Figure 170

This will perform the drill-across, by *Calendar Year/Month*, and the selected characteristic will be added to the report, as shown on Figure 171.

Figure 171

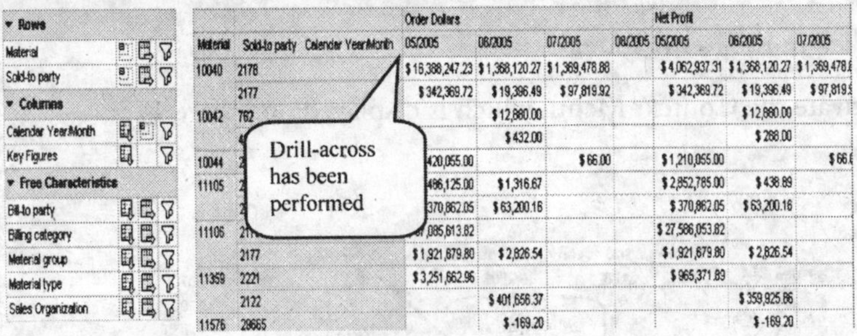

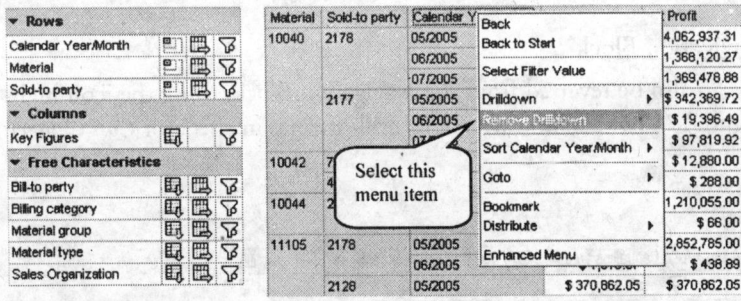

Copyright SAP AG

How to remove drill-down or drill-across

A drill-down or drill-across in effect can be removed using the following methods:

Using the Context Menu

To remove a drill-down:

- Right-click on the characteristic header *Calendar Year/Month*, for which the drill-down is to be removed

This will activate the Context Menu, which is displayed on Figure 172.

Figure 172

Copyright SAP AG

- Select the menu item *Remove drilldown*, as shown on Figure 172, which will remove the drill-down

Another method can also be used to remove a drill-down (Figure 173):

- Right-click in the Results Area

This will activate the Context Menu, which is displayed on Figure 173:

Figure 173

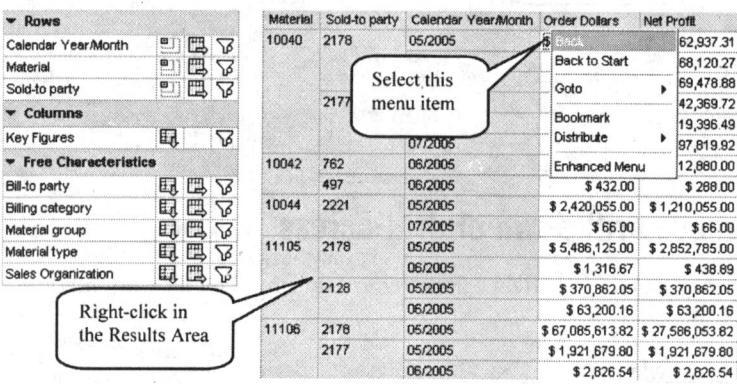

Copyright SAP AG

- Select the menu item *Back*, as shown on Figure 173

This will reverse the previous step (drill-down). If the *Back to Start* item is selected, instead of *Back*, the report will revert to the initial query results (when the report was first executed) and any drilling performed during the navigation process will be reversed.

Using the Navigation Block

A drill-down can also be reversed from the Navigation Block, using the icon highlighted on Figure 174 (which indicates that a drill-down is in effect for *Cost Center*).

Figure 174

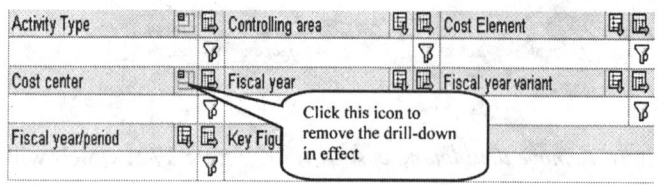

Copyright SAP AG

To remove the drill-down on *Cost Center*:

- Click the icon next to the relevant item, *Cost Center*, which is highlighted on Figure 174

This will reverse the drill-down for the *Cost Center* characteristic.

How to filter by a characteristic

The two methods which can be used to apply various filtering functions in BEx are:

- Context Menu
- Navigation Block

Using the Context Menu to filter

The Context Menu can be used to execute various filtering functions, such as *Keep filter Value*, *Select Filter Value*, and *Filter and drilldown according to*. To specify a filter for the report displayed on Figure 175:

- Right-click the key figure column header (*Calendar Year/Month*)

This will cause the Context Menu to pop-up, which is displayed on Figure 175.

Figure 175

Rows		Material	Sold-to party	Order Dollars	Net Profit
Material		10040	2178	$ 17,756,367.50	$ 5,431,057.58
Sold-to party			2128	$ 364,107.48	$ 364,107.48
Columns				$ 12,880.00	$ 12,880.00
Key Figures				$ 432.00	$ 288.00
				$ 2,420,055.00	$ 1,210,055.00
Free Characteristics				$ 5,487,441.67	$ 2,853,223.89
Bill-to party				$ 434,062.21	$ 434,062.21
Billing category		11106	2178	$ 67,085,613.82	$ 27,586,053.82
Calendar Year/Mo	Back		2177	$ 1,924,506.34	$ 1,924,506.34
Material group	Back to Start		2221	$ 3,251,662.96	$ 965,371.89
Material type			2122	$ 401,656.37	$ 359,925.86
Sales Organization	Select Filter Value			$ -169.20	$ -169.20
	Drilldown ▶			$ -1,829.01	$ -1,829.01
	Sort Calendar Year/Month ▶			$ 702.87	$ 702.87
				$ 0.00	$ 0.00
	Goto ▶		29632	$ 3,932.56	$ 3,932.56
	Bookmark		604	$ 937.12	$ 937.12
	Distribute ▶		2177	$ 33,736.32	$ 33,736.32
			833	$ 6,152.84	$ 6,152.84
	Enhanced Menu		2130	$ -2,244.36	$ -2,244.36

Right-click the characteristic to activate the Context Menu

Select this menu item

Copyright SAP AG

- Select the menu item *Select Filter value*, as shown on Figure 175.

This will cause the next window, *Select Filter Value for Calendar Year/Month*, to pop-up (Figure 176):

Figure 176

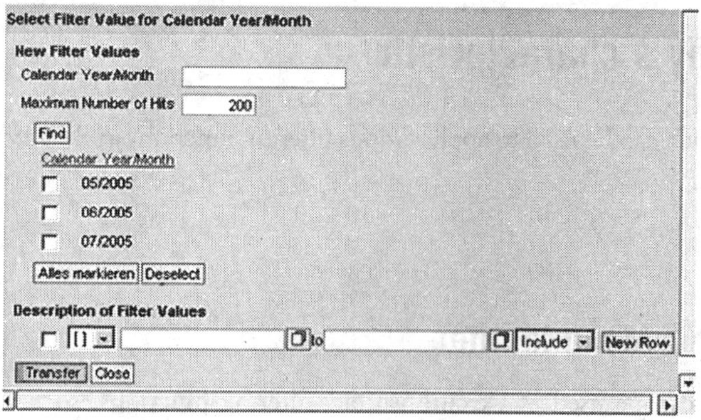

```
Select Filter Value for Calendar Year/Month
New Filter Values
  Calendar Year/Month      [         ]
  Maximum Number of Hits   [ 200 ]
  [Find]
    Calendar Year/Month
    ☐  05/2005
    ☐  06/2005
    ☐  07/2005
  [Alles markieren] [Deselect]
Description of Filter Values
  ☐ [1]▼ [         ] [▣]to[         ] [▣] Include ▼ [New Row]
  [Transfer] [Close]
```

Copyright SAP AG

On the *Select Filter Value* window, filter vales for a specific characteristic can be specified. On Figure 176, three values can be selected for *Calendar Year/Month* (05/2005, 06/2005, and 07/2005). To select two months (May and June) as filter values:

- Click the checkboxes for the required two values, 05/2005 and 06/2005, as shown on Figure 177

Figure 177

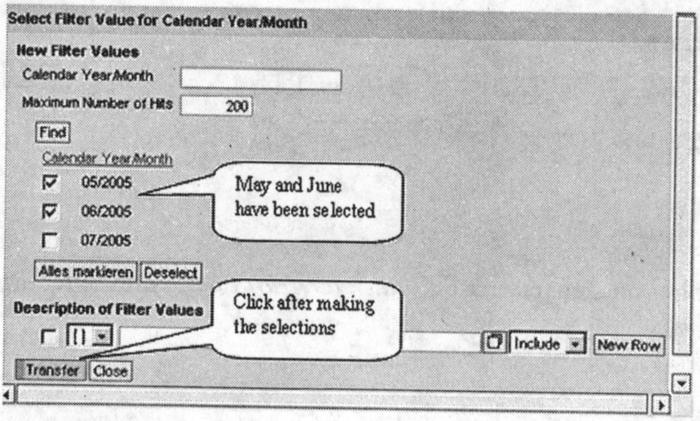

```
Select Filter Value for Calendar Year/Month
New Filter Values
  Calendar Year/Month  [          ]
  Maximum Number of Hits  [ 200 ]
  Find
  Calendar Year/Month
  ☑  05/2005          ┌─────────────────┐
  ☑  06/2005          │ May and June    │
  ☐  07/2005          │ have been selected│
                      └─────────────────┘
  Alles markieren  Deselect
Description of Filter Values  ┌─────────────────┐
  ☐ [1] ▼                     │ Click after making│
                              │ the selections  │
                              └─────────────────┘         [ ] Include ▼  New Row
  Transfer  Close
```

Copyright SAP AG

- Click the *Transfer* button

This will lead to the next window, Figure 178, where the specified filter is displayed.

Figure 178

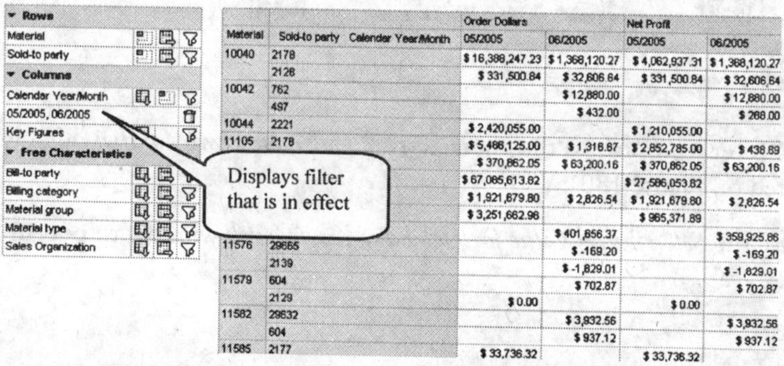

				Order Dollars		Net Profit	
▼ Rows		Material	Sold-to party	Calendar Year/Month	05/2005	06/2005	05/2005	06/2005
Material		10040	2178		$16,388,247.23	$1,368,120.27	$4,062,937.31	$1,368,120.27
Sold-to party			2126		$331,500.84	$32,606.64	$331,500.84	$32,606.64
▼ Columns		10042	762			$12,880.00		$12,880.00
Calendar Year/Month			497			$432.00		$268.00
05/2005, 06/2005		10044	2221		$2,420,055.00		$1,210,055.00	
Key Figures		11105	2178		$5,468,125.00	$1,318.67	$2,852,785.00	$438.89
▼ Free Characteristics					$370,862.05	$63,200.16	$370,862.05	$63,200.16
Bill-to party					$67,085,613.82		$27,586,053.82	
Billing category					$1,921,879.80	$2,826.54	$1,921,879.80	$2,826.54
Material group					$3,251,682.98		$965,371.89	
Material type		11576	29665			$401,856.37		$359,925.86
Sales Organization			2139			$-169.20		$-169.20
		11579	604			$-1,829.01		$-1,829.01
			2129			$702.87		$702.87
		11582	29632		$0.00		$0.00	
			604			$3,932.56		$3,932.56
		11585	2177			$937.12		$937.12
					$33,736.32		$33,736.32	

Copyright SAP AG

Using the Navigation Block to filter

The Navigation Block can also be used to specify the filter values for a characteristic or key figure. To specify a filter, click the appropriate filter icon on the Navigation Block, such as the *Fiscal year* icon, which has been highlighted on Figure 179.

Figure 179

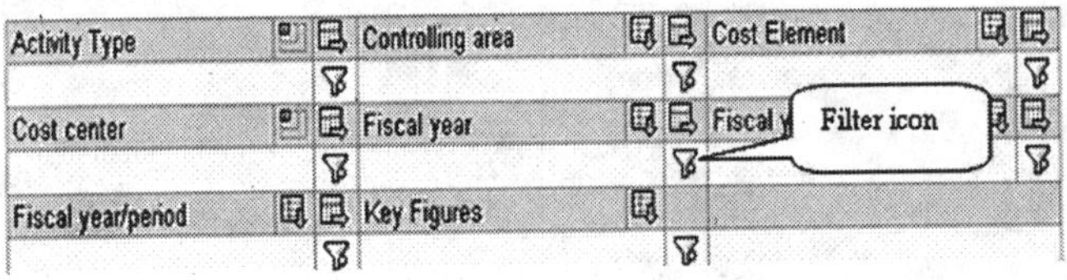

Activity Type		Controlling area		Cost Element	
Cost center		Fiscal year		Fiscal y... [Filter icon]	
Fiscal year/period		Key Figures			

Copyright SAP AG

We will now place a filter on a characteristic, *Calendar Year/Month*, on the report displayed on Figure 180.

Figure 180

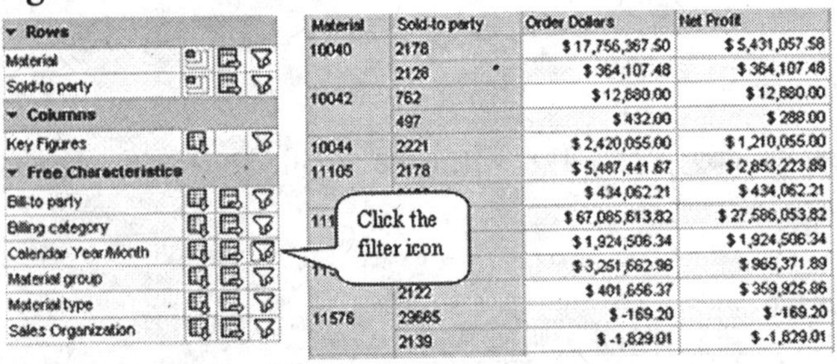

Rows			Material	Sold-to party	Order Dollars	Net Profit
Material			10040	2178	$17,756,367.50	$5,431,057.58
Sold-to party				2128	$364,107.48	$364,107.48
Columns			10042	762	$12,880.00	$12,880.00
Key Figures				497	$432.00	$288.00
Free Characteristics			10044	2221	$2,420,055.00	$1,210,055.00
Bill-to party			11105	2178	$5,487,441.67	$2,853,223.89
Billing category			11... [Click the filter icon]		$434,062.21	$434,062.21
Calendar Year/Month					$67,085,613.82	$27,586,053.82
Material group					$1,924,506.34	$1,924,506.34
Material type				2122	$3,251,662.96	$965,371.89
Sales Organization			11576	29665	$401,656.37	$359,925.86
					$-169.20	$-169.20
				2139	$-1,829.01	$-1,829.01

Copyright SAP AG

- Click the filter icon next to the characteristic *Calendar Year/Month*, which is highlighted on Figure 180

This will cause the *Select Filter Value for Calendar Year/Month* window to pop-up (Figure 181).

Figure 181

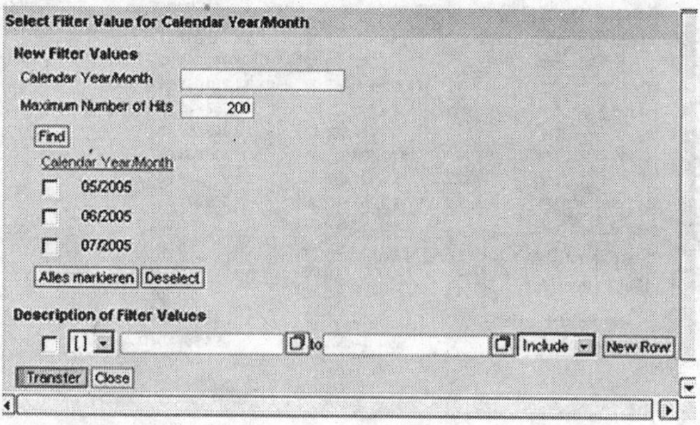

Copyright SAP AG

On the *Select Filter Value* window, filter vales for a specific characteristic can be specified. On Figure 181, three values can be selected for *Calendar Year/Month* (05/2005, 06/2005, and 07/2005). To select *May 2005* as the filter value:

- Click the checkbox next to the desired month, as shown on Figure 182

Figure 182

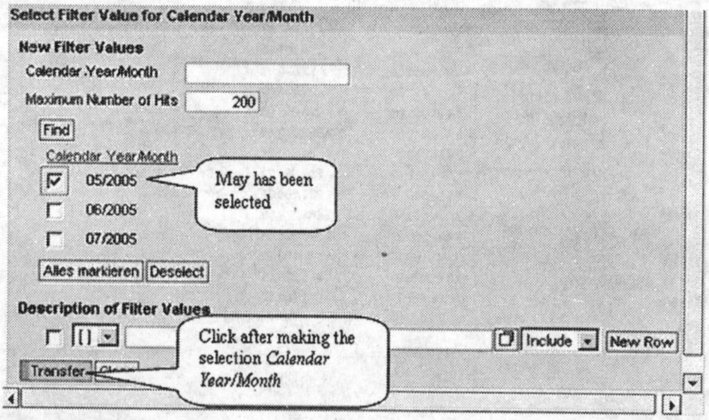

Copyright SAP AG

- Click the *Transfer* button

This will lead to the next window, Figure 183, where the specified filter is displayed.

Figure 183

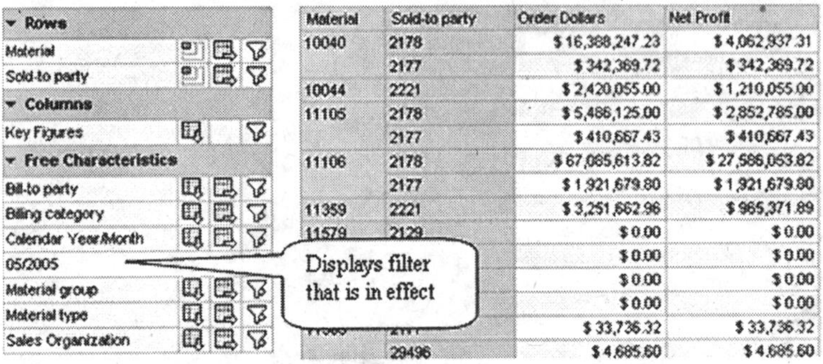

Material	Sold-to party	Order Dollars	Net Profit
10040	2178	$ 16,388,247.23	$ 4,062,937.31
	2177	$ 342,369.72	$ 342,369.72
10044	2221	$ 2,420,055.00	$ 1,210,055.00
11105	2178	$ 5,486,125.00	$ 2,852,785.00
	2177	$ 410,667.43	$ 410,667.43
11106	2178	$ 67,085,613.82	$ 27,586,053.82
	2177	$ 1,921,679.80	$ 1,921,679.80
11359	2221	$ 3,251,662.96	$ 965,371.89
11579	2129	$ 0.00	$ 0.00
		$ 0.00	$ 0.00
		$ 0.00	$ 0.00
		$ 0.00	$ 0.00
		$ 0.00	$ 0.00
		$ 33,736.32	$ 33,736.32
	29496	$ 4,685.60	$ 4,685.60

Displays filter that is in effect

Copyright SAP AG

How to filter and drilldown according to

To execute the *Filter and drilldown according to* function, we will start with the following report, Figure 184, where we will apply it to *Calendar Year/Month* for *Material 10040*.

Figure 184

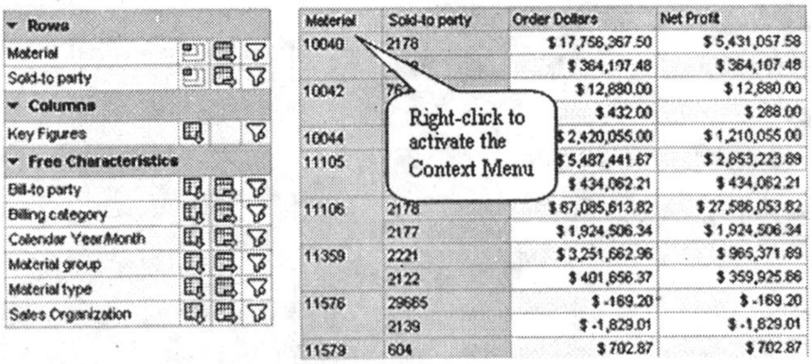

Material	Sold-to party	Order Dollars	Net Profit
10040	2178	$ 17,758,367.50	$ 5,431,057.58
		$ 364,197.48	$ 364,107.48
10042	762	$ 12,880.00	$ 12,880.00
		$ 432.00	$ 288.00
10044		$ 2,420,055.00	$ 1,210,055.00
11105		$ 5,487,441.67	$ 2,853,223.89
		$ 434,062.21	$ 434,062.21
11106	2178	$ 67,085,613.82	$ 27,586,053.82
	2177	$ 1,924,506.34	$ 1,924,506.34
11359	2221	$ 3,251,662.96	$ 965,371.89
	2122	$ 401,656.37	$ 359,925.86
11576	29665	$ -169.20	$ -169.20
	2139	$ -1,829.01	$ -1,829.01
11579	604	$ 702.87	$ 702.87

Right-click to activate the Context Menu

Copyright SAP AG

To start the process:

- Right-click on *Material 10040*, as shown on Figure 184

This will activate the Context Menu, which is displayed on the next window (Figure 185).

Figure 185

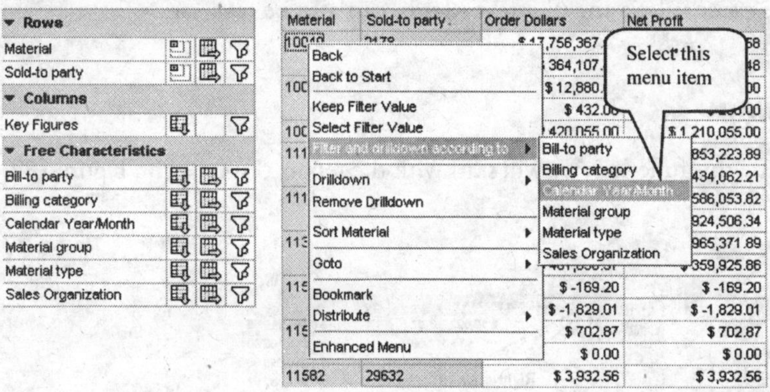

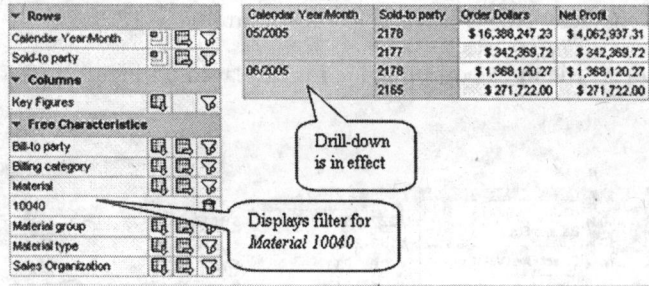

Copyright SAP AG

- Navigate via the menu path *Filter and drilldown according to* > *Calendar Year/Month*, as shown on Figure 185

This will execute the function and lead to the results displayed on Figure 186.

Figure 186

Copyright SAP AG

How to swap axes

What is swapping

The swap function enables a report layout to be changed by switching rows with columns. For example, if the characteristics are displayed in the rows and key figures in the columns, executing the swap function will cause the characteristics to be displayed in the columns and the key figures in the rows. Like a pivot table in

Excel, this function enables analysis from different angles. The swap function, which can be executed via the Context Menu, can also be reversed.

How to swap

To demonstrate this function, we will start with the report displayed on Figure 187:

Figure 187

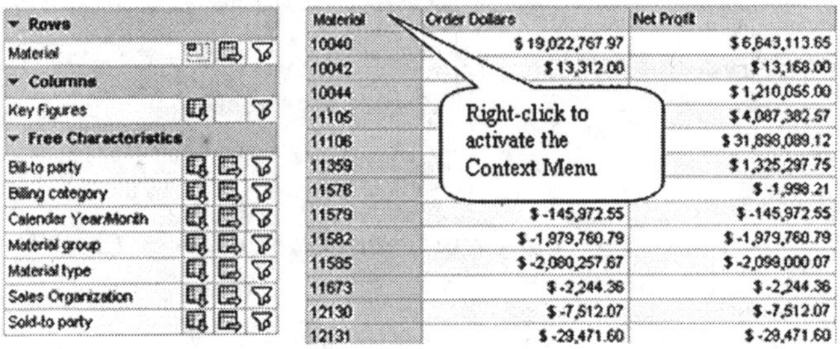

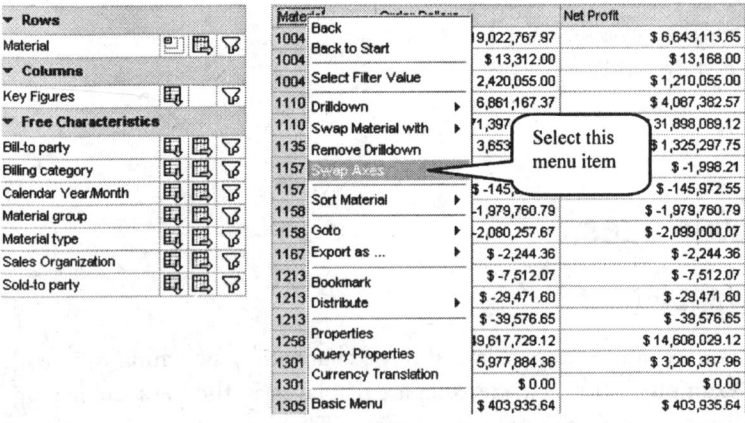

Copyright SAP AG

To perform a swap for the characteristic *Material*:

- Right-click on the characteristic (*Material*), as shown on Figure 187

This will cause the Context Menu to pop-up, which is displayed on Figure 188.

Figure 188

Copyright SAP AG

- Select the menu item *Swap Axes*

This will execute the swap function and lead to the results displayed on Figure 189, where the rows have been switched with the columns.

Figure 189

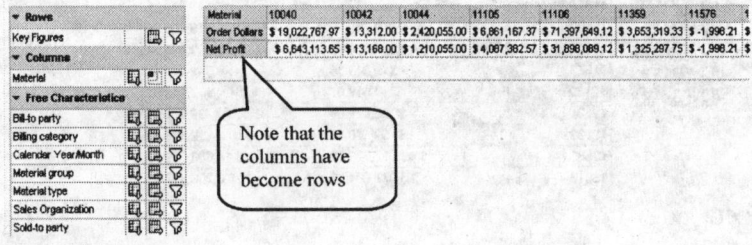

Copyright SAP AG

How to sort

The sort function is used to organize data with the objective of analyzing report results from a different perspective. In BEx, a sort can be performed on a key figure or a characteristic. A key figure can be sorted in ascending or descending order. A characteristic can be sorted by its key or description in either ascending or descending order.

To sort a characteristic in descending order, we will start with the following report (Figure 190):

Figure 190

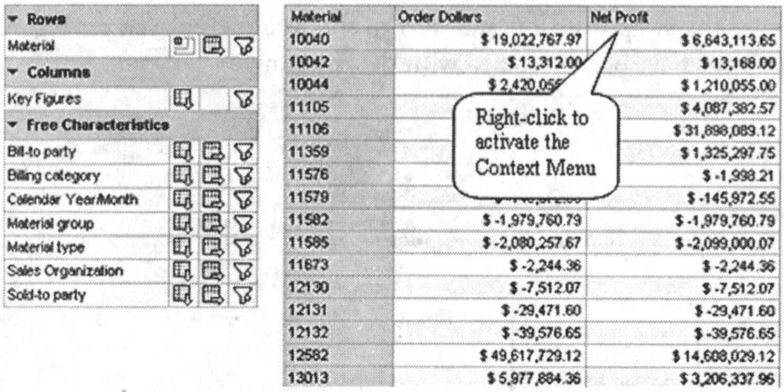

Copyright SAP AG

- Right-click on the column heading of the characteristic (*Net Profit*), as shown on Figure 190

This will cause the Context Menu to pop-up, which is displayed on Figure 191.

Figure 191

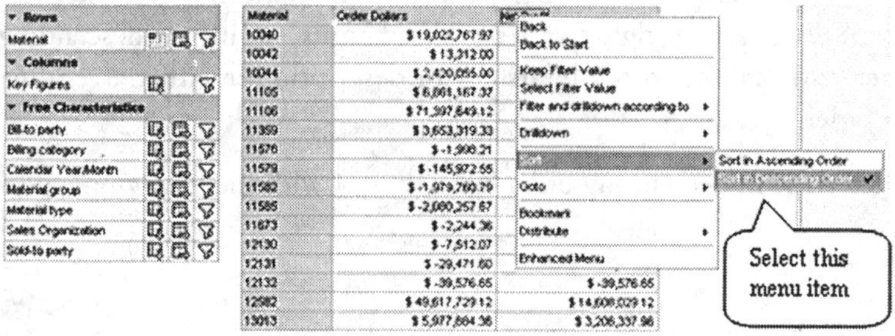

Copyright SAP AG

- Navigate via the menu path *Sort > Sort in Descending Order*, as shown on Figure 191

This will execute the sort function and the results will be displayed, with *Net Profit* in descending order, as shown on Figure 192.

Figure 192

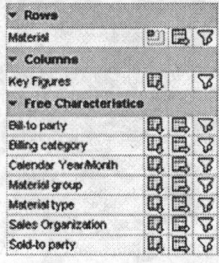

Copyright SAP AG

Working with hierarchies

What is a hierarchy

This feature was explained earlier in Chapter 11, which you should review in order to understand hierarchies prior to following the step-by-step instructions contained in the following sections. Even though Chapter 11 is based on the Analyzer, the same principles govern hierarchies in both Excel and web reports.

Expanding a hierarchy

To expand a hierarchy:

- Right-click in the Results Area

This will activate the Context Menu, which is displayed on Figure 193:

Figure 193

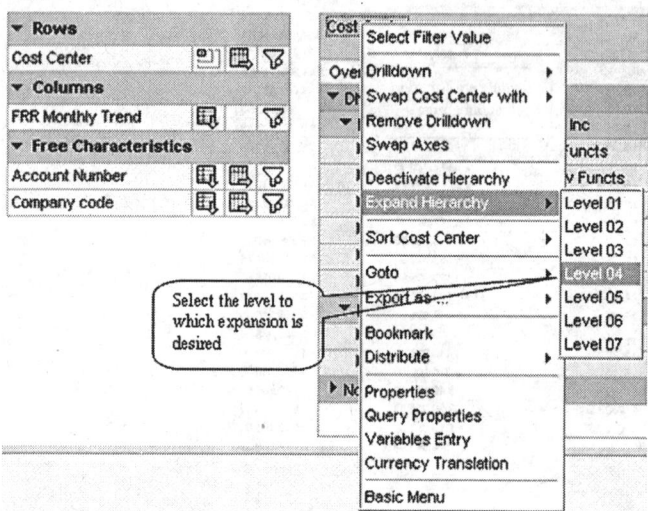

Copyright SAP AG

You can now navigate to the desired hierarchy level. To expand the hierarchy to Level 04:

- Navigate via the menu path *Expand Hierarchy > Level 04*, as shown on Figure 193

This will cause the hierarchy to expand to the specified level.

Expanding a hierarchy node

To expand a hierarchy node:

- Right-click to activate the Context Menu, as shown on Figure 194

Figure 194

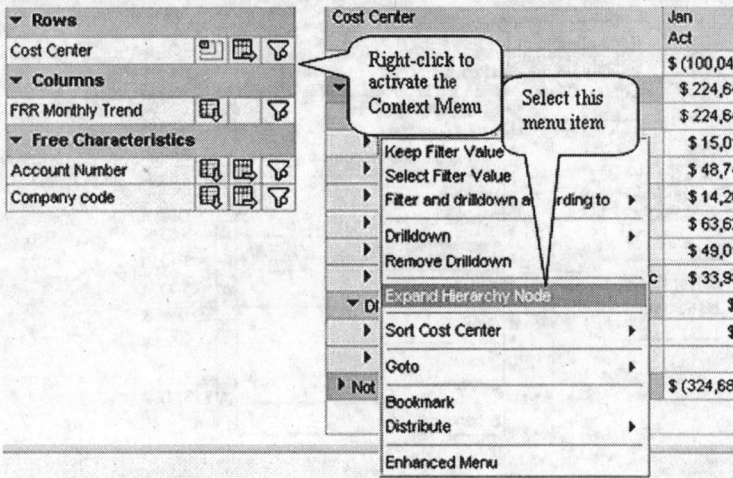

Copyright SAP AG

- Select the menu item *Expand Hierarchy Node*, as shown on Figure 194

This will expand the hierarchy node.

Collapsing a hierarchy node

To collapse a hierarchy node:

- Right-click to activate the Context Menu, as shown on Figure 195

Figure 195

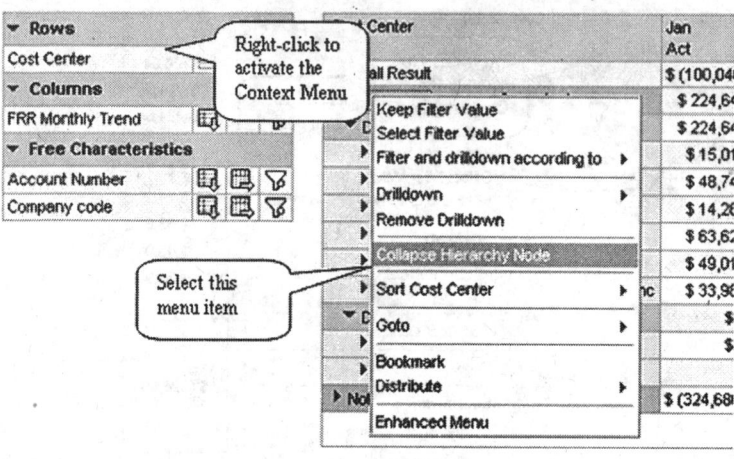

Copyright SAP AG

- Select the menu item *Collapse Hierarchy Node*, as shown on Figure 195 This will collapse the hierarchy node.

Deactivating a hierarchy

To deactivate a hierarchy:

- Right-click to activate the Context Menu, as shown on Figure 196

Figure 196

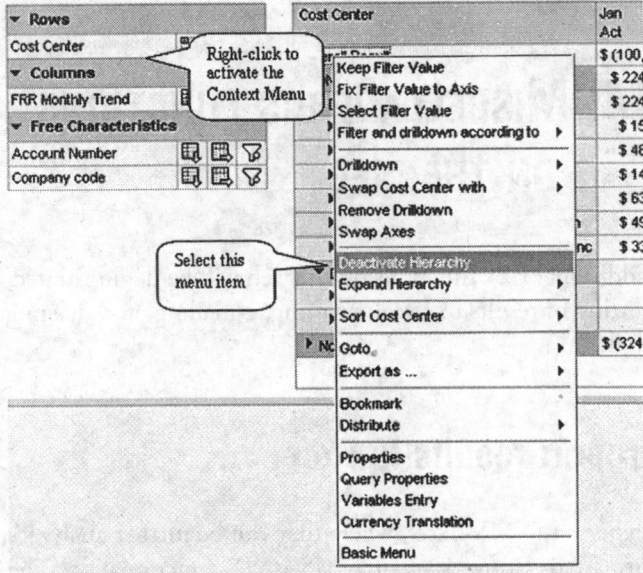

Copyright SAP AG

- Select the menu item *Deactivate Hierarchy*, as shown on Figure 196

This will deactivate the hierarchy.

How to use the jump function

This function was described earlier in Chapter 11. To activate the jump feature:

- Right-click the mouse

This will activate the Context Menu.

- Select the appropriate menu item, *Jump*, on the Context Menu
- Navigate to and select the specific secondary report that you want to execute and review

CHAPTER 14: MISCELLANEOUS FUNCTIONS ON THE WEB

In this chapter, some additional BEx functions on the web will be demonstrated. These include the exporting of results to Excel, printing, e-mailing, and deleting reports from the favorites.

How to export report results to Excel

Report results can be exported to MS-Excel, where they can be further analyzed, manipulated, or reformatted using standard MS-Excel functionality. The exported Excel file can be saved to the local drive or a shared drive.

To export report results:

- Right-click to activate the Context Menu, which is displayed on Figure 197

Figure 197

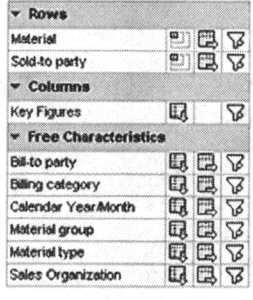

Copyright SAP AG

- Navigate via the menu path *Export as* > *MS Excel 2000 File*, as shown on Figure 197

This will initiate the download process and the following window will pop-up (Figure 198):

Figure 198

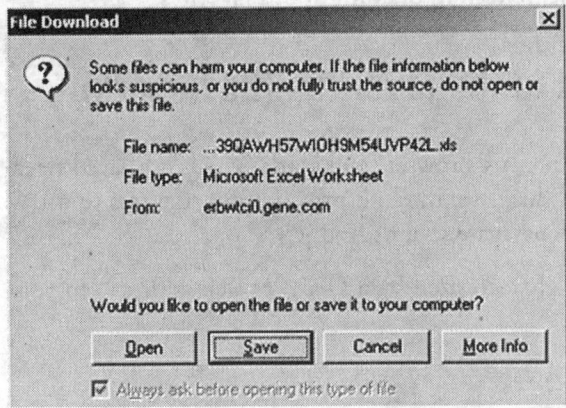

- Click the *Save* button

This will start the download process and lead to the *Save as* window, Figure 199, where the save options (directory, file name, and file type) are to be specified:

Figure 199

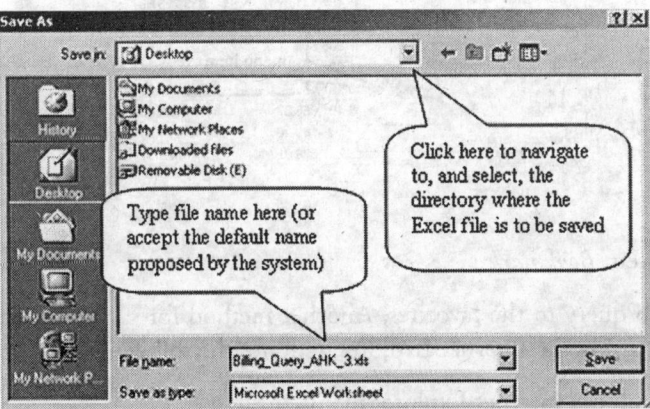

- Select the directory where the Excel file is to be saved, as shown on Figure 199
- Type the name of the file that you want to save (or accept the default file name proposed by the system)
- Click the *Save* button

The saved Excel file can be e-mailed to other BW and non-BW users as an attachment. A non-BW user can modify such a file but cannot refresh it. However, a BW user can modify such a file, refresh it, or add it to his favorites.

How to add a report to the favorites (Bookmark)

A BW favorite is just like an Internet browser bookmark, which is a saved reference in the form of a link. In this case, the link provides direct access to a BW report, eliminating the need to navigate to it or find it.

To add a web query, which is characterized by a URL (or web address), to your favorites:

- Right-click in the Results Area

This will cause the Context Menu to pop-up, which is displayed on Figure 200.

Figure 200

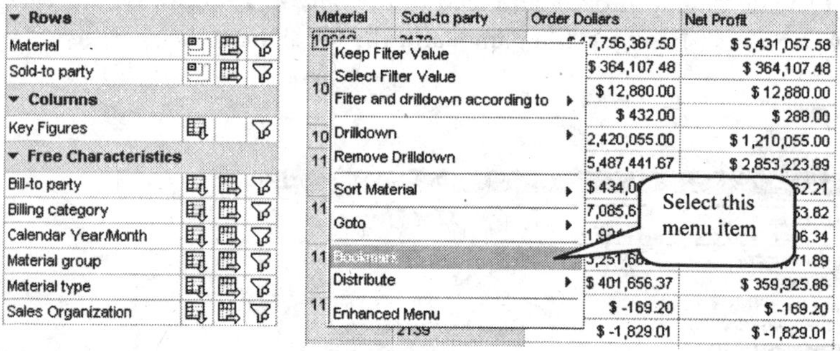

Copyright SAP AG

- Select the menu item *Bookmark*

This will save the web query to the favorites. Another method for saving a web query to the favorites, using the Internet Explorer, requires the following steps:

- Select *Favorites* from the Internet Explorer menu
- Select the menu item *Add to favorites*

This will cause the next window, *Add Favorite*, to pop-up (Figure 201):

Figure 201

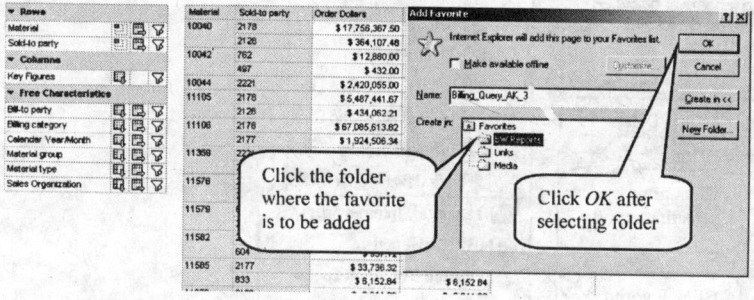

Copyright SAP AG

- Click the appropriate folder, where the favorite is to be added, to select it
- Click the *OK* button

This will save the web query to the Internet Explorer favorites. A similar procedure can be followed for others browsers, such as Firefox or Netscape.

How to delete a report from the favorites folder

A web report can be deleted easily from the favorites. To delete a favorite:

- Navigate via the Internet Explorer menu path *Favorites* > *Organize Favorites*

This will cause the following window to pop-up (Figure 202):

Figure 202

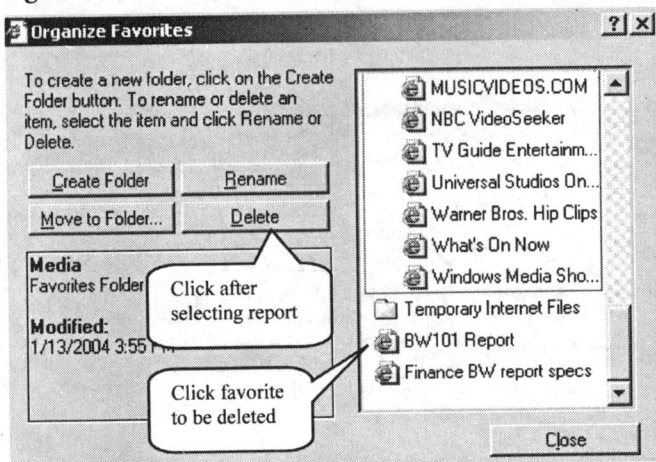

- Click the report to be deleted from the favorites, *BW101 Report*, which is highlighted on Figure 202
- Click the *Delete* button

How to print a report

A web report can be printed using standard browser printing functionality. To print the report displayed on Figure 203, proceed as follows:

- Navigate via the Internet Explorer menu path *File > Print*, as shown on Figure 203

Figure 203

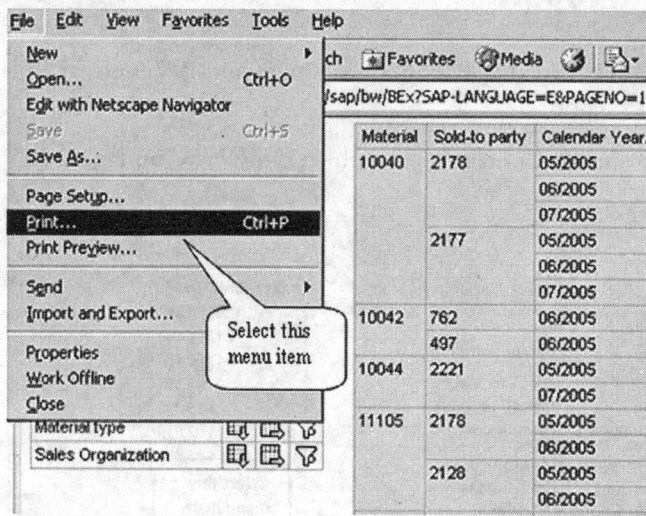

Copyright SAP AG

This will cause the next window, *Print*, to pop-up (Figure 204):

Figure 204

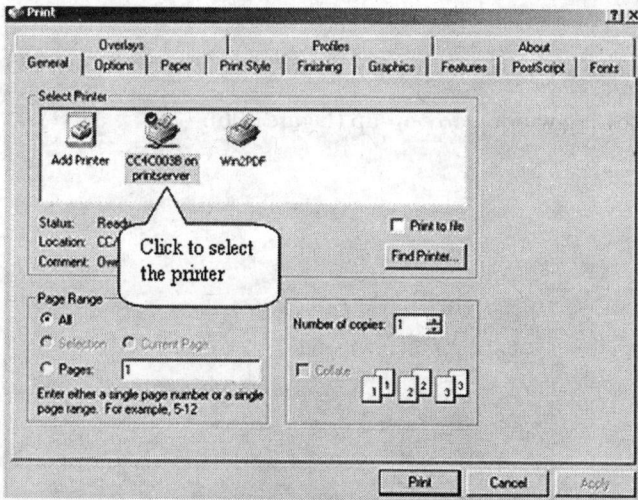

- Click the printer where the report is to be printed, which selects it, as shown on Figure 204
- Click the *Print* button

How to e-mail a report

A BW web report can be e-mailed to BW users, as well as non-BW users, as a file attachment. To e-mail a report:

- Right-click to activate the Context Menu, which is displayed on Figure 205

Figure 205

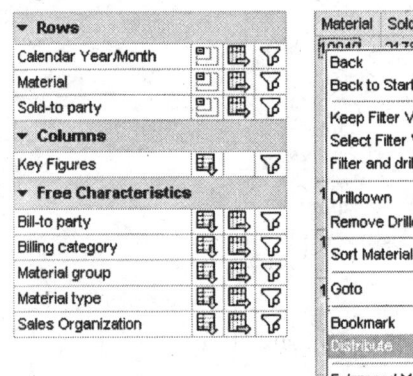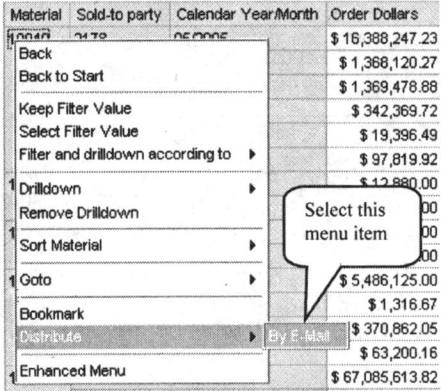

Copyright SAP AG

- Navigate via the menu path *Distribute > By E-mail*, as shown on Figure 205

This will cause the following window to pop-up (Figure 206):

Figure 206

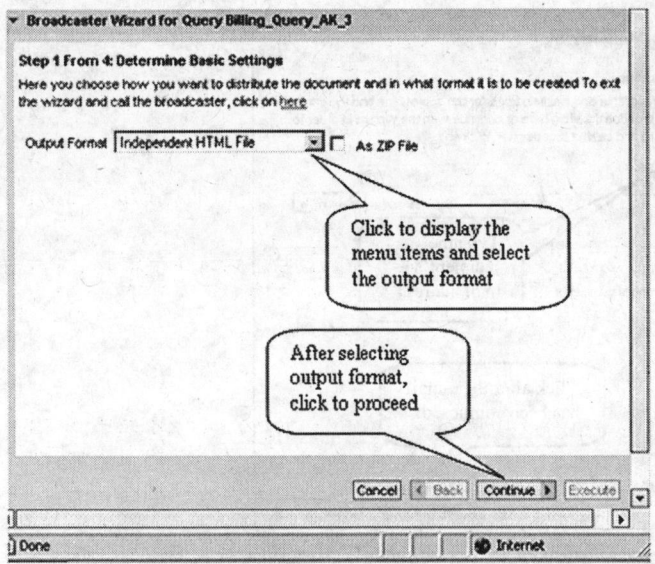

Copyright SAP AG

- Select the *Output Format* (or accept the default—*Independent HTML file*), as shown on Figure 206
- Click the *Continue* button

This will cause the following window to pop-up (Figure 207):

Figure 207

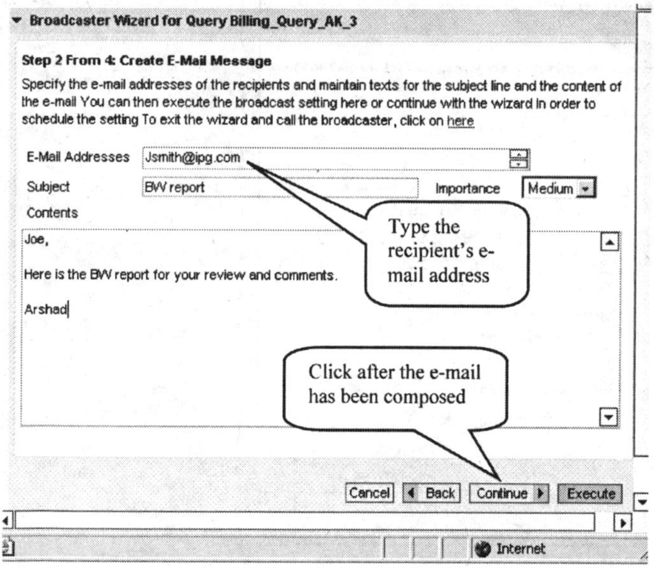

Copyright SAP AG

On Figure 207, enter the required data, which includes the:

- Recipient's e-mail address
- Subject
- Message for the recipient

After the e-mail has been composed:

- Click the *Continue* button (Figure 207)

This will lead to the next window (Figure 208):

Figure 208

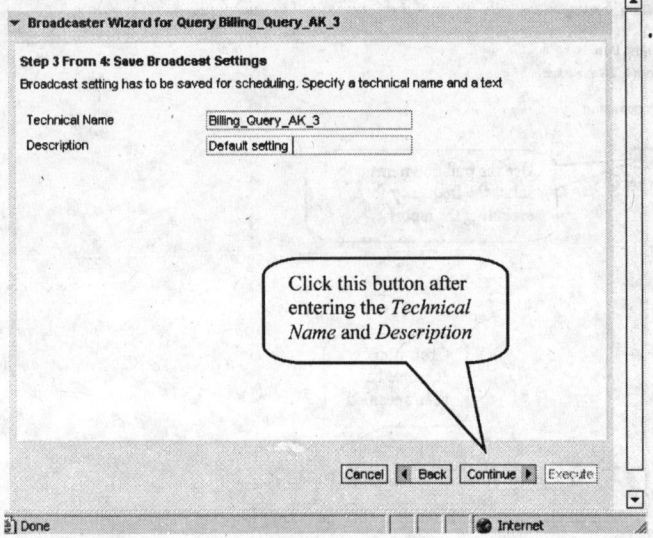

Copyright SAP AG

- Enter the *Technical Name* (query name)
- Enter the *Description* (query description)
- Click the *Continue* button

This will lead to the next window (Figure 209):

Figure 209

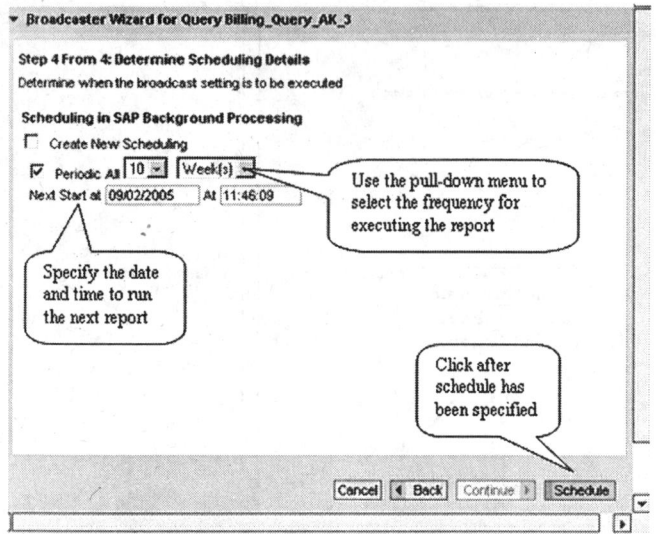

Copyright SAP AG

- Enter the scheduling information in the appropriate fields (frequency, start date, timing), as shown on Figure 209
- Click the *Schedule* button

How to logoff

To logoff, simply close the Browser window in which the web report is being displayed.

How to create, retrieve, and delete a variant

These topics have been described in detail in Chapter12.

Chapter 15: Changing properties (Excel)

BW report displays can be enhanced by modifying default settings for the properties of key figures and characteristics. Such changes can enable easier and more effective analysis. Modifications can include the addition of attributes, such as adding the address attribute to the vendor characteristic. Query properties can be modified using the Query Designer tool.

Query Designer

The Query Designer is a powerful and versatile tool that can define and/or change BW queries. It can execute various functions, such as working with queries (open, create, change, save, delete, etc.), with the help of the Query Designer Toolbar. The Query Designer functions that BW end-users are allowed to execute are very limited compared to BW developers and power-users. This chapter covers the functions that end-users will typically be allowed to execute at most sites.

Launching the Query Designer

Figure 210 displays an Analyzer report, which will be the starting point for our exercise.

Figure 210

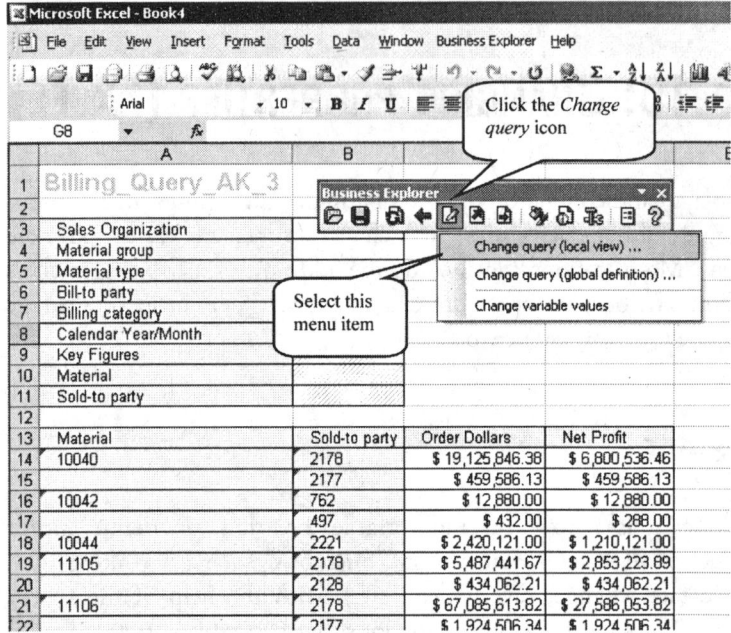

Copyright SAP AG

To launch the Query Designer:

- Execute the report that is to be modified

After the report is displayed (Figure 210):

- Click the *Change query* icon on the BEx Toolbar

This will display the menu, which is shown on Figure 210.

- Select the menu item *Change query (local view)*

This will launch the Query Designer and lead to the next window (Figure 211).

Query Designer windows

Figure 211 displays the structure (key figures, characteristics, and free characteristics) of the report from which the Query Designer was launched.

Figure 211

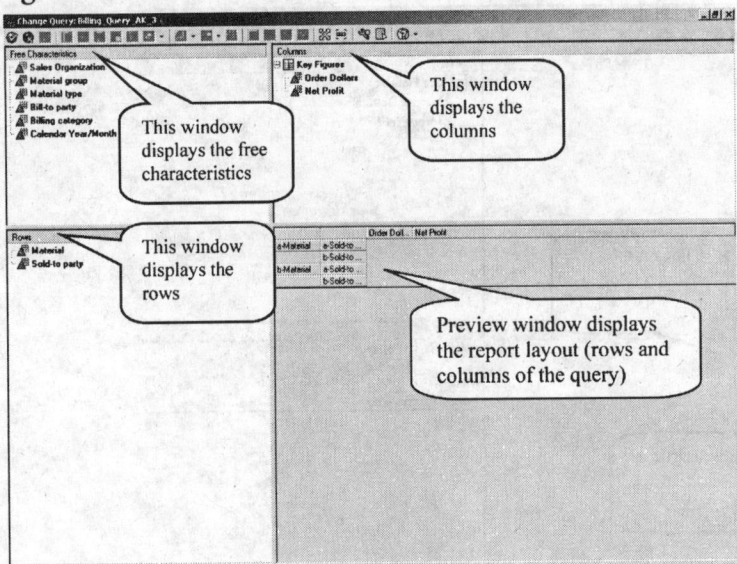

Copyright SAP AG

Figure 211 is split into four distinct windows:

- Rows: Lists the report's rows
- Columns: Lists the report's columns
- Free characteristics: Lists the report's free characteristics. Free characteristic is a BW term for a characteristic or dimensional attribute that can be used in a query. Free characteristics are excluded in the initial query results to be displayed. Subsequently, they can be incorporated into the results by using interactive navigation functions.
- Preview: Provides a preview of the query result format (based on the selections in the other windows)

How to change properties

How to change the properties of characteristics

We will now change the properties of the *Sold-to-party* characteristic, which is displayed in the Query Designer row window (Figure 212):

Figure 212

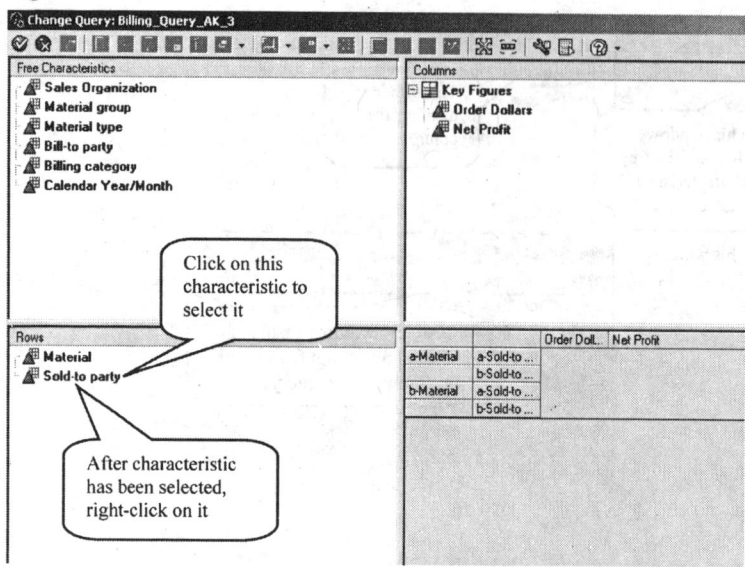

Copyright SAP AG

- Click the *Sold-to-party* characteristic in order to select it
- Right-click on the row item *Sold-to-party*

This will lead to the next window, Figure 213, where a menu is displayed:

Figure 213

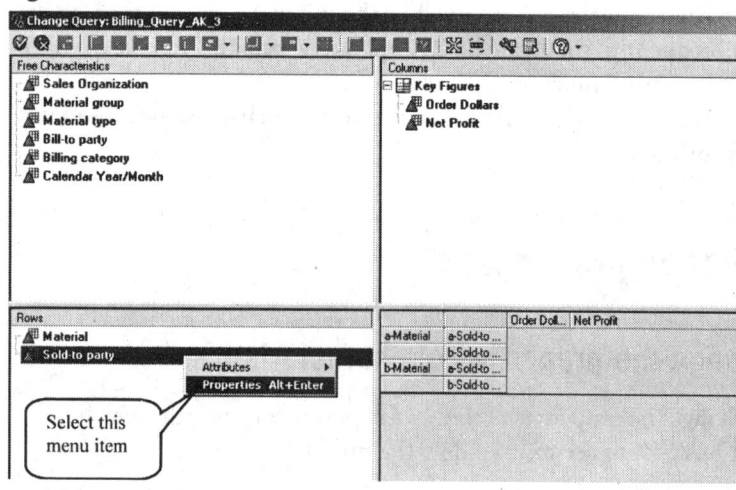

Copyright SAP AG

- Select the menu item *Properties*

This will cause the next window, *Properties of Characteristic Sold-to-party*, to pop-up (Figure 214):

Figure 214

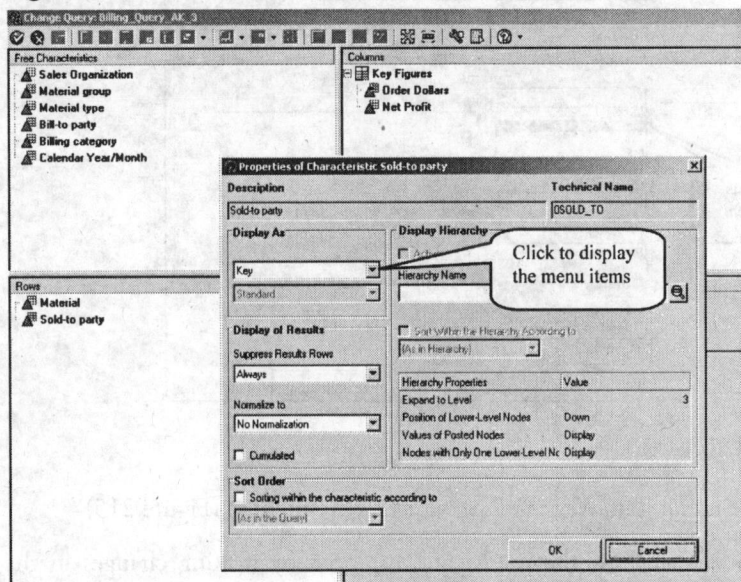

Copyright SAP AG

We can now make the desired changes for the various properties of the characteristic *Sold-to-party*, which are displayed on Figure 214.

To change the *Display As* property from *Key* to *Key and Text*:

- Click the pull-down menu for *Display As*, as shown on Figure 214

This will display the menu items, which are shown on Figure 215:

Figure 215

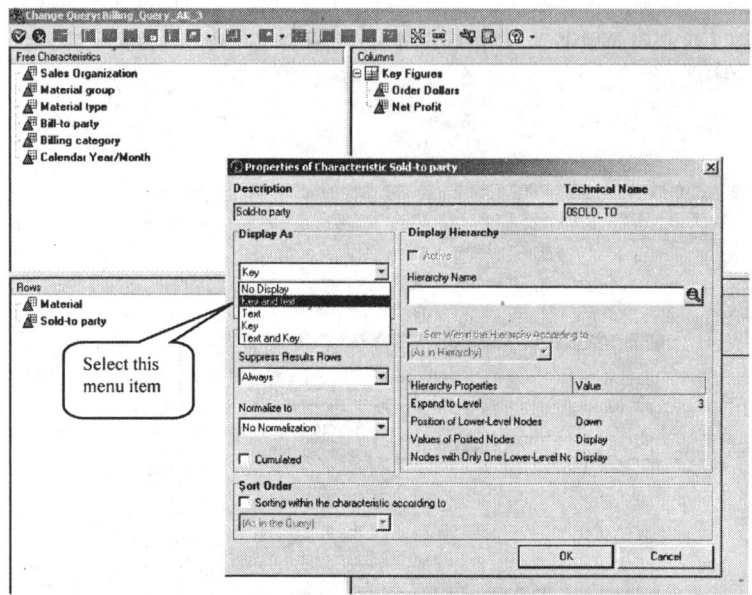

Copyright SAP AG

- Select the menu item *Key and Text*, which is highlighted (Figure 215)

We will now change how the results are displayed by making changes in the *Display of Results* section. Specifically, we will select an option for the *Suppress Results Rows*. This function is used to control or suppress a report's display of sub-totals. The options are:

- Never: Sub-totals are never suppressed
- With only one value: Sub-totals are suppressed for sub-groups with only a single row's results
- Always: Sub-totals are always suppressed

To change the *Suppress Results Rows* property (Figure 214):

- Click the pull-down menu for *Suppress Results Rows*

This will display the menu items, which are shown on Figure 216.

Figure 216

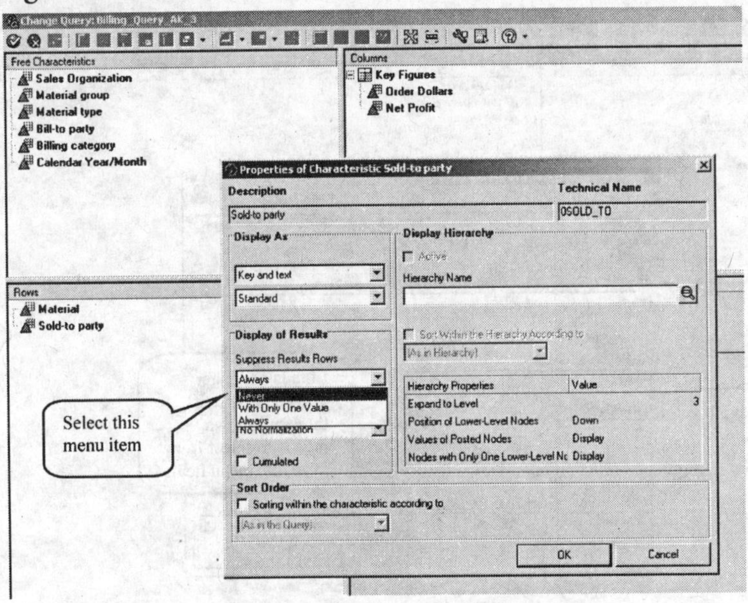

Copyright SAP AG

- Select the menu item *Never*, which is highlighted (Figure 216)

To specify the *Sort Order:*

- Click to place a checkmark next to *Sorting within the characteristic according to*, as shown on Figure 217

This will cause the previously grayed out line, below *Sorting within the characteristic according to*, to change as highlighted on Figure 217.

Figure 217

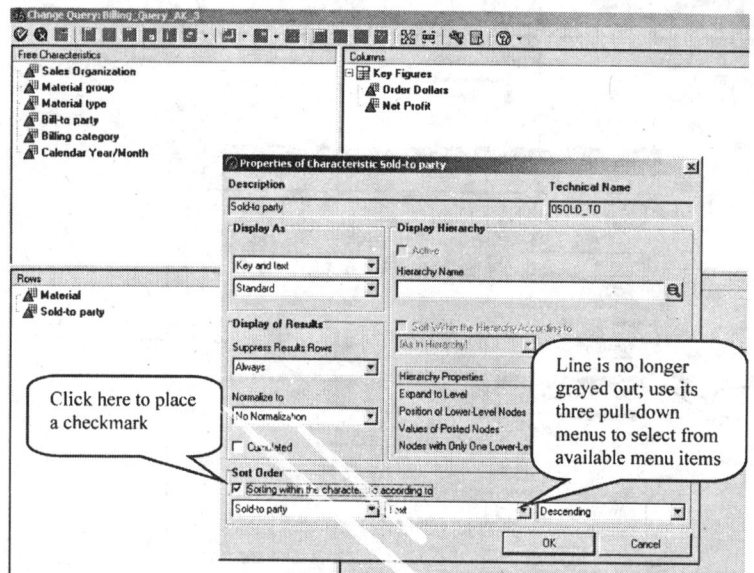

Copyright SAP AG

- Click the three pull-down menus (*Sold-to-party, Text, Descending*), highlighted on Figure 217, to display their menu items
- Select the desired menu item for each of the three menus

After all the property changes have been made:

- Click the *OK* button

This will implement the characteristic property changes.

How to change the properties of key figures

We will now change the properties of the *Order Dollars* key figure, which is displayed in the Query Designer columns window (Figure 218):

Figure 218

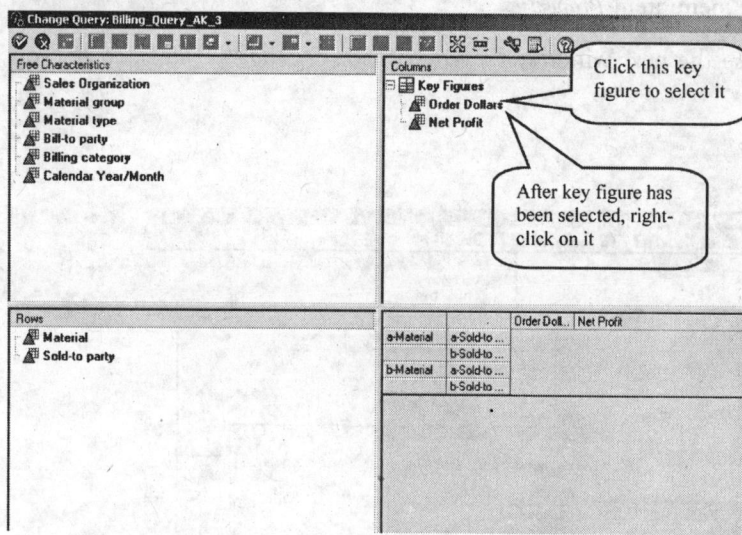

Copyright SAP AG

- Click the *Order Dollars* key figure in order to select it
- Right-click on the column item *Order Dollars*

This will lead to the next window (Figure 219):

Figure 219

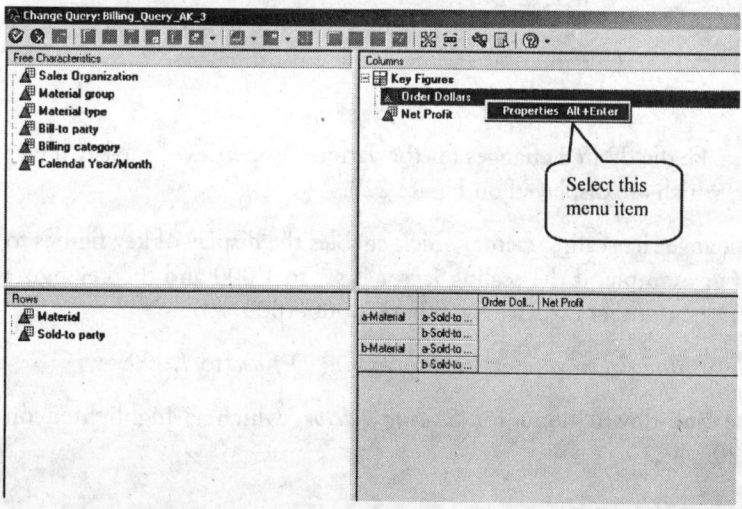

Copyright SAP AG

- Select the menu item *Properties*

This will cause the next window, *Properties of the Selection/Formula*, to pop-up (Figure 220):

Figure 220

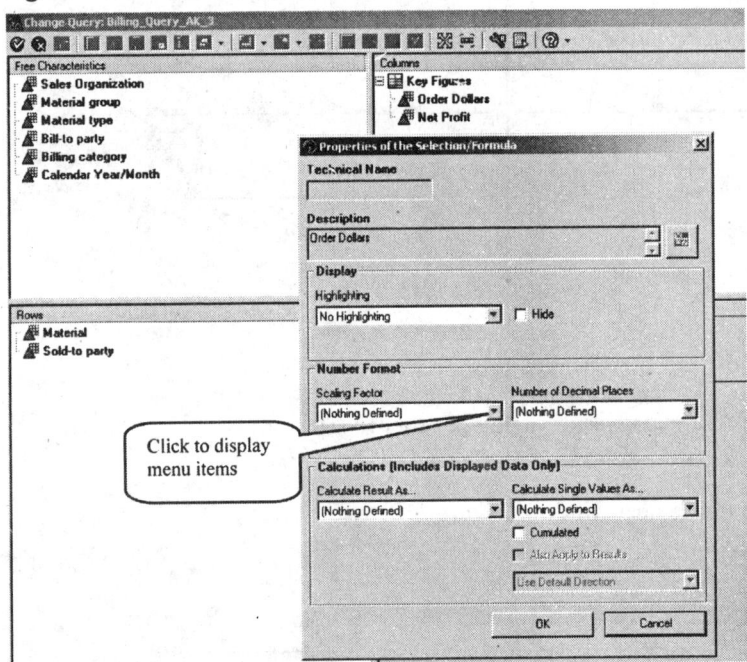

Copyright SAP AG

We can now make the desired changes for the various properties of the key figure *Order Dollars*, which are displayed on Figure 220.

We will first change the scaling factor, which enables the display of key figures to be adjusted. For example, if the scaling factor is set to 1,000 and the key figure value is 3,000, the number displayed will be 3 (3000/1000 = 3).

To change the *Scaling Factor* property from *Nothing Defined* to *1,000*:

- Click the pull-down menu for *Scaling Factor*, which is highlighted on Figure 220

This will display the *Scaling Factor* menu items, which are shown on Figure 221:

Figure 221

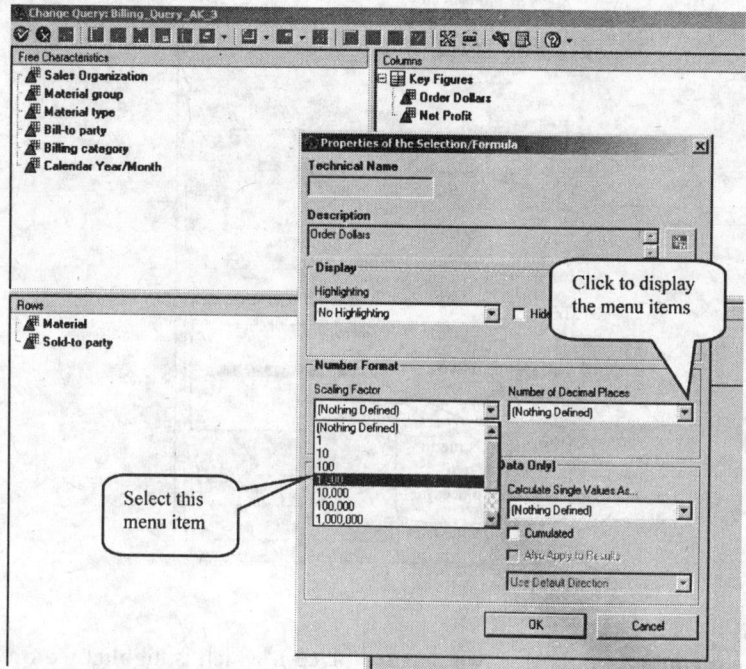

Copyright SAP AG

- Select the menu item *1,000*, which is highlighted (Figure 221)

To change the *Number of Decimal Places* property:

- Click the pull-down menu for *Number of Decimal Places*, which is also highlighted on Figure 221.

This will display the *Number of Decimal Places* menu items, which are shown on Figure 222:

Figure 222

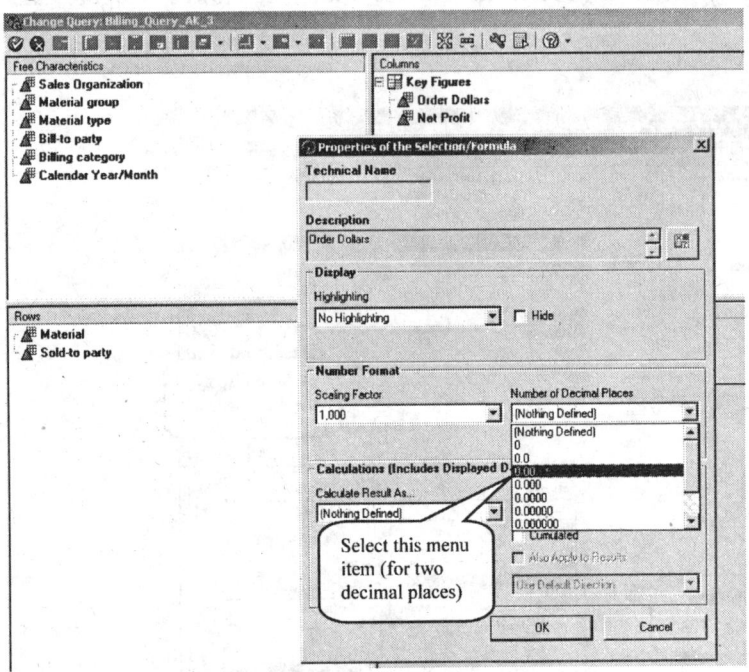

Copyright SAP AG

- Select the menu item *0.00* (for two decimal places), which is highlighted on Figure 222

This will lead to the next window, Figure 223, where the selected items for the key figure are displayed:

Figure 223

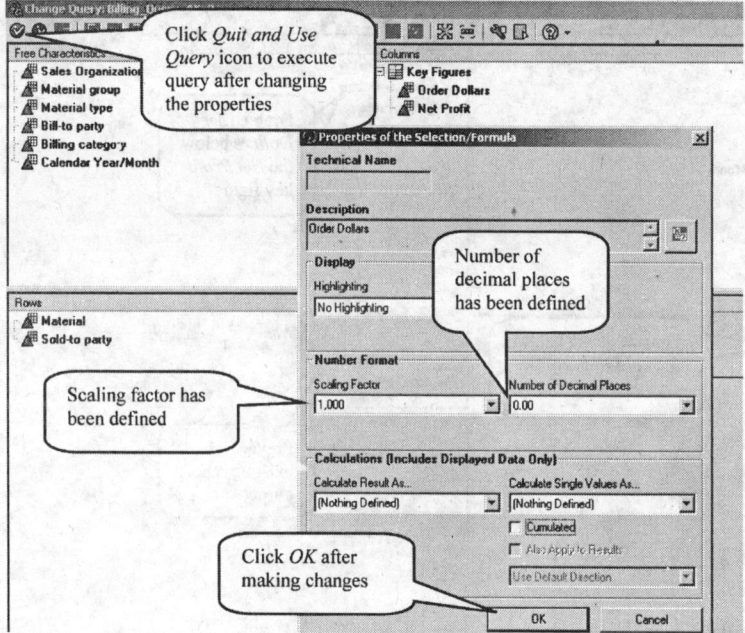

Copyright SAP AG

- Click the *OK* button

To execute the query after the key figure property changes have been implemented:

- Click the *Quit and Use Query* icon, on the Query Designer Toolbar, which is highlighted on Figure 223

This will execute the report and display the results.

How to change the row display order

The display arrangement of rows and columns can be modified through a simple drag and drop operation. We will now change the row sequence which, currently, is *Material* and *Sold-to-party* (Figure 224). We will also change the column sequence which, currently, is *Order Dollars* and *Net Profit* (Figure 224).

Figure 224

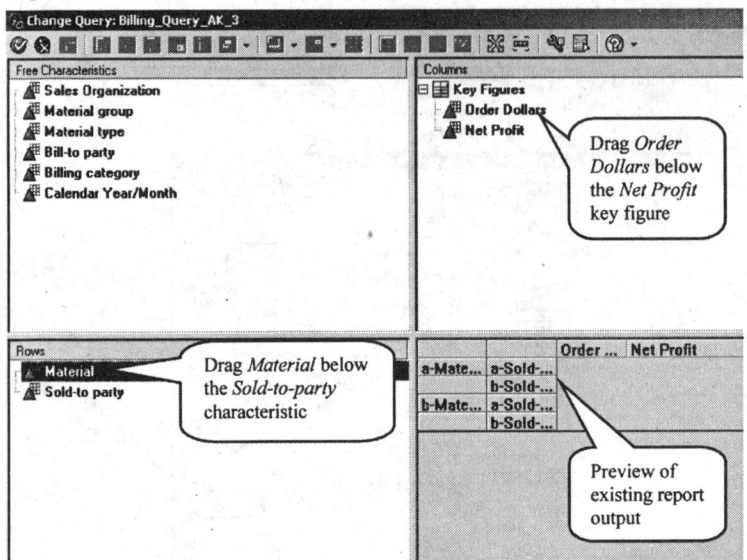

Copyright SAP AG

Using the mouse:

- Drag and drop the *Material* characteristic below the *Sold-to-party* characteristic
- Drag and drop the *Order Dollars* key figure below the *Net Profit* key figure

These operations will change the report display sequence for two characteristics (*Material* and *Sold-to-party*) and two key figures (*Order Dollars* and *Net Profit*), as shown on Figure 225.

Figure 225

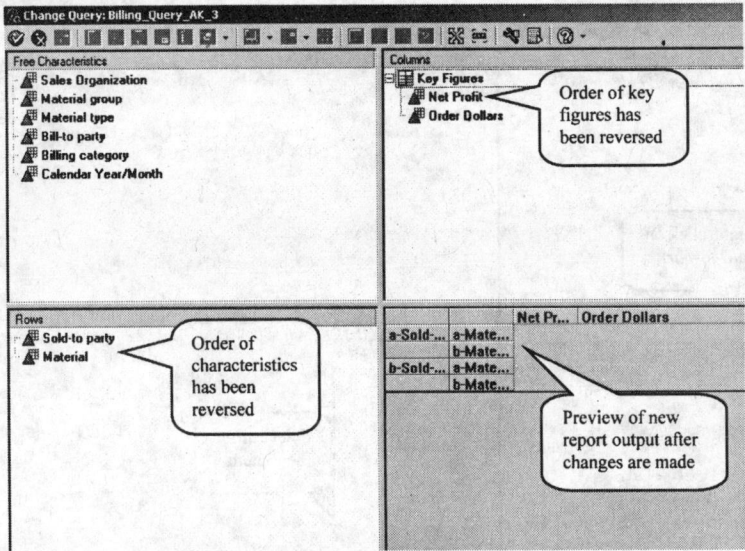

Copyright SAP AG

How to add an attribute

Attributes can be added to a characteristic to make its display more meaningful. In the following example, we will add *Postal Code* to the *Sold-to-party* characteristic by executing the following steps, which are highlighted on Figure 226:

- Right-click the row item *Sold-to-party*
- Navigate via the menu path *Sold-to-party > Attributes > Name 2—Call frequency > Postal Code*

Figure 226

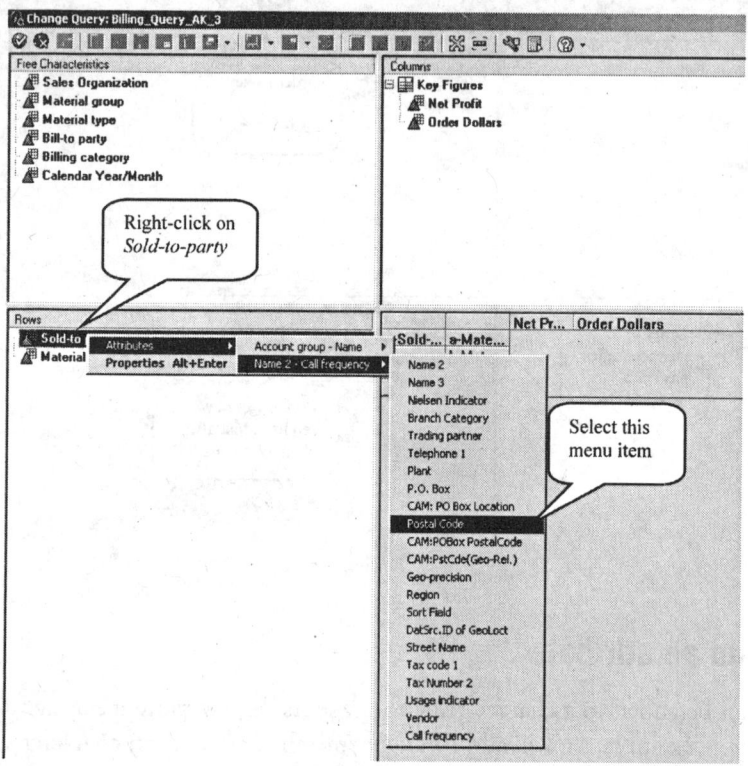

Copyright SAP AG

This will cause the *Postal Code* attribute to be added to the *Sold-to-party* characteristic, as shown on Figure 227.

Figure 227

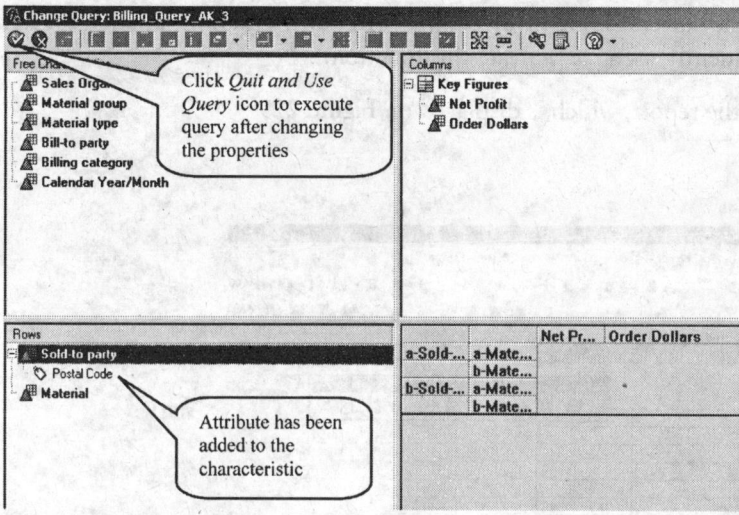

Copyright SAP AG

To execute the report after the property changes have been implemented:

- Click the *Quit and Use Query* icon, on the Query Designer Toolbar, which is highlighted on Figure 227

This will execute the report and display the results (Figure 228).

Figure 228

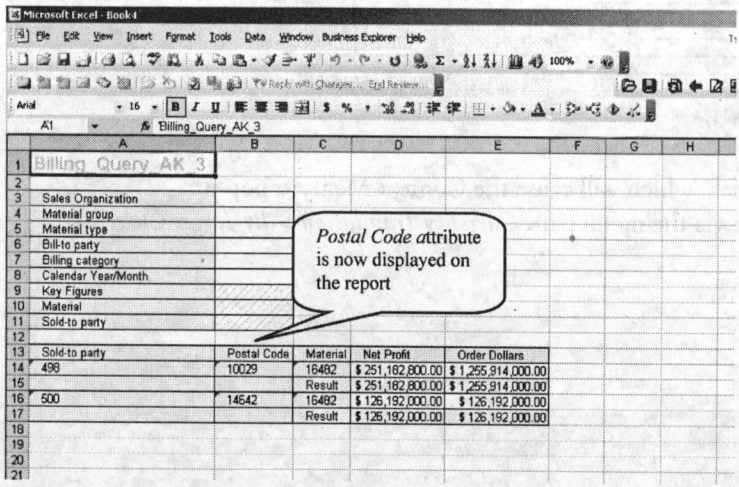

Currency translation

When multiple currencies are involved, the currency translation function for key figures is frequently used. To activate this function:

- Execute the report, which is displayed on Figure 229

Figure 229

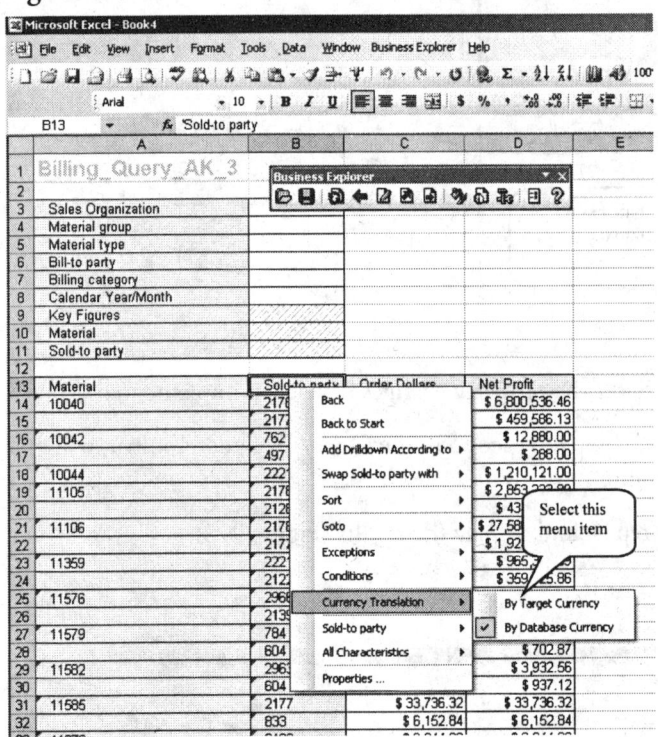

Copyright SAP AG

- Right-click, which will cause the Context Menu to pop-up
- Navigate via the menu path *Currency Translation > By Target Currency*

Chapter 16: Changing properties (Web)

In Chapter 15, various exercises demonstrated how to enhance Excel report displays by modifying default settings for the properties of key figures and characteristics. Such functions can also be executed on the web, which are demonstrated in this chapter.

How to change properties

How to change the properties of characteristics

We will start with the original report results, which are displayed on Figure 230.

Figure 230

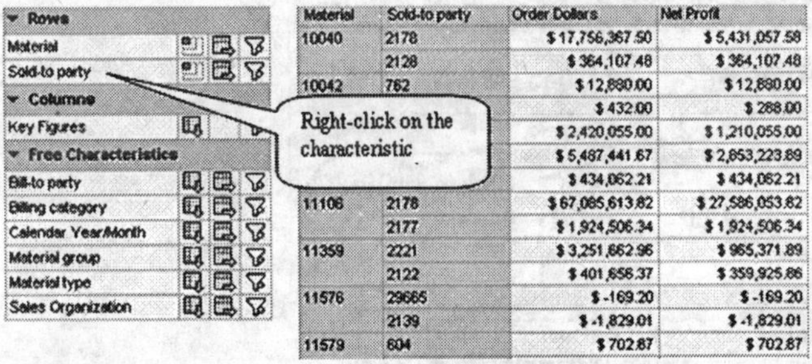

Rows			Material	Sold-to party	Order Dollars	Net Profit
Material			10040	2178	$17,756,367.50	$5,431,057.58
Sold-to party				2128	$364,107.48	$364,107.48
Columns			10042	762	$12,880.00	$12,880.00
Key Figures					$432.00	$288.00
Free Characteristics					$2,420,055.00	$1,210,055.00
					$5,487,441.67	$2,853,223.89
Bill-to party					$434,062.21	$434,062.21
Billing category			11106	2178	$67,085,613.82	$27,586,053.82
Calendar Year/Month				2177	$1,924,506.34	$1,924,506.34
Material group			11359	2221	$3,251,662.96	$965,371.89
Material type				2122	$401,656.37	$359,925.86
Sales Organization			11576	29665	$-169.20	$-169.20
				2139	$-1,829.01	$-1,829.01
			11579	604	$702.87	$702.87

(Callout: Right-click on the characteristic)

Copyright SAP AG

To change the properties of the characteristic *Sold-to-party*:

- Right-click on *Sold-to-party*

This will cause the Context Menu to pop-up, which is displayed on Figure 231.

Figure 231

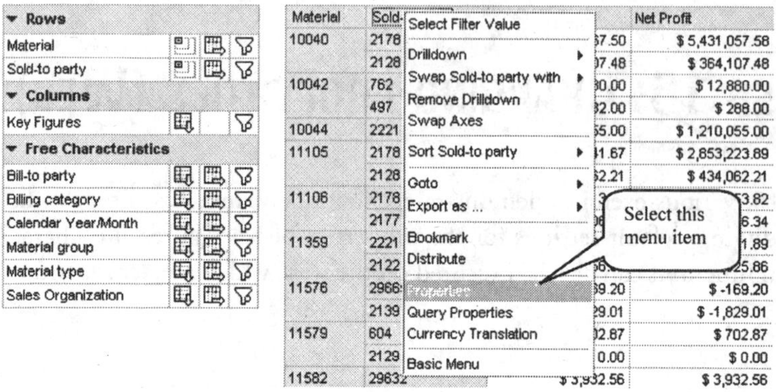

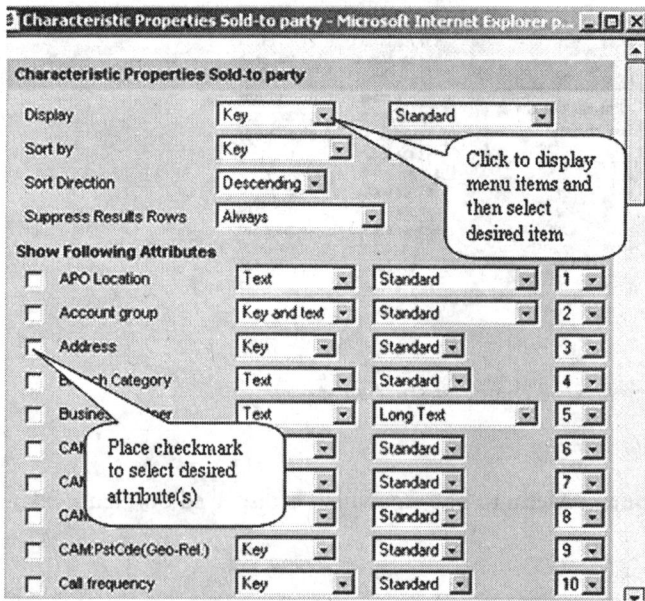

Copyright SAP AG

- Select the menu item *Properties*

This will cause the next window to pop-up, Figure 232, where the various characteristic properties can be modified:

Figure 232

Copyright SAP AG

To change a characteristic property displayed on Figure 232:

- Click the pull-down menu to display the menu items for the applicable property
- Select the desired menu item

To display/change an attribute:

- Place a checkmark next to the appropriate attribute
- Click the pull-down menu for the selected attribute
- Select the desired item from the displayed menu items

Figure 233 provides examples of how some properties have been, or can be, modified.

Figure 233

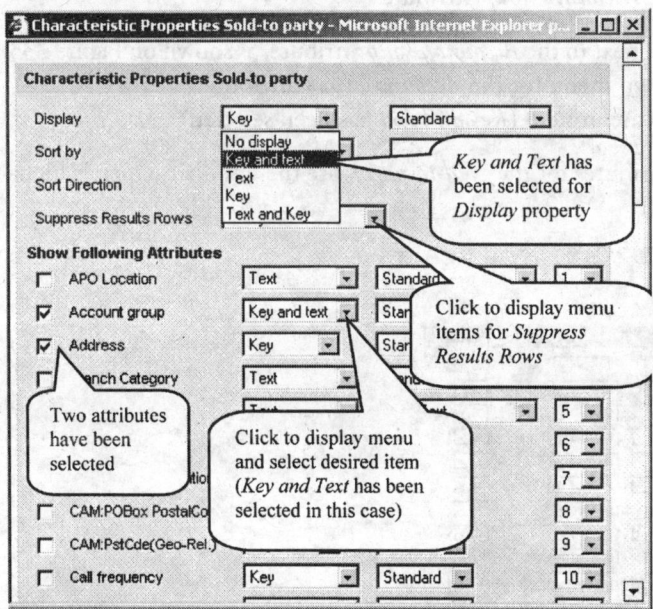

Copyright SAP AG

To change the *Display* properties on Figure 233:

- Click the pull-down menu for the *Display* property
- Select the desired menu item from the displayed list (menu item *Key and Text* has been highlighted)

The *Suppress Result Rows* function, a commonly used function, is used to control or suppress a report's display of sub-totals. The options are:

- Never: Sub-totals are never suppressed
- With only one value: Sub-totals are suppressed for sub-groups with only a single row's results
- Always: Sub-totals are always suppressed

The menu items for *Suppress Result Rows* can be displayed by clicking on the appropriate pull-down menu, which is highlighted on Figure 233. After the menu is displayed, select the appropriate menu item (*never, with only one value, always*).

To display/change the *Account Group* attribute:

- Place a checkmark next to the *Account Group* attribute, as shown on Figure 233
- Click the pull-down menu for the *Account Group* attribute
- Select the desired menu item (*Key and text* has been selected)

To view additional attributes for the *Sold-to-party*, use the scrollbar which is highlighted on Figure 234.

Figure 234

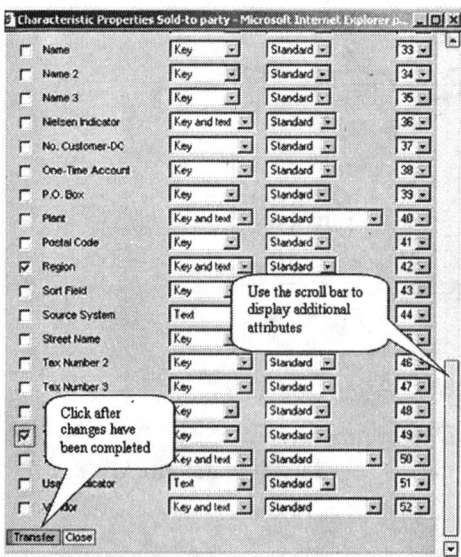

Copyright SAP AG

After all the selections and changes have been completed:

- Click the *Transfer* button

This will implement the changes made to the *Sold-to-party* characteristic.

How to change the properties of key figures

In addition to modifying the properties of characteristics, the properties of key figures can also be changed. We will now change the properties of the *Order Dollars* key figure for the following report (Figure 235):

Figure 235

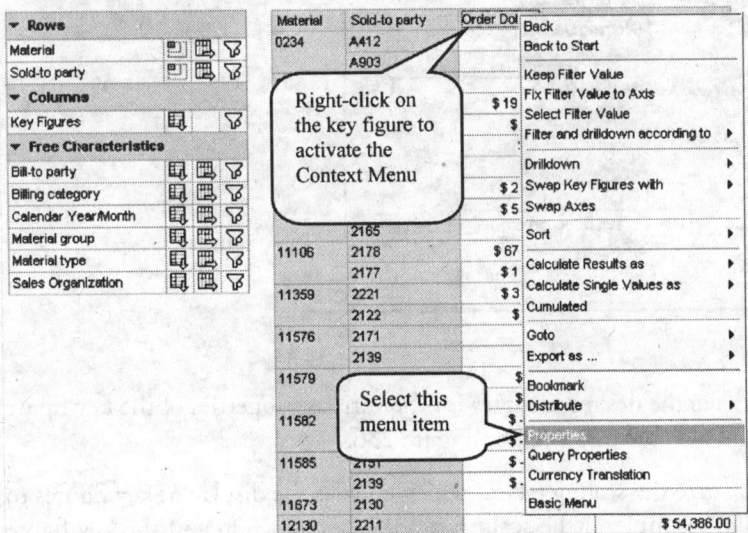

Copyright SAP AG

To change the properties for the *Order Dollars* key figure (Figure 235):

- Right-click on key figure *Order Dollars*

This will activate the Context Menu, which is displayed on Figure 235.

- Select the menu item *Properties*

This will cause the next window, *Properties for Order Dollars*, to pop-up (Figure 236):

Figure 236

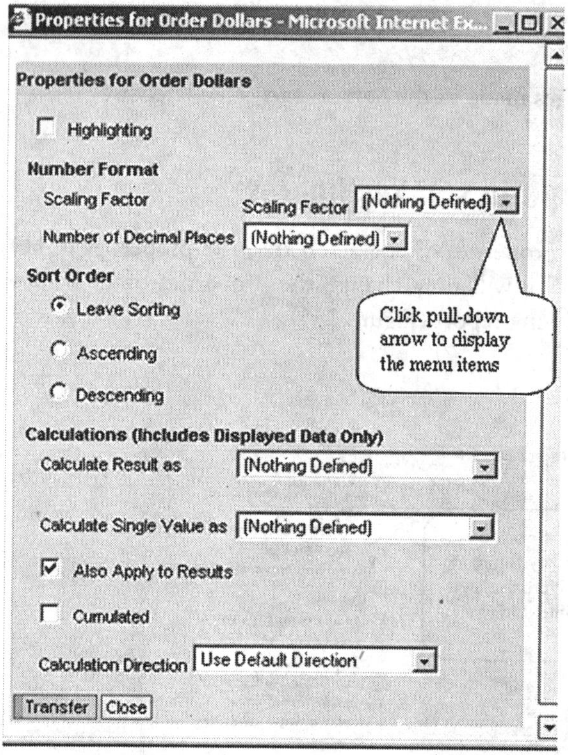

Properties for Order Dollars - Microsoft Internet Ex...

Properties for Order Dollars

☐ Highlighting

Number Format
Scaling Factor   Scaling Factor [Nothing Defined] ▼
Number of Decimal Places [Nothing Defined] ▼

Click pull-down arrow to display the menu items

Sort Order
◉ Leave Sorting
○ Ascending
○ Descending

Calculations (Includes Displayed Data Only)
Calculate Result as   [Nothing Defined] ▼

Calculate Single Value as [Nothing Defined] ▼

☑ Also Apply to Results

☐ Cumulated

Calculation Direction [Use Default Direction] ▼

[Transfer] [Close]

Copyright SAP AG

We can now make the desired changes for the various properties of the key figure *Order Dollars*, which are displayed on Figure 236.

We will first change the scaling factor, which enables the display of key figures to be adjusted. For example, if the scaling factor is set to 1,000 and the key figure value is 3,000, the number displayed on the report will be 3 (3000/1000 = 3).

To change the *Scaling Factor* property from *Nothing Defined* to *1,000*:

- Click the pull-down menu for *Scaling Factor*, which is highlighted on Figure 236

This will display the *Scaling Factor* menu items, which are displayed on Figure 237:

Figure 237

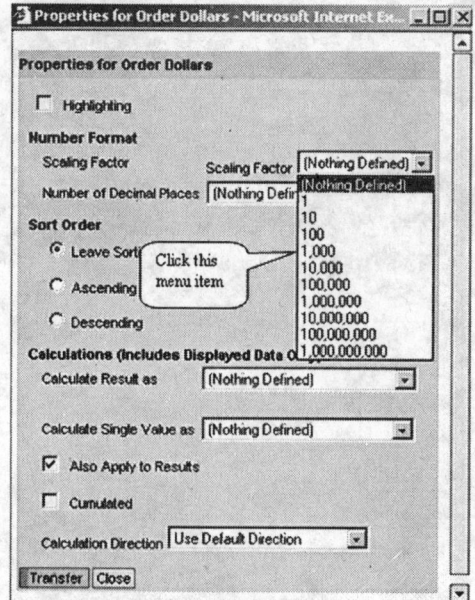

Copyright SAP AG

- Select the menu item *1,000*, which is highlighted (Figure 237)

This will lead to the next window (Figure 238):

Figure 238

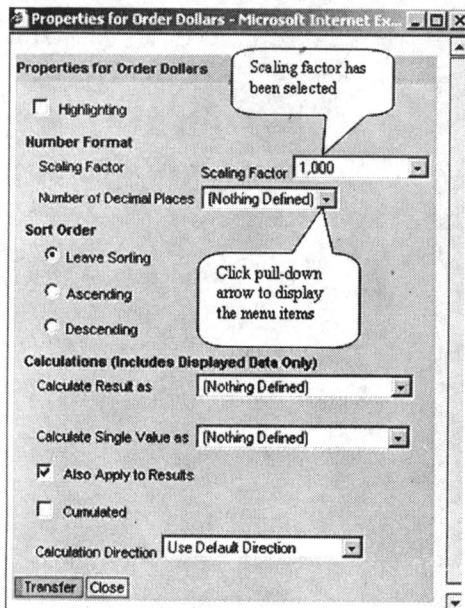

Copyright SAP AG

To change the *Number of Decimal Places* property:

- Click the pull-down menu for *Number of Decimal Places*, which is highlighted on Figure 238

This will display the *Number of Decimal Places* menu items, which are displayed on Figure 239:

Figure 239

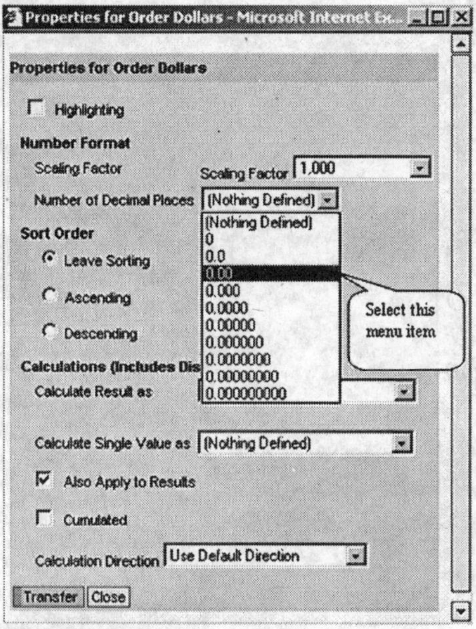

Properties for Order Dollars dialog showing Number Format with Scaling Factor 1,000 and Number of Decimal Places dropdown expanded showing: (Nothing Defined), 0, 0.0, **0.00**, 0.000, 0.0000, 0.00000, 0.000000, 0.0000000, 0.00000000, 0.000000000. Callout: "Select this menu item"

Copyright SAP AG

- Select the menu item *0.00* (for two decimal places), which is highlighted on Figure 239

This will lead to the next window, Figure 240, where the selected items for the key figure are displayed:

Figure 240

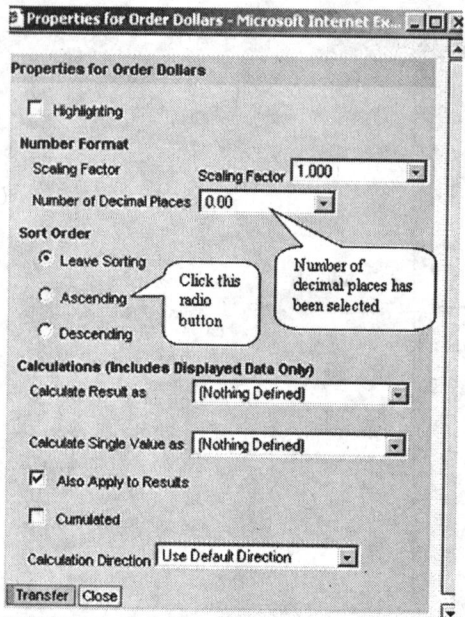

Copyright SAP AG

To specify an ascending sort order:

- Click the radio button for *Ascending*, which is highlighted on Figure 240

This will lead to the next window (Figure 241):

Figure 241

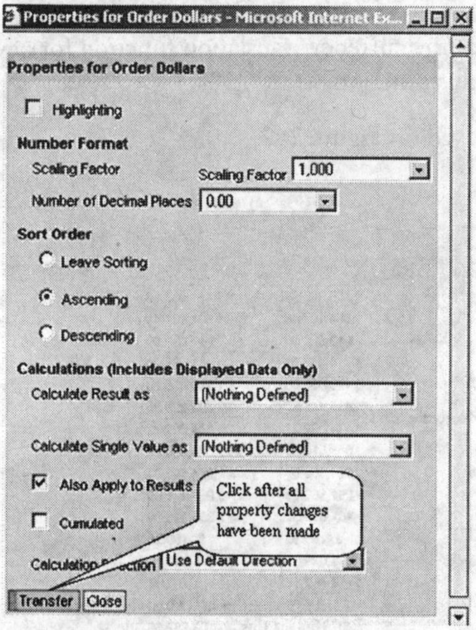

```
Properties for Order Dollars - Microsoft Internet Ex...  _ □ ×

Properties for Order Dollars

  ☐ Highlighting
Number Format
  Scaling Factor          Scaling Factor  1,000
  Number of Decimal Places  0.00
Sort Order
  ○ Leave Sorting
  ● Ascending
  ○ Descending
Calculations (Includes Displayed Data Only)
  Calculate Result as     [Nothing Defined]
  Calculate Single Value as  [Nothing Defined]
  ☑ Also Apply to Results      Click after all
  ☐ Cumulated                  property changes
                               have been made
  Calculation ...ection  Use Default Direction

  [Transfer] [Close]
```

Copyright SAP AG

After all the required property changes have been made:

- Click the *Transfer* button

This will implement the changes made to the *Order Dollars* key figure.

Currency translation

When multiple currencies are involved, the currency translation function for key figures is frequently used. To activate this function:

- Execute the report, which is displayed on Figure 242

Figure 242

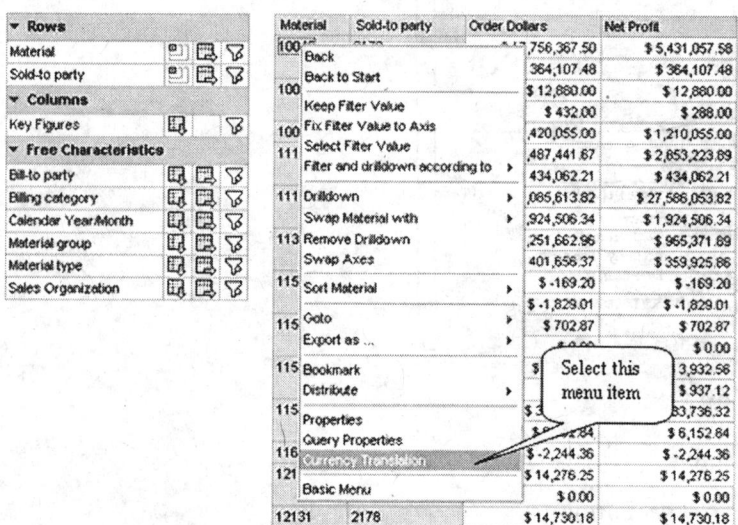

Copyright SAP AG

- Right-click, which will cause the Context Menu to pop-up
- Select the menu item *Currency Translation*

Notes

Notes